INTRODUCTION TO MUSIC APPRECIATION

By Bethanie Hansen, David Whitehouse,
and Cathy Silverman

Edited by Kimberly Jacobs

American Public University System ePress

2012

Revised 2014

Authors: Bethanie Hansen, David Whitehouse, and Cathy Silverman
Content Editor: Kimberly Jacobs
Acquisitions Editor: Judith Novak
Production Editor: Molly Fischer
Copy Editor: Missy Sheehan
Editor in Chief: Fred Stielow

Cover Illustration: Jessica Radlich,
American Public University System Visual Arts

Printed in the United States of America
This text was compiled in Charles Town, West Virginia by the APUS ePress.

This book uses constantly changing technologies, and is frequently updated to
ensure links are accessible.

ISBNs: 978-1-937381-08-0 (e-book)
978-1-937381-05-9 (print book)

American Public University System ePress
111 West Congress Street
Charles Town, WV 25414

www.apus.edu http://apus.campusguides.com/APUS_ePress

ABOUT THE PRINT EDITION OF THIS BOOK

This textbook was created first and foremost to be an interactive e-book.

Consequently, some of the interactivity is lost in the printed version. In this version,

hyperlinks and URLs are underlined and shown in gray. Visit

http://ezproxy.apus.edu/login?url=http://ebooks.apus.edu/MUSI200/Hansen_2012_Introd

uction to Music Appreciation.pdf and log in to access the e-book version.

Table of Contents

Chapter 1

Music Elements, Critical Listening, and Course Overview

By Bethanie L. Hansen and Cathy Silverman

Figure 1.1 Clip art image of a man wearing headphones, used with permission from Microsoft.

"The whole problem can be stated quite simply by asking, 'Is there a meaning to music?' My answer would be, 'Yes.' And 'Can you state in so many words what the meaning is?' My answer to that would be, 'No.'"

– Aaron Copland

(Copland, Rich, and Schuman 9)

Figure 1.2 Clip art image of sheet music, used with permission from Microsoft.

This book is about listening, appreciating, understanding, and discussing music; it will explore the history, aesthetics, and criticism of music so that you will better understand the background and meaning of Western music. In studying this book and the supplementary listening examples, you will come away a more informed music-listener who can enjoy a broader spectrum of music from both the past and the present.

The musical world is full of so many selections that we could not possibly cover them all in this book. However, by completing this course of study, you will gain the tools and skills needed to critically listen to and consider a variety of musical aspects that can apply to any musical style. These tools include contextual information about composers, history, and musical styles. A solid foundation of musical terms and concepts, allow you to listen for key ideas in the music and to discuss what you are hearing.

Music is a product of its time. To understand music from the past, one must first learn to think like the people of its age. In fact, if music is the outward expression of the composers and cultures that shaped it, a solid understanding of historical context is necessary in order to appreciate the music of any era outside our own. In the chapters to come, you will learn about the middle ages through the twenty-first century. As you study this text and listen to the music examples, you will survey a broad overview of music in history and learn how cultural contexts can offer the perspective necessary to understand great music from any era.

During the next eight weeks in this music appreciation course, you will explore the following areas of music: Early Music (to 1600), the Baroque Era (1600-1750), the Classical Era (1750-1820), the Romantic Era (1800s), the Twentieth Century, Jazz, and World Music. You will find pieces you enjoy and pieces you do not; however, each chapter will help to facilitate listening comprehension and allow you to speak about music in a common language understood by professionals, enthusiasts, and amateurs alike.

What is Music?

Music is a language of its own with expressive and communicative elements. Music has been studied as an art, a science, a therapy, and a power. **Music** is sound organized in a meaningful way, and may include a melody, harmony, rhythm, and form. Music can be performed by one voice or instrument, or by many—and it can even be performed as silence. John Cage was a modern composer who created his piece 4'33" based on silence.

The ancient Greeks believed music was cosmically related to science and culture. They asserted that mathematical laws of music were the same as the laws that regulated harmony in all matters—from the spiral growth patterns seen in nature to geometry and good government. This magical connection between sound and form was thought to be integral in maintaining harmony at all levels of society. Various musical modes were used to create desired moods such as calming or stimulating. Believing these modes resonated within the endocrine system in the human body, the ancient Greeks embraced music as much more than an expressive art.

The power of music is not merely abstract but is also physical. Physicists and other scientists have concluded that all matter is composed of energy or vibration. The air vibrations of sound are real and measurable, capable of shattering glass. Music and other sounds cause all kinds of sympathetic vibratory resonances within objects at a distance. Contemporary research into sounds of a lower frequency than is audible to the human ear suggests that nausea or headaches can be caused by sounds produced by industrial machinery from a distance. Rhythm, another measurable force, is the rationale behind commanding officers' ordering troops to break step when crossing a bridge marching in unison. The rhythmic effect of marching in step can lead to the collapse of the bridge. For more information about the science of music, please visit The Exploratorium.

Although music therapy is a new concept to the West, music has been used as a healing power for thousands of years by non-Western traditional cultures. Most evidence of the use of music in primitive/archaic cultures demonstrates that music was primarily used in sacred rituals. These rituals were intended to attract the attention of nature's spirits, to heal the sick, to bring good fortune, and to repel negative forces. The shaman could be called humanity's original "multimedia artist," using music, dance, visual art, and theatre to bring balance to communities and the environment. Today, music is used in developed societies as a clinical therapy to promote wellness, manage stress, alleviate pain, express feelings, enhance memory, improve concentration, and promote physical rehabilitation (American Music Therapy Association). For more information about the healing power of music and modern music therapy, please visit the <u>American Music Therapy Association's website</u>.

Music Elements

To understand various musical aspects throughout *Music Appreciation*, you must first understand the language of music. You will need to know several key terms and be comfortable using them throughout this course. Practice and use these terms during your listening exercises, this will help you become skillful at using them to discuss music in an intelligent way.

In the following section, music terms are presented, along with links to audio examples. As you read about these terms, consider listening to the related sound clips for illustrations of their meaning. Then, complete the self-check exercises to verify your understanding of key terms. Practice describing music using these terms any time you listen to music.

Clip art image of tools, used with permission from Microsoft.

Throughout this book, you will find the tool symbol to highlight specific terms or tools to describe music listening. If you lose track of a music term, just look for these symbols.

Music Terms

Instrumentation describes what kind of instrument or voice produced the music. It may be a solo piano or an entire orchestra of wind instruments, string instruments, and percussion. Each instrument or voice has unique and recognizable sounds or qualities.

Listen to audio or video introductions to a few instruments, presented by the Dallas Symphony Orchestra Kids Club, by clicking the following instrument terms to follow the hyperlink.

Oboe

Figure 1.3 Clip art image of an oboe, used with permission from Microsoft.

Flute

Figure 1.4 Clip art image of a child playing a flute, used with permission from Microsoft.

Clarinet

Figure 1.5 Clip art of the midsection of clarinet, used with permission from Microsoft.

Saxophone

Figure 1.6 Clip art image of an alto saxophone, used with permission from Microsoft.

Trumpet

Figure 1.7 Clip art image of a trumpet, used with permission from Microsoft.

Trombone

Figure 1.8 Clip art image of a trombone, used with permission from Microsoft.

Tuba

Figure 1.9 Clip art image of a tuba, used with permission from Microsoft.

<u>Violin</u>

Figure 1.10 Clip art image of a violin, used with permission from Microsoft.

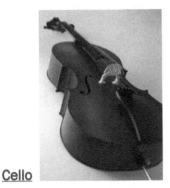

<u>Cello</u>

Figure 1.11 Clip art image of a cello, used with permission from Microsoft.

<u>Bass</u>

Figure 1.12 Clip art image of a man playing string bass, used with permission from Microsoft.

Each instrument belongs to a family: <u>woodwinds, brass, strings, percussion, or keyboards</u>. To view an (optional) interactive map with sound clips of the instruments in an orchestra, visit <u>Bedford/St. Martin's website</u> and load the viewer.

The Kennedy Center has an excellent interactive tool to help you explore the instruments of the orchestra from the Baroque period through the present. The tool is engaging and interesting, using a baseball game metaphor. Try The Kennedy Center's "Perfect Pitch" tool to learn more.

 Musical expression generally refers to the communicative power in music. This communication is best conveyed through changing tempos, meaning that the music gradually or suddenly changes speeds, dynamics, or both.

 Timbre, or tone quality, describes the quality of a musical sound. Timbre is generally discussed using adjectives, like "bright," "dark," "buzzy," "airy," "thin," and "smooth." Many different adjectives can be effectively used to describe timbre, based on your perceptions and opinions about what you hear in the sound. Not everyone will describe specific instrumental or vocal timbres the same way.

Figure 1.13 Clip art image of a woman playing classical guitar, used with permission from Microsoft.

The difference between a nylon-stringed classical guitar and an electric guitar with the distortion knob turned up provides a tangible illustration of timbre. The classical guitar produces a mellow, warm timbre. One might describe it as peaceful-sounding and smooth. Classical guitars are often associated with folk music and formal concerts.

In contrast, the distorted electric guitar produces a bright, cold, and edgy timbre. One could even describe it as rough sounding or aggressive. Electric guitars are most often associated with rock and alternative music.

Figure 1.14 Clip art image of a man with an electric guitar, used with permission from Microsoft.

Both classical guitar and electric guitar timbres are easily recognized and distinctly different from each other. Yet, the terms used to describe these two different timbres may vary from one person to the next.

 Texture is a term that describes what is going on in the music at any moment. Musical texture is the way that melody, harmony, and rhythm work together. Texture can be described in musical terms, such as monophonic, homophonic, and polyphonic—or with adjectives, like "thin," "thick," and "rich."

 A melody is a recognizable line of music that includes different notes, or pitches, and rhythms in an organized way. A melody may be simple or complex, and it may be comprised of smaller pieces called "motifs." Beethoven's Symphony no. 5, for example, includes a melody based on repeated motifs. Listen to an example of the allegro con brio from Beethoven's Symphony no. 5 in C minor, and take notice of the motif "da-da-da-daaaaa," (the first four notes of the symphony) as you hear it pass by. After several statements of this smaller motif, the smaller motivic pieces begin to form a recognizable melody. The melody stands out from the background musical material because it is stronger, louder, and played more aggressively.

 Harmony refers to the vertical relationship between pitches and is created when two or more notes are sounded at the same time. Two main types of harmony generally exist in Western music—homophony and polyphony. One additional musical texture, monophony, does not include any harmony.

- Monophonic texture, also called monophony, involves only one melody with no harmony. For example some types of early chant, a solo singer, or an unaccompanied instrument—like a trumpet or flute. Listen to "Gute Nacht for Trumpet (Good Night)," an example of monophony, performed on solo trumpet by Brian McWhorter.

- Homophonic texture, also called homophony, involves one clear melody with harmony or background material. In homophony, both the melody and its harmony can share similar rhythms. An example of homophony would be a church hymn arranged for four voices, a Scott Joplin rag such as "The Easy Winners," or a pop song with a solo vocalist. In homophony, the background material may be a chord accompaniment or harmony designed to support the main melody as background material. Listen to a performance of Handel's "Hallelujah" chorus. The chorus begins with a short orchestra introduction, followed by the choir singing "Hallelujah" in homophony.

- Polyphonic texture, also called polyphony, involves more than one specific melody. Two or more melodies may compete for importance. Rounds, canons, fugues, and many selections from the Baroque period, provide good examples of polyphony. Listen to a Bach fugue. In this fugue, you will hear a single melody on the piano. Shortly after it begins, another melody of equal importance will begin. Soon, there are several melodies played at the same time, and it will become increasingly difficult to identify which melody is more important.

When considering **musical texture**, ask yourself these questions:

- What instruments or voices am I hearing?
- Do I hear one melody, or more than one?
- Are the extra voices or instruments changing together or at different times?

- Is it difficult to identify the melody, perhaps because there are several melodies happening at once?

Tempo/time is the speed of the music. Tempo can change during a piece to add expression, such as a rubato, or slowing of the tempo. Speeding up the tempo is called an accelerando, and slowing down gradually is called a ritardando. Time signature is a related concept that explains which pulses are emphasized or "heavier" than others are. In this piece, *Carmina Burana: "Chramer, gip die varwe mir*, by Carl Orff, high choir voices sing at a fast tempo. Then, after the short statement of the melody, voices stop singing and instruments play briefly. During the instrumental section, the tempo seems to slow down. If you would like an additional example, watch a performance of Orff's *Carmina Burana: "O Fortuna."* In this example, singers begin at a slow tempo and then suddenly speed up to a much faster tempo. This second example is also a great illustration of sudden dynamic changes, because the singers move from a loud volume to a much softer one, then back to a louder volume.

Dynamics refer to the changing volume levels of musical sounds. Dynamics can range from softer than piano (soft or quiet) to fortissimo possibile (loudest possible). Dynamics can also change, getting louder (crescendo) and getting softer (diminuendo). Dynamics and changing dynamics give the music expression, make it interesting, and add variety. For an example of sudden dynamic changes, listen to Joseph Haydn's *Finale: Allegro con spirito from Symphony no. 88*. The symphony begins softly (*piano*). After a few statements of the melody, the entire orchestra suddenly plays more loudly (*forte*).

Form is the organization and structure of a musical selection. The form of a work may include repeating large sections, repeating a theme or motif, or non-repeating sections. Large parts within a musical form are usually labeled with capital letters, like "A" and "B," so we can discuss them. Within these larger sections, smaller parts may be labeled with lower-case letters, like "a" and "b" to further designate repeated and non-repeated sections. Form will be presented in all sections of this book because the form of musical works has changed often over time.

Music Notation

Music notation allows different people to reproduce musical sounds and musical works written by others. Notes and rhythms tell musicians what to play and how long to play it. Articulation markings give performers direction about how the note or rhythm should be played more specifically, and dynamic markings tell musicians what volume to play (or sing). Throughout this text, music theory is presented, as needed, to give you increased understandings of musical examples. Music theory, however, is a subject of its own and is not the emphasis of *Music Appreciation*.

Visit MusicTheory.net to explore the following music topics:

- The staff, clef, and ledger lines

- Note duration

- Measures and time signatures

- Rest duration

- Dots and ties

- Simple and compound meter

- Odd meter

Genres

Musical genres are broad categories used to classify music. Some genres that will be presented in *Music Appreciation* include Western classical and art music, world music, jazz, rock, pop, and other modern genres. Sometimes, music is grouped by instrumentation as a genre, such as "symphony" or "string quartet."

Styles

Within musical genres, music can be further classified into specific styles. Western classical music is not all from the Classic era. In fact, Western classical music includes medieval and early music, Renaissance music, Baroque music, Classical music, Romantic period music, and other period-specific music. Within each period, many styles may exist including ballads, operas, concertos, solo works, and more. Music styles consist of combined musical elements, instrumentation, timbre, texture, tempo, dynamics, form, and mood. As you read this text, you will learn about many styles of music that were new in their cultural contexts and have endured as specific musical styles through the present day.

Self-Check Exercises

Complete the following self-check exercises to verify your mastery of key music terms presented in this chapter.

1. Which new term could be used to discuss all of the following actions: slowing down, speeding up, and getting louder or softer in the music?
   a. Form
   b. Texture
   c. Expression
   d. Timbre

2. Which term is used to discuss the way the melody, harmony, and rhythm combine in music?
   a. Form
   b. Texture
   c. Expression
   d. Timbre

3. Which term is used to discuss the way the music is organized into repeated or non-repeated sections, so listeners can better understand or enjoy it?
   a. Form
   b. Texture
   c. Expression
   d. Timbre

4. Which term is used to discuss the quality of sounds, or what different tone qualities are?
   a. Form
   b. Texture
   c. Expression
   d. Timbre

Your understanding of these basic terms is essential to critical listening throughout this course. If you would like additional information about these terms, please review before proceeding.

After you have read the questions above, check your answers at the bottom of this page.

Self-check quiz answers:
1. c. 2. b. 3. a. 4. d.

Critical Listening

Before you begin to listen, set yourself up for success by obtaining a quality pair of headphones, speakers, or related

amplification devices. Laptop speakers are not made for a quality music listening experience, so carefully consider what equipment you will use throughout this course.

Figure 1.15 Clip art image of a man wearing headphones and seated in front of a computer, used with permission from Microsoft.

There is a difference between hearing and listening. Hearing means that sound enters the ear, but the brain does not necessarily process its meaning. When the brain is engaged, noticing, and attending to the sound, critical listening can happen. The best way to listen to music throughout this course is to use your growing skills to identify specific music elements and to follow these throughout a listening selection.

Listening Goals

Each week, specific listening goals will be presented along with music terms and a listening map. Review the terms listed and use the listening map as a tool to meet listening goals.

Figure 1.16 Clip art image of a woman wearing headphones, used with permission from Microsoft.

What are listening maps? Listening maps are written tools used to explain the form of a piece of music, so that listeners understand what they are hearing in a given piece. As you listen to music examples, follow the listening maps illustrated throughout the text. Some listening maps are simple charts to help guide listening, like the following chart produced by the Atlanta Symphony. Listen to the first movement of Dmitri Shostakovich's <u>Symphony no. 9 in E flat</u> while following the listening map.

Activity: Follow this map of the 1st movement of the Shostakovich 9th Symphony. The recapitulation of the themes is not an exact repeat, but you'll know them when you hear them. (Read left to right.)

I. EXPOSITION:

A THEME:

a	b	a
strings	oboe	strings

B THEME:

a	a	b	a
piccolo	piccolo	woodwinds	brass

II. DEVELOPMENT:

A THEME (NEW KEYS):

a	b	a
high strings upside down	high strings	low strings

B THEME (NEW KEYS):

a	b
woodwinds	horn and bassoon

RECAPITULATION:

A THEME (HOME KEY):

a	b	a
strings	strings	bassoon

B THEME:

a	b
violin solo	trombones

A THEME:

a
clarinet solo

B THEME:

a
high strings

A THEME:

a
clarinet, oboe and trumpet small fragment

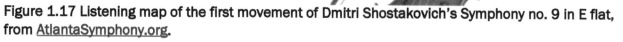

Figure 1.17 Listening map of the first movement of Dmitri Shostakovich's Symphony no. 9 in E flat, from AtlantaSymphony.org.

How do I make connections to my own ideas about music and my modern music listening?

Each time you learn a new musical concept in this course, practice listening for that concept in one of the assigned listening examples. Then, try listening for the same concept in a modern or popular piece of music during the week. For example, after you listen to identify the sounds of specific instruments during our course, see how many instruments you can identify in your favorite rock, country, hip-hop, rap, or other musical selection. By applying music listening skills to your favorite music, you will become more comfortable and adept at using your new skills.

Closing

Music Appreciation is organized chronologically, presenting a brief overview of music in its context throughout history. As you move through this course, you will read about history and culture, composers, and major musical works to form a more complete picture of what influenced a composer, a community, and a historical period. With history as your tool, you can try to listen as a member of the composer's community, with the mentality of the people of its era. This kind of perspective could lead you to feel the excitement and joy a musical work can inspire. Learn the music terms as they are introduced, and listen to musical examples as much as possible to practice using these tools. Get involved in your class, and participate in discussions about the music. Before you know it, you will be able to discuss music with confidence.

Sound, Music, and the Environment

This week, watch the 25-minute video "Sound, Music, and the Environment," part of the Annenberg Learner video series we will be viewing throughout the text.

Additional Resources

This web resource list was adapted from Bedford/St. Martin's website:

Alabama

Alabama Symphony Orchestra, Birmingham
http://www.alabamasymphony.org/

Mobile Symphony Orchestra
http://www.mobilesymphony.org/

Alaska

Anchorage Symphony Orchestra
http://www.anchoragesymphony.org/

Fairbanks Symphony Orchestra
http://www.fairbankssymphony.org/

Juneau Symphony
http://www.juneausymphony.org/

Arizona

Flagstaff Symphony Orchestra
http://www.flagstaffsymphony.org/

The Phoenix Symphony
http://www.phoenixsymphony.org/

Tucson Symphony Orchestra
http://www.tucsonsymphony.org/

Arkansas

Arkansas Symphony Orchestra, Little Rock
http://www.arkansassymphony.org/

California

Los Angeles Philharmonic
http://www.laphil.com/

Sacramento Philharmonic Orchestra & Opera
http://2intune.org/

San Diego Symphony
http://www.sandiegosymphony.org/

San Francisco Symphony
http://www.sfsymphony.org/

Colorado

Colorado Springs Philharmonic
http://www.csphilharmonic.org/

Colorado Symphony Orchestra, Denver
http://www.coloradosymphony.org/

Connecticut

Hartford Symphony Orchestra
http://www.hartfordsymphony.org/

Delaware

Delaware Symphony Orchestra, Wilmington
http://www.delawaresymphony.org/

District of Columbia

National Symphony Orchestra, Washington, DC
http://www.kennedy-center.org/nso/

Florida

Miami Symphony Orchestra
http://www.miamisymphony.org/

Florida Orchestra, Tampa Bay area
http://www.floridaorchestra.org/

Jacksonville Symphony Orchestra
http://www.jaxsymphony.org/

Orlando Philharmonic Orchestra
http://www.orlandophil.org/

Pensacola Symphony Orchestra
http://www.pensacolasymphony.com/

Georgia

Atlanta Symphony Orchestra
http://www.atlantasymphony.org/

Hawaii

Hawaii Symphony Orchestra
http://hawaiisymphonyorchestra.org/

Idaho

Boise Philharmonic
http://www.boisephilharmonic.org/

Illinois

Chicago Symphony Orchestra
http://www.cso.org/

Illinois Symphony Orchestra
http://www.ilsymphony.org/

Indiana

Indianapolis Symphony Orchestra
http://www.indianapolissymphony.org/

Iowa

Orchestra Iowa (Eastern Iowa)
http://www.artsiowa.com/orchestra/

Des Moines Symphony
http://www.dmsymphony.org/

Sioux City Symphony Orchestra
http://www.siouxcitysymphony.org/

Kansas

Wichita Symphony Orchestra
http://wichitasymphony.org/

Kentucky

Louisville Orchestra
http://www.louisvilleorchestra.org/

Louisiana

Louisiana Philharmonic Orchestra, New Orleans
http://www.lpomusic.com/

Shreveport Symphony Orchestra
http://www.shreveportsymphony.com/

Maine

Bangor Symphony Orchestra
http://www.bangorsymphony.org/

Portland Symphony Orchestra
http://www.portlandsymphony.org/

Maryland

Baltimore Symphony Orchestra
http://www.bsomusic.org/

Massachusetts

Boston Classical Orchestra
http://www.bostonclassicalorchestra.org/

Boston Symphony Orchestra
http://www.bso.org/

Boston Philharmonic
http://www.bostonphil.org

Springfield Symphony Orchestra
http://www.springfieldsymphony.org/

Michigan

Detroit Symphony Orchestra
http://www.dso.org/

Minnesota

Minnesota Orchestra
http://www.minnesotaorchestra.org/

Saint Paul Chamber Orchestra
http://www.thespco.org/

Mississippi

Mississippi Symphony Orchestra, Jackson
http://www.msorchestra.com/

Missouri

Kansas City Symphony
http://www.kcsymphony.org/

Saint Louis Symphony Orchestra
http://www.stlsymphony.org/

Montana

Billings Symphony Orchestra & Chorale
http://www.billingssymphony.org/

Helena Symphony
http://www.helenasymphony.org/

Nebraska

Omaha Symphony
http://www.omahasymphony.org/

Nevada

Las Vegas Philharmonic
http://lvphil.org/

New Hampshire

New Hampshire Philharmonic Orchestra, Manchester
http://www.nhphil.org/

New Jersey

New Jersey Symphony Orchestra, Newark
http://www.njsymphony.org/

New Mexico

New Mexico Philharmonic
http://www.nmphil.org/

New York

Albany Symphony
http://www.albanysymphony.com/

Buffalo Philharmonic Orchestra
http://www.bpo.org/

New York Philharmonic
http://nyphil.org/

Symphony Syracuse
http://www.symphonysyracuse.org/

North Carolina

Charlotte Symphony
http://www.charlottesymphony.org/

North Carolina Symphony, Raleigh
http://www.ncsymphony.org/

Ohio

Cincinnati Symphony Orchestra
http://www.cincinnatisymphony.org/

Cleveland Orchestra
http://www.clevelandorchestra.com/

Columbus Symphony Orchestra
http://www.columbussymphony.com/

Oklahoma

Oklahoma City Philharmonic
http://www.okcphilharmonic.org/

Oregon

Oregon Symphony, Portland
http://www.orsymphony.org/

Pennsylvania

Philadelphia Orchestra
http://www.philorch.org/

Pittsburgh Symphony
http://www.pittsburghsymphony.org/

Rhode Island

Rhode Island Philharmonic, Providence
http://www.ri-philharmonic.org/

South Carolina

Charleston Symphony Orchestra
http://www.charlestonsymphony.com/

South Dakota

South Dakota Symphony Orchestra, Sioux Falls
http://www.sdsymphony.org/

Tennessee

Knoxville Symphony Orchestra
http://www.knoxvillesymphony.com/

Memphis Symphony Orchestra
http://www.memphissymphony.org/

Nashville Symphony
http://www.nashvillesymphony.org/

Texas

Dallas Symphony Orchestra
http://www.dallassymphony.com/

El Paso Symphony Orchestra
http://www.epso.org/

Houston Symphony
http://www.houstonsymphony.org/

Utah

Utah Symphony and Opera, Salt Lake City
http://www.usuo.org/

Vermont

Vermont Symphony Orchestra, Burlington
http://www.vso.org/

Virginia

Richmond Symphony
http://www.richmondsymphony.com/

Washington

Seattle Symphony
http://www.seattlesymphony.org/

Spokane Symphony Orchestra
http://www.spokanesymphony.org/

West Virginia

West Virginia Symphony Orchestra, Charleston
http://www.wvsymphony.org/

Wisconsin

Madison Symphony Orchestra
https://www.madisonsymphony.org/

Milwaukee Symphony Orchestra
http://www.mso.org/

Wyoming

Cheyenne Symphony Orchestra
http://www.cheyennesymphony.org/

Wyoming Symphony Orchestra, Casper
http://www.wyomingsymphony.org/

Arizona

Tucson Jazz Society
http://www.tucsonjazz.org/

Arkansas

Arkansas Jazz Heritage Foundation (Little Rock based)
http://www.arjazz.org/home/

California

Royal Society Jazz Orchestra (San Francisco based)
http://www.rsjo.com/

Monterey Hot Jazz Society
http://www.montereyhotjazzsociety.org/

Colorado

Northern Colorado Traditional Jazz Society (Fort Collins based)
http://www.fortnet.org/tradjazz/

Connecticut

Hartford Jazz Society
http://www.hartfordjazzsociety.com/index.html

District of Columbia

Smithsonian Jazz Masterworks Orchestra
http://smithsonianassociates.org/ticketing/landing/jazz-masterworks-orchestra.aspx

Potomac River Jazz Club (DC/Baltimore area)
http://www.prjc.org/

Florida

South Florida Jazz (Plantation based)
http://www.southfloridajazz.org/index.php

Georgia

Jazz Orchestra Atlanta
http://www.orchestraatlanta.org/

Idaho

Boise Jazz Society
http://www.boisejazzsociety.org/

Illinois

Chicago Jazz
http://www.jazzinstituteof
chicago.org/

Indiana

The Jazz Arts Society of
Indiana
http://www.indianapolisja
zzorchestra.org/

Iowa

Bix Beiderbecke
Memorial Society
(Davenport)
http://www.bixsociety.org
/

Kentucky

Louisville Jazz Society
http://www.louisvillejazz.
org/

Louisiana

New Orleans Jazz
Orchestra
http://www.thenojo.com/

Maryland

Baltimorejazz.com
http://baltimorejazz.com/

Potomac River Jazz Club
(DC/Baltimore area)
http://www.prjc.org/

Massachusetts

JazzBoston
http://www.jazzboston.or
g/

Michigan

West Michigan Jazz
Society (Grand Rapids
based)
http://www.wmichjazz.org
/

Paul Keller Orchestra
http://www.pkorecords.c
om/about.html

Minnesota

Minnesota Jazz Orchestra
http://www.minnesotajaz
zorchestra.com/

Twin Cities Jazz Society
http://www.tcjs.org/

Missouri

St. Louis Jazz Club
http://www.stlouisjazzclu
b.org/index.htm

Kansas City Jazz
Orchestra
http://www.kcjazzorchest
ra.org/

Montana

Montana Jazz
http://www.montanajazz.
com/index.html

Nebraska

Nebraska Jazz Orchestra
(Lincoln based)
http://artsincorporated.or
g/njo/

Nevada

Reno Jazz Orchestra
http://renojazzorchestra.
org/

New Jersey

Vanguard Jazz Orchestra
(NY/NJ)
http://www.vanguardjazz
orchestra.com/

New Mexico

New Mexico Jazz
Workshop (Albuquerque
based)
http://www.nmjazz.org/

New York

Jazz at Lincoln Center
Orchestra
http://www.jazz.org/

Central New York Jazz
Orchestra
https://www.cnyjazz.org/

North Carolina

North Carolina Jazz
Repertory Orchestra
http://www.ncjro.org/ind
ex.html

Ohio

Jazz Arts Group
(Columbus)
http://www.jazzartsgroup.
org/

Cleveland Jazz Orchestra
http://www.clevelandjazz.
org/

Oklahoma

Oklahoma Jazz Hall of
Fame (Tulsa)
http://www.okjazz.org/

Oregon

Jazz Society of Oregon (Portland based)
http://www.jsojazzscene.org/

Pennsylvania

Philadelphia Legends of Jazz Orchestra
http://www.phillylegendsofjazz.com/

Pittsburgh Jazz Society
http://www.pittsburghjazz.org/

South Carolina

Jazz Artists of Charleston
http://jazzartistsofcharleston.org/

South Dakota

Sioux Falls Jazz & Blues Society
http://www.sfjb.org/

Tennessee

Knoxville Jazz Orchestra
http://www.knoxjazz.org/

Tennessee Jazz & Blues Society (Nashville based)
http://www.jazzblues.org/

Texas

Austin Traditional Jazz Society
http://www.atjs.org/

Utah

Jazz Arts of the Mountain West (Ogden based)
http://www.jamnational.org/

Vermont

Vermont Jazz Ensemble
http://www.vermontjazzensemble.com/

Virginia

Richmond Jazz Society
http://www.vajazz.org/

Washington

Seattle Repertory Jazz Orchestra
http://www.srjo.org/

Seattle Women's Jazz Orchestra
http://www.swojo.com/

Spokane Jazz Society and Orchestra
http://www.spokanejazz.org/spokane-jazz-society

West Virginia

West Virginia Jazz Society
http://www.wvjazzsociety.com/

Wisconsin

Madison Jazz Society
http://www.madisonjazz.com

Madison Jazz Orchestra
http://www.madisonjazzorchestra.com

Works Consulted

Adams, Ricci. *MusicTheory.net*. MusicTheory.net, LLC, 2012. Web. 11 Sept. 2012. <http://www.musictheory.net/>.

Alto saxophone, used with permission from Microsoft. "Images." *Office*. Web. 4 Sept. 2012. <http://office.microsoft.com/en-us/images/results.aspx?qu=saxophone&ctt=1#ai:MP900384844|mt:2|>.

American Music Therapy Association. *American Music Therapy Association Website*. American Music Therapy Association, 2011. Web. 17 Mar. 2012. <http://www.musictherapy.org/>.

Bach, Johann Sebastian. *Fugue in B-flat major (after J.C. Erselius), BMV 955*. Perf. C. Breemer. *Piano Society*, 30 July 2012. Web. 30 Aug. 2012. <http://server3.pianosociety.com/protected/bach-bwv954-breemer.mp3>.

Beethoven, Ludwig Van. *Symphony No. 5 in C Minor, Op. 67*. 1808. Cond. Fernando Lozano. Perf. Orquestra Filarmónica De La Ciudad de México. 2009. *Music Online: Classical Music Library*. Alexander Street Press. Web. 2 Oct. 2014. <http://ezproxy.apus.edu/login?url=http://search.alexanderstreet.com/view/work/76036>.

Berio, Luciano. *Gute Nacht for Trumpet*. 1986. Perf. Brian McWhorter. 2006. *Music Online: Classical Music Library*. Alexander Street Press. Web. 2 Oct. 2014. <http://ezproxy.apus.edu/login?url=http://search.alexanderstreet.com/view/work/757095>.

"Cello, Instrument." *DSO Kids*. Dallas Symphony Association. Web. 9 Apr. 2014. <http://dsokids.com/listen/by-instrument/cello.aspx>.

Cello, used with permission from Microsoft. "Images." *Office*. Web. 4 Sept. 2012. <http://office.microsoft.com/en-us/images/results.aspx?qu=cello&ctt=1#ai:MP900385375|mt:2|>.

Child playing a flute, used with permission from Microsoft. "Images." *Office*. Web. 4 Sept. 2012. <http://office.microsoft.com/en-us/images/results.aspx?qu=flute&ctt=1#ai:MP900227714|mt:2|>.

"Clarinet, Instrument." *DSO Kids*. Dallas Symphony Association. Web. 9 Apr. 2014. <http://dsokids.com/listen/by-instrument/clarinet.aspx>.

Classic Guitar Sample. *Internet Archive*. Internet Archive, n.d. Web. 18 Mar. 2012. <http://archive.org/details/ClassicGuitar>.

Construction tools sign, used with permission from Microsoft. "Images." *Office*. Web. 4 Sept. 2012. <http://office.microsoft.com/en-us/images/results.aspx?ex=2&qu=tools#ai:MC900432556|mt:0|>.

Copland, Aaron, Alan Rich, and William Schuman. *What To Listen For In Music*. New York,
    NY: Signet Classics, 1999. Print.

Crookes, Luke. *A Listening Guide to Beethoven's Symphony No. 9*. YouTube. 28 Aug. 2007.
    Web. 30 Aug. 2012. <http://youtu.be/SLCXgZOGLVo>.

Distorted Guitar Sample. Internet Archive. Internet Archive, n.d. Web. 18 Mar. 2012.
    <http://archive.org/details/DistortedGuitarSample>.

"Double Bass, Instrument." *DSO Kids*. Dallas Symphony Association. Web. 9 Apr. 2014.
    <http://dsokids.com/listen/by-instrument/double-bass.aspx>.

Ewell, Terry B. "Introduction to Pitch Notation in Music." *Connexions*. Rice University, 4 May
    2009. Web. 2 Oct. 2014. <http://cnx.org/contents/c5ca8b28-7879-493c-8125-
    2b26ea2a5454@1/Introduction_to_Pitch_Notation>.

"Flute, Instrument." *DSO Kids*. Dallas Symphony Association. Web. 9 Apr. 2014.
    <http://dsokids.com/listen/by-instrument/flute.aspx>.

Handel, George Frideric. "Hallelujah." *The Messiah*. 1741. Cond. Stephen Simon. Perf.
    Handel Festival Orchestra of Washington D.C & Howard University Choir. 1985. *Music
    Online: Classical Music Library*. Alexander Street Press. Web. 2 Oct. 2014.
    <http://ezproxy.apus.edu/login?url=http://search.alexanderstreet.com/view/work/1
    78837>.

Haydn, Franz Joseph. *Symphony No. 88 in G Major*. 1787. Perf. London Mozart Players.
    1989. *Music Online: Classical Music Library*. Alexander Street Press. Web. 2 Oct.
    2014.
    <http://ezproxy.apus.edu/login?url=http://search.alexanderstreet.com/view/work/1
    79287>.

Kerman, Joseph and Gary Tomlinson. "Instruments of the Orchestra." *Listen: Brief Fifth
    Edition*. Bedford/St. Martin's, n.d. Web. 30 Aug. 2012.
    <http://bcs.bedfordstmartins.com/listen/pages/bcs-
    main.asp?s=00030&n=99000&i=99030.01&v=category&o=&ns=0&uid=0&rau=0>
    .

Listening map of Shostakovich's Symphony no. 9 in E flat. *Listen! A Guide to the Atlanta
    Symphony Orchestra: 2003-2004 Young People's Concerts. Atlanta Symphony
    Orchestra*. 15. Web. 31 July 2012.
    <http://www.atlantasymphony.org/aso/asoassets/downloadcenter/ASOstudent030
    4_000.pdf>.

Man playing string bass, used with permission from Microsoft. "Images." *Office*. Web. 4
    Sept. 2012. <http://office.microsoft.com/en-
    us/images/results.aspx?qu=bass&ctt=1#ai:MP900400108|mt:2|>.

Man wearing headphones and seated in front of a computer, used with permission from
    Microsoft. "Images." *Office*. Web. 4 Sept. 2012. <http://office.microsoft.com/en-

us/images/results.aspx?qu=listening%20to%20headphones&ctt=1#ai:MP9004225
41|mt:2|>.

Man wearing headphones, used with permission from Microsoft. "Images." *Office*. Web. 4
Sept. 2012. <http://office.microsoft.com/en-
us/images/results.aspx?ex=2&qu=listening to music#ai:MP900442510|mt:2|>.

Man with an electric guitar, used with permission from Microsoft. "Images." *Office*. Web. 4
Sept. 2012. <http://office.microsoft.com/en-
us/images/results.aspx?qu=electric%20guitar&ctt=1#ai:MP900422708|mt:2|>.

Midsection of clarinet, used with permission from Microsoft. "Images." *Office*. Web. 4 Sept.
2012. <http://office.microsoft.com/en-
us/images/results.aspx?qu=clarinet&ctt=1#ai:MP900182841|mt:2|>.

Music Genres List. N.p., 2012. Web. 11 Sept. 2012. <http://musicgenreslist.com/>.

Oboe, used with permission from Microsoft. "Images." *Office*. Web. 4 Sept. 2012.
<http://office.microsoft.com/en-
us/images/results.aspx?qu=oboe&ctt=1#ai:MP900175040|mt:2|>.

"Oboe, Instrument." *DSO Kids*. Dallas Symphony Association. Web. 9 Apr. 2014.
<http://dsokids.com/listen/by-instrument/oboe.aspx>.

Orff, Carl. "Chramer, gip die varwe mir." *Carmina Burana*. 1936. Cond. Riccardo Muti. Perf.
Philharmonia Chorus and Philharmonia Orchestra. 2005. *Music Online: Classical
Music Library*. Alexander Street Press. Web. 2 Oct. 2014.
<http://ezproxy.apus.edu/login?url=http://search.alexanderstreet.com/view/work/9
31082>.

—. "O Fortuna." *Carmina Burana*. 1936. Cond. David Hill. Perf. Bournemouth Symphony
Chorus. 2008. *Music Online: Classical Music Library*. Alexander Street Press. Web. 2
Oct. 2014.
<http://ezproxy.apus.edu/login?url=http://search.alexanderstreet.com/music-
performing-arts/view/work/962896>.

"Perfect Pitch." *ArtsEdge*. The Kennedy Center. Web. 31 July 2012.
<http://artsedge.kennedy-center.org/interactives/perfectpitch/>.

"Saxophone, Instrument." *DSO Kids*. Dallas Symphony Association. Web. 9 Apr. 2014.
<http://dsokids.com/listen/by-instrument/saxophone.aspx>.

Schmidt-Jones, Catherine. "Dynamics and Accents in Music." *Connexions*. Rice University, 15
Feb. 2013. Web. 2 Oct. 2014. <http://cnx.org/contents/b9f0594e-2995-4ce7-970e-
7a17ba38905e@13/Dynamics_and_Accents_in_Music>.

—. "Form in Music." *Connexions*. Rice University, 15 Feb. 2013. Web. 2 Oct. 2014.
<http://cnx.org/contents/689c1edd-5d25-4430-9108-
735cc9035c18@17/Form_in_Music>.

—. "Harmony." *Connexions*. Rice University, 15 Feb. 2013. Web. 2 Oct. 2014.
<http://cnx.org/contents/9b86eea1-acee-487a-93e5-46b71222ab1e@13/Harmony>.

—. "Melody." *Connexions*. Rice University, 15 Feb. 2013. Web. 2 Oct. 2012.
<http://cnx.org/contents/4336d682-7b96-46af-8d34-3b4f2d50dd1b@12/Melody>.

—. "Tempo." *Connexions*. Rice University, 15 Feb. 2013. Web. 2 Oct. 2014.
<http://cnx.org/contents/0d0a576a-f615-4847-a456-fe74e7a1a09a@11/Tempo>.

—. "The Textures of Music." *Connexions*. Rice University, 14 Nov. 2013. Web. 2 Oct. 2014.
<http://cnx.org/contents/04ac529b-2695-4994-b5a6-22a3776d69e3@14/The_Textures_of_Music>.

—. "Timbre: The Color of Music." *Connexions*. Rice University, 15 Feb. 2013. Web. 2 Oct.
2014. <http://cnx.org/contents/f306fb29-f034-4a34-99d5-a44adf8ae813@15/Timbre:_The_Color_of_Music>.

"Science of Music: Accidental Scientist." *The Exploratorium: the Museum of Science, Art and Human Perception*. The Exploratorium, 2011. Web. 30 Aug. 2012.
<http://www.exploratorium.edu/music/index.html>.

Sheet music, used with permission from Microsoft. "Images." *Office*. Web. 4 Sept. 2012.
<http://office.microsoft.com/en-us/images/results.aspx?ex=2&qu=muscial notes#ai:MP900438700|mt:2|>.

Shostakovich, Dmitri. *Symphony no. 9 in E flat, Op. 70*. 1945. Perf. Munich Philharmonic Orchestra and Sergiu Celibidache. *Music Online: Classical Music Library*. Alexander Street Press. Web. 2 Oct. 2014.
<http://ezproxy.apus.edu/login?url=http://search.alexanderstreet.com/view/work/944477>.

"Sound, Music, and the Environment." Prod. Pacific Street Films and the Educational Film Center. "Exploring the World of Music." *Annenberg Learner*. Web. 31 July 2012.
<http://www.learner.org/resources/series105.html#>.

"Trombone, Instrument." *DSO Kids*. Dallas Symphony Association. Web. 9 Apr. 2014.
<http://dsokids.com/listen/by-instrument/trombone.aspx>.

Trombone, used with permission from Microsoft. "Images." *Office*. Web. 4 Sept. 2012.
<http://office.microsoft.com/en-us/images/results.aspx?qu=trombone&ctt=1#ai:MP900175048|mt:2|>.

"Trumpet, Instrument." *DSO Kids*. Dallas Symphony Association. Web. 9 Apr. 2014.
<http://dsokids.com/listen/by-instrument/trumpet.aspx>.

Trumpet, used with permission from Microsoft. "Images." *Office*. Web. 4 Sept. 2012.
<http://office.microsoft.com/en-us/images/results.aspx?qu=trumpet&ctt=1#ai:MP900289688|mt:2|>.

"Tuba, Instrument." *DSO Kids*. Dallas Symphony Association. Web. 9 Apr. 2014. <http://dsokids.com/listen/by-instrument/tuba.aspx>.

Tuba, used with permission from Microsoft. "Images." *Office*. Web. 4 Sept. 2012. <http://office.microsoft.com/en-us/images/results.aspx?qu=tuba&ctt=1#ai:MP900385292|mt:2|>.

Violin, used with permission from Microsoft. "Images." *Office*. Web. 4 Sept. 2012. <http://office.microsoft.com/en-us/images/results.aspx?qu=violin&ctt=1#ai:MP900405478|mt:2|>.

"Violin, Instrument." *DSO Kids*. Dallas Symphony Association. Web. 9 Apr. 2014. <http://dsokids.com/listen/by-instrument/violin.aspx>.

Woman playing classical guitar, used with permission from Microsoft. "Images." *Office*. Web. 4 Sept. 2012. <http://office.microsoft.com/en-us/images/results.aspx?qu=guitar&ctt=1#ai:MP900227430|mt:2|>.

Woman wearing headphones, used with permission from Microsoft. "Images." *Office*. Web. 4 Sept. 2012. <http://office.microsoft.com/en-us/images/results.aspx?qu=listening%20to%20headphones&ctt=1#ai:MP900422199|mt:2|>.

Chapter 2

Early Western Art Music

By David Whitehouse

Figure 2.1 Phintias, Music Lesson, ca. 510 BCE. The teacher is on the right, the student on the left. Between them a boy reads from a text.

The Western music known today has its roots in the musical practices found in Europe and the Middle East over twenty centuries ago. These musical practices, in turn, have their roots in ancient Greek and Roman practices which are detailed in musical and philosophical treatises of the time. Greek civilization, with its political structures, its architectural and musical attainments, and its great achievements in philosophy and poetry, has influenced European culture and in turn American culture.

Music from these two ancient civilizations cannot be heard or faithfully reconstructed because the historical records are sparse and incomplete. The Greeks produced a rich trove of writings about music. What is known of the Greek practices of music come from philosophical works such as Plato's Republic, Aristotle's Politics, and from thinkers such as Pythagoras. Pythagoras was the first to note the relationship of the intervals of music to mathematics. Greek writers thought that music influenced morals, and was a reflection of the order found in the universe. Over the long period of Greek civilization, many writers emerged with differing viewpoints.

These viewpoints include the relationship of musical rhythm to poetic rhythm. They delineate precise definitions of melody, intervals, scales, and modes. This last term, mode, means the relationship of notes in a scale. Much of Western Art Music uses the two modes called major and minor. The Greeks had several further modes which reflected the practices of the time. These ideas, while forgotten and disused after the ascendance of Roman dominance, were nevertheless rediscovered in later centuries and formed the basis of musical practice. Listen to a recreation of the oldest known complete song from Greek civilization called, "Song of Seikilos." **Please note that for this chapter, transcripts of song and music lyrics are not necessary to gain an understanding of the material.**

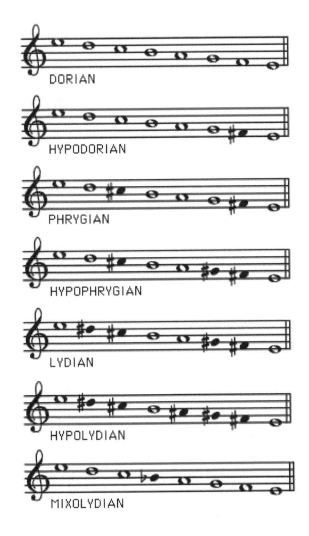

DORIAN

HYPODORIAN

PHRYGIAN

HYPOPHRYGIAN

LYDIAN

HYPOLYDIAN

MIXOLYDIAN

Figure 2.2 Seven Greek modes in modern notation showing the whole and half-step patterns which characterize each. The modes shown are Dorian, Hypodorian, Phrygian, Hypophrygian, Lydian, Hypolydian, and Mixolydian.

Less is known of Roman music. After the Greek islands became a Roman province in

146 BCE, music played an important function at festivals, state occasions, religious rites,

and in warfare. Writers of the time tell of large gatherings of musicians and of music

competitions, and depict choruses and orchestras. Emperors improved their image by

funding music and other arts. However, Roman musical practices had no direct bearing on

the development of European culture.

After the fall of Rome, generally ascribed to the year 476 CE, civilization in this part of the world entered the "Middle Ages". Extending for a thousand years, the first five hundred years of the *Middle Ages* has until recently been described as the "*Dark Ages*" or the *Gothic Period*. These years were actually a time of the coalescing of societal forces that serve as the basis of our understanding of music, art, architecture, literature, and politics. The Church developed its *liturgy* and codified the music it used. Visual art moved toward expressions of realism—the attempt to depict subjects as they appear objectively, without interpretation.

Literature developed and language was becoming standardized in many countries. Kings and noblemen began sharing power with the authorities of the Church. Politics was in a nascent stage with the advent of barons of commerce who, with their control of resources and trade, formed guilds. All of these developments had consequences for the development of music.

Gregorian Chant and the Liturgy

As the Church spread over the continent of Europe the basic shape of its worship services formed. In the monasteries that were founded, the monks and nuns lived their lives around a daily rendering of worship in the church. There were, and are still, eight of these worship services called *offices*, and a ninth chief service called the **Mass**. All services had as their basis readings from the Bible, weekly recitation of the Psalms, and regular prayers. Over time these texts were sung, rather than simply recited. This singing was most likely an outgrowth of the society in which early Christians found themselves, with influences from Jewish, Hebrew, and Middle Eastern cultures. Scholars debate how the melodies for these texts, referred to as *Gregorian chant, plainsong,* or *plainchant,* came into being. All three of these terms refer to the same thing. They are called plain because their chief characteristic is a one-line melody, called ***monophony***, described by the term ***monophonic***. Many hundreds of these melodies developed by the middle of the sixth century. They can be classified as ***sacred*** as opposed to ***secular***.

Figure 2.3 Sadler, Joseph Ignatz. *Saint Gregory the Great*, eighteenth century. In this fresco from a church in the Czech Republic, Pope Saint Gregory the Great is shown receiving inspiration from a dove, the representation of the Holy Spirit of the Christian church. This is an inspiring if apocryphal story.

Pope Gregory the Great (who held papacy from 590 to 604 CE) began the process of collecting and codifying these chants in order to bring stability to what was allowed in the services; thus they acquired the name Gregorian. Many plainchants in the same style came into use after the time of St. Gregory. The schola cantorum that Gregory founded trained singers in this body of chant and sent them to teach it in disparate lands. Later, Pope Stephen II and French kings Pepin the Short and Charlemagne also encouraged the spreading of these chants to a much wider area, at some times by force.

Monophony in the chant was aided by other characteristics, including free flow of the melody with no perceivable rhythm. Cadences, musical sequences that provide resolution to phrases, occurred at advantageous points in the text to add an understanding of what was being sung; introductory and ending notes provided starting and ending points. Chanting, i.e. the singing of words, provides a heightened sense of the text's importance, and an understanding that is not as readily available when speaking the text. Church leaders deemed it appropriate to the intent of the worship services to have the texts, which were entirely in Latin, sung and not merely spoken.

An example of one of the most famous of these chants is called "Dies Irae", or "Day of Wrath".

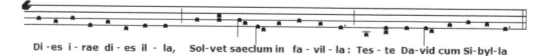
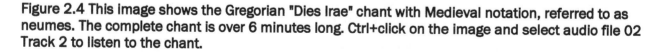

Figure 2.4 This image shows the Gregorian "Dies Irae" chant with Medieval notation, referred to as neumes. The complete chant is over 6 minutes long. Ctrl+click on the image and select audio file 02 Track 2 to listen to the chant.

Di - es i - rae, di - es il - la,   Sol - vet__ sae__- clum__ in fa - vil - la: Tes - te__ Da - vid__ cum Sy - bil - la.

Figure 2.5 This image shows the Gregorian Chant "Dies Irae" in modern notation. .Ctrl+click on the image and select audio file 02 Track 2 to listen to the chant.

In listening to the chant, it helps to remove any distractions that modern life has given us; chants were sung in formal worship with nothing else going on, except the actions of the clergy in the services. "Dies Irae" is a text that was sung during a special version of the *Mass* called a Requiem Mass, or Mass of the Dead. It depicts what was extant in theology of the time: the day of wrath and mourning when the soul is judged. The chant reveals the typical progression of plainchant, with nuanced melodic contours inspired by the text itself. There is no foot-tapping rhythm. Each phrase of text is marked by longer notes, starting and ending as if from the ether. This chant will reappear several hundreds of years later when it is used by Hector Berlioz in his *Symphonie Fantastique* in the early nineteenth century.

By the time Gregory was working, ca. 600 CE, many chants were in use and a system of notation had developed for accurate learning and rendition. Shown above are "Dies Irae" two examples of the same music; the first is the music as it appeared in the Middle Ages, the second is a modern notation.

As you listen notice the main characteristics of the music: 1. there is no strict rhythm—the music flows in a gentle manner with no beat; 2. the words are set almost always one syllable to a note but some syllables have more than a few notes, called *melisma*; 3. there is no accompaniment or other voice—this is strictly a one-line melodic progression of notes referred to earlier called *monophony*.

Secular Music

Music outside of churches in the Middle Ages was not written down. Music in societies where the majority of the population was non-literate was passed down orally, and this music has been almost entirely lost. Known to us are wandering *minstrels* who were the professional musicians of their day. They would provide music for tournaments, feasts, weddings, hunts, and almost any gathering of the day. Minstrels performed plays, and they would also carry with them news of surrounding areas. Often they would be employed by lords of the manors that made up medieval society. *Troubadours* (feminine *trobairitz*) were active in the south of France, *trouviers* in the north. In German lands the same type of musicians were referred to as *minnesingers*.

Figure 2.6 These two troubadours play stringed instruments, one strummed and one bowed; Figure 2.7 The troubadour calling is alive in modern times.

Texts of these musicians often revolved around human love, especially unrequited love. The exploits of knights, the virtues of the ruling class, and the glories of nature were among other themes. The musicians most often composed their own poetry.

These songs were accompanied by instruments such as the vielle, the hurdy-gurdy (for the remainder of the links in this section, click the image on the web page to hear an example), and the psaltery.

**Figure 2.8 This is a modern reproduction of a Medieval fiddle or vielle which is played with a bow.
Figure 2.9 This woman is playing a psaltery shown held in her lap and bowed.**

Rhythm instruments such as the ***side drum*** and the ***tabor*** (usually played by one person with the ***pipe***) provided rhythmic underpinnings. Other Medieval instruments include the ***recorder*** and ***transverse flute***, the ***shawm***, the ***bladder pipe***, the ***serpent***, and the ***lizard***.

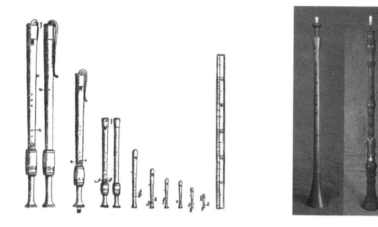

Figure 2.10 This image shows several sizes of the Renaissance recorder. Figure 2.11 From left to right: shawm, Baroque oboe, modern oboe.

The Beginnings of Polyphony

From the single-line chanting of the monks and nuns, music gradually came to be

polyphonic, meaning more than one line of music playing simultaneously. The simplest form

of adding another voice is to use a device called a **drone**. This is a note or notes that are

held while the melody plays. This musical arrangement is found in many European and Asian

cultures in their folk music, suggesting a long history. Our example of "Columba Aspexit"

("The dove peered in"—for interested students, a translation of the lyrics can be accessed at

the Columbia History of Music website) composed by Hildegard of Bingen shows the

amazing complexity that the vocal lines achieve while still relating to the background drone.

Another device used in oral traditions in the Church was **organum**. Organum is the

singing of chant with another voice singing exactly the same chant only at differing intervals

(an interval being the difference in pitch between two notes). The second voice follows the

chant in exact parallel motion. In the ninth century the **fifth** (notes at the interval of five

steps) was considered a perfect interval, pleasing and harmonious. Therefore the movement

of the two voices, while it may sound dry and uninteresting to the modern ear, was pleasing

and reassuring to medieval listeners.

Music moving along in parallel fifths was not the only way organum was practiced. In order to avoid certain intervals while the chant progressed, the singers of the accompanying voice had to alter certain notes, move in contrary motion, or stay on the same note until the chant moved past the note that would have created a forbidden interval. For example, the tritone (an interval of two notes with six half steps or semitones between them) was considered an unstable, dangerous interval. It was said to personify the devil and was avoided in sacred music—and in some cases specifically forbidden under Canon law. Changing the chant to avoid certain intervals such as the tritone provided the beginning of *oblique* and *contrary* motion. This development led the way to thinking of music as a combination of voices rather than a single line. *Polyphony* can be said to have arisen from this practice.

Figure 2.12 This music shows oblique motion where one voice remains on the same note.

Figure 2.13 This music shows the two voices moving in opposite direction called contrary motion.

How did this come about? It is good to place ourselves in the context of plainchant music creation in order to understand the genesis. As stated earlier, debate continues over exactly when these practices began, but they most likely have their roots in the Byzantine, Hebrew, and Jewish chants in which Christianity itself has its roots. Gregory's attempt to codify and restrict music in the Church was circumvented by the process of singing dozens

of chants and lengthy texts nine times a day, 365 days a year. The chants were passed

down orally. New monks and nuns would learn the chanting by rehearsing and singing the

nine services. Chants were sung from memory. As the Mass was the chief service of the

church, it was performed with increasing ritual, ornamentation, and pageantry. Music also

became more complex. The addition of a second voice singing at the fifth (or fourth) would

have enriched the resonance in the large acoustic spaces of the monasteries and

cathedrals that began construction in the Medieval era. The addition of polyphony took

place gradually over long periods of time so that each succeeding generation would accept

and enlarge upon concepts they automatically learned when entering into a religious order.

From the auspicious beginnings of organum (parallel, oblique, and contrary motion of

the chants with one added voice), new styles developed. One of the most important places

of further development came in Paris at Notre Dame Cathedral. Reflecting the magnificence

of the building, the rich stained glass windows, and the ornate style of decorative stone, the

music developed in proportion and complexity. Two significant practitioners emerged from

this place and time: **_Leoninus_** (or Leonin, active ca.

1150-1201) and **_Perotinus_** (or Perotin, active late

twelfth and early thirteenth centuries).

These two musicians were part of a tradition of

musical practice that might be called "collective

composition." This means that the musical

performance of orally transmitted chant

Figure 2.14 Notre Dame Cathedral in Paris is shown from across the Seine river.

acquired variations, with each musician writing down their own musical preferences. This style of music has as its basis the chants of the Church. The chant was sung to long, sustained pitches while another melody was sung above it. The chant melody, the ***tenor***, becomes like a drone in this music because of the length of each note. The melody which flows along on top of each note of the tenor, called the ***duplum***, had many notes to each note of the tenor. Much subtlety of rhythm and the beginnings of form are contained in these versions of the chants. Leoninus is credited with first composing organa (plural of organum) that had more than a few notes in the duplum to each note of the chant. This enrichment of the chant itself may have been inspired by the magnificence of Notre Dame Cathedral, and provided further enrichment of the most important liturgy of the church, the Mass.

Perotinus extended and developed even further the advances notated by Leoninus. Above the chant, he added more than a single voice. He composed chant with one, two, and three voices accompanying it. Chant with one voice added is called ***organum duplum***, with two voices added, organum triplum (***triplum*** for short), and with three voices added, ***quadruplum***. Perotinus' music achieved a complexity of texture, rhythm, and harmonic implication that resonated throughout the known Christian world. Our example is two separate settings of the opening of the chant "Viderunt Omnes." The first setting, sung by the Choir of the Monks of the Benedictine Abbey of St. Martin, Beuron is monophonic—a single line, sung with all voices on the same note. The second setting is polyphonic, with four different voices performing different lines simultaneously (ctrl+click on the image to listen to this example).

Figure 2.15 Perotinus, "Viderunt Omnes," ca. 1200. This image shows the polyphonic chant, with four melodic lines singing simultaneously. The large "V" is from the first word, "Viderunt". Ctrl+click the image to hear an example of this chant.

The chanters sing an opening pitch together. Listen to how the lowest part keeps singing as the upper parts take a breath and begin long melismas above the drone-like note of the lower part (as a reminder, melismas are simply multiple notes sung to one syllable of text). The lower part is actually singing the chant melody, but now in lengthy, drawn-out notes. The flexibility of rhythms and the interplay of the upper voices, imitating each other and crossing lines, influenced music-making in the wider culture.

Motet

In addition to setting liturgical texts with the added voices of duplum, triplum, and quadruplum, musicians at this time began using other Latin texts, some newly written, with the added vocal parts. This resulted in a new way of thinking about what type of texts would be used with the new musical style. Chant was the official music of the Church, and sacred composers were seeking new ways of expressing the developments of society at the time. They were also aware that the Church authorities were using different tactics to mark the Mass as the most significant service of the church. New architectural grandeur, highly stylized clerical attire, ornate decorations of wood and stone, and the growing complexity of chant practices all reflected the significance of the Mass. While retaining the official chant, composers were responding to a concomitant blend of richness and complexity all around them.

The addition of voices to a chant—and the idea of setting new words to those voices—resulted in the ***motet***. The words used were fit for various occasions: regular services of the church, special days such as Christmas and Easter, and special local circumstances, such as the founding anniversary of a church or the crowning of a monarch. Eventually, other subjects were used for the accompanying voices, including love poems. The liturgical chants on which they were layered also came to be optional, with the composer either writing a new chant or adapting an existing one rhythmically.

Mention must be made here of a special type of polyphonic work called the ***round***. "Sumer Is Icumen In" is a round that was written sometime after 1250 by an anonymous composer. It is for four voices singing one after the other in continuous fashion, with two more voices in the background repeating "sing cuckoo" repeatedly. The text praises the coming of summer. The tone is bright and happy. The two background voices are called the *pes*, Latin for "foot".

Figure 2.16 "Sumer Is Icumen In", a 13th century round, is shown in modern notation. The bottom two lines, Pes I and II, are sung as background. New voices enter from the beginning at +. Ctrl+click on image to listen to an example.

As the 1300s began, polyphony became increasingly complex. Rhythm became a predominant feature of a new style of composing called *Ars Nova*. This "new art" was characterized by greater rhythmic variety, melodies that were longer and more shapely, and increasing independence of individual lines of music.

Ways of writing music developed that showed division of longer notes into shorter values (breve, to semibreve, to its smallest division, the minim). The use of a device called *isorhythm* ("equal rhythm") came into more complex practice with the motets of Philippe de Vitry (1291-1361). This extended practices found at Notre Dame and in earlier motets, increasing the rhythmic complexity and extending the melodic pattern of lines. For an example of isorhythm's use, listen to Vitry's "Vos Qui Admiramini/Gratissima Virginis/Gaude Gloriosa".

While listening to the interweaving melodies, notice recurring rhythmic patterns occurring within longer melodic segments. These may or may not coincide, sometimes beginning together, sometimes overlapping, and not always ending together. Also notice that the melodic range—the distance between the melody's lowest and highest notes—is wider than previously encountered in the earlier Medieval period (compare the relative closeness of the intervals of Perotinus' "Viderunt Omnes" or the stepwise motion of the "Dies Irae" chant). The lower two voices have longer rhythmic units of their own and provide a sonic backdrop to the upper parts.

Listening Objectives

Listening objectives during this unit are to:

1. Listen for fluidity in the melody of Gregorian chant. Listen for the lack of rhythmic beat.

2. Listen to early examples of polyphony including:

   a) instrumental drone with human voices;

   b) human voices singing in parallel fifths no instruments; and

   c) human voices singing long drone notes (which are notes of the chant) while other human voices sing in and around each other along with the drone notes.

3. Listen for differences in energy and mood between sacred and secular music.

4. Listen for how instruments are used both in conjunction with human voices and independently.

Key Music Terms

Instrumentation The Renaissance (ca. 1400-1600) was a time of developing human musical potential. The human voice was considered the prime musical instrument, and all other instruments strove to emulate its expressive capability. Humans have four general ranges of singing: the higher soprano and lower alto for women, and the higher tenor and lower bass for men. Instruments developed in ways that corresponded to these designations. These are called families of instruments, such as the viol family. Keyboard instruments also developed highs and lows by simply extending the keyboard; the harpsichord and organ became the principal Renaissance keyboard instruments.

Instruments are classified by how they are played. Strings are bowed and plucked, woodwinds are blown with reeds and varying mouthpieces to produce sound, and brass instruments are blown with lips against a rounded mouthpiece. In this period, designations were rarely given for the musical part that would be played by a specific instrument. Can you name instruments from each of these classes from the Renaissance?

Timbre or *Tone Quality* The sound of Renaissance instruments is "thin" to our ears. Details of design and materials of construction gave limited results. The preferred timbre of human voices can only be guessed at because there are no recordings, methods of vocal production were different, and the sound of vowels and other elements of local languages for which music was written are unknown. "Haut" and "bois" were terms used for instruments suited for outdoors (haut/high) and for indoors (bois/low). In this case, high and low refer to the strength of the tone.

Texture Textures varied from solo instruments such as the lute, harpsichord, and organ, to massed choirs with brass and other instrumental accompaniment. During the Renaissance, accompaniment referred to doubling the human voices with the instruments, not playing an independent instrumental accompaniment. Texture in the Renaissance had a solemn, other-worldly quality, especially in sacred music. Secular music generally sounds thin, as opposed to resonant, and does not carry far.

Harmony During the Renaissance, harmony moved in blockish groups. Individual lines of music moved with each other to produce modal effects. Not until the Baroque Era did each line of music became equally important, relating to the other lines of music in rhythmic collusion toward tighter harmonic schemes. All modes were still used in the Renaissance. These gradually gave way to only two modes, major and minor, by the end of the Baroque Era.

 Tempo Tempos (tempi) in the years preceding the Baroque Era were generally slower. Sixteenth notes were not unheard of, especially for solo lute and keyboard pieces, but were unusual for chorus and ensemble writing.

 Dynamics Dynamics were generally not designated during the Renaissance. Because music written at this time was not created for wide dissemination, the composer and those performing it would have known what they preferred in terms of dynamics and thus they were not recorded.

 Form Forms were the province of both sacred and secular music in the Renaissance. Popular musicians, called troubadors, trouviers, and minnesingers among others, sang popular songs such as the villancico (a song style used in the Iberian peninsula) and frottola (a popular Italian secular song), with the most enduring of all being the Italian madrigal. Sacred music included forms such as the motet and the sections of the Mass (*kyrie, gloria, sanctus, credo,* and *agnus dei*), and forms that grew out of other parts of the divine service.

The Renaissance

The Renaissance is a designation that historians have used to cover the period of roughly 1400 to 1600, although the exact dates have been debated. Every historical period must be seen in the light of ongoing developments in all aspects of society; the Renaissance is no exception. While composers, performers, theorists, makers of musical instruments, sculptors, painters, writers of all types, philosophers, scientists, and merchants were all making advances, they were not doing so in sudden, entirely new ways. "Renaissance" is a term meaning "rebirth," which implies that things were born anew, with no regard to what had come before. In the case of the Renaissance, this not precisely accurate. The rebirth that is suggested is the rediscovery of Greek and Roman civilization—their treatises and philosophies, their ways of governing. In actuality, leading figures of the time took ideas from the Greek and Roman civilizations and applied them to contemporary currents of thought and practice. Renaissance people had no desire to rid themselves of their religion. They rather had the desire to elevate their faith in reason and in the abilities of humans alongside their faith in the divine.

The art of music was influenced by many historical and artistic advances during this period, including the fall of Constantinople in 1453, the invention of printing and paper around the year 1440, Michelangelo's way of depicting the human form as in his statue of David and in his painting of the Sistine Chapel ceiling, and the writings of Michel de Montaigne, Miguel de Cervantes, and Dante Alighieri. In music, the practices of old continued and were updated, while international styles were being cross-bred by musicians travelling and mixing local practices. Late in the fifteenth century two characteristics of music emerged and came to predominate. *Imitative counterpoint* (when two voices repeat a specific melodic element) and *homophony* (when two or more parts move in the same rhythm and in harmony) are found in much music composed and performed in the Renaissance.

Printed music was developed by 1501 and made dissemination and availability much wider. Styles were no longer confined to one particular place with little chance of reaching a wider populace. The increasing relative wealth of the average person now allowed for access to printed scores, instruments on which to play those scores, and the time to enjoy them.

Upheavals in the Church affected music in diverse ways. The Protestant Reformation began when Martin Luther nailed his Ninety-Five Theses on the door of the Castle Church in Wittenberg in the year 1517. As other countries saw reactions against the authority and profligacy of the Catholic Church, the Church launched its own counteroffensive in what is called the ***Counter Reformation***. The Council of Trent was held intermittently for a very long period, from 1545-63. Discussion concerning the purification of music that was allowed in church services took place during this Council. There was talk of purging the services of any polyphonic music, primarily because the words had become difficult to hear. A legend arose surrounding an acknowledged master of ***high Renaissance polyphony***, Giovanni Pierluigi da Palestrina (1525/1526-94). According to the legend, Palestrina wrote the "Missa Papae Marcelli" ("Pope Marcellus Mass") to argue for keeping polyphony in the Church.

Palestrina was in service to church music almost his entire life, spending over forty years in churches in Rome. He became renowned especially for his Masses and motets. For an example, listen to a section from the legendary "Mass for Pope Marcellus."

The "Gloria" is one of the five sections of the Mass. In this music, one can hear a many-layered texture. Beginning with jubilation, the voices sing in rhythmic equality. The mood is at times solemn, and the effect is serene. The tone is one of humility yet grandeur, a fascinating combination of the attitude that the worshiper was encouraged to have when approaching the divine in liturgy. The listener senses the importance of the words, yet is never bogged down. There is regular pulse, yet the feeling of meter is just out of reach. The music flows in stepwise fashion for the most part. There are regular cadences that conform to the phrases of the text.

Palestrina holds a distinct place in sacred music of the Renaissance, but what of the music-making at court and in the countryside? Two main developments during the Renaissance are the *madrigal* and *secular song*.

Printing music made written music less expensive, as less labor was involved. Formerly the province of rich households, the nobility, and those working with the resources of the Church, printed music became in demand from humbler households during the sixteenth century. Types of popular song became widespread in composition and use—in Spain, the *villancico*, in Italy, the *frottola*, and in other styles in other countries. Most enduring of all popular music at this time, however, is the Italian madrigal. All popular music sought to express varieties of emotion, imagery, and specific themes, and to experiment with *declamation,* expressing character and drama.

The Italian madrigal reigned supreme in its achievements in these areas. Poetry of various types was set to *through-composed* music. Through-composed refers to a style of composition where new music is used for each line of poetry. In the first half of the 1500s, most madrigals were composed for four voices; later five became the norm, with six not unheard of. Composers sought to express the themes of the poems, individual ideas of each line, and even single words. While "voices" here can mean human singers, using instruments on the vocal parts was standard practice, especially if a human to sing the voice part was missing.

One example of the spread of the Italian madrigal style is by Bavarian Orlande de Lassus. Entitled "Eco," it is a light-hearted take on words that tell of an echo. One can readily hear the effects of the word painting. This is but one of an infinite variety of examples of how madrigals are expressive, contrasting, and imitative, conveying intensity of feeling in an open, robust way.

Italian madrigals foremost, with French *chansons* and German *Lieder* (both terms mean "song" in those languages), and English madrigals, set the stage for the birth of ***opera***. Techniques found in madrigals, chansons, and lieder of the time were also found in music used in the presentation of plays. Discussion of these will continue in Chapter 3. Since the majority of this chapter has concerned music for voices, discussion turns now to the instrumental music that preceded the full flowering of the Baroque orchestra.

Renaissance musicians played a variety of instruments. Modern musicians typically specialize in one instrument and possibly closely related ones as well, but it was expected of a musician in this time to be proficient at more than a few. These can be broadly classified into *haut* (high) and *bas* (low) instruments—that is, loud and soft. *Haut* instruments would be suitable for playing outdoors, *bas* for indoors. Until the end of the sixteenth century, composers did not specify which instruments to use. There were varieties of ensembles, depending upon what was available or working at any given point. Wind instruments include the recorder, transverse flute, shawm, cornett, and trumpet. The ***sackbut*** (precursor to the trombone) and the ***crumhorn*** (double reed, but still a *haut* instrument) were additions of the Renaissance. To add percussive effects, the tabor, side drum, kettledrums, cymbals, triangles, and bells were played, though parts for these were not written. (See the discussion of these instruments with examples above.)

The *lute* gained particular favor, as the modern guitar is favored today. It was a five-stringed instrument with a pear shape. Leather straps around the neck to tell the player where to place his or her fingers. Great varieties of effect could be produced, with lutenists playing solo, accompanying singing, and playing in groups.

Among the string group of instruments is the *viol,* or ***viol da gamba***. This is a bowed instrument which is the precursor to the modern violin. The **viol** family contains instruments in every range, from soprano as the highest to bass as the lowest. A group of viols playing together was referred to as a consort of viols. The **violin** was present at this time as a three-stringed instrument used to accompany dancing, tuned in intervals of fifths rather than the fourths of the viol.

Keyboard instruments included the ***pipe organ***, which was growing in size and complexity. From the portative (small organ that can be carried) and positive organs (larger version of the portative and on wheels) of the Middle Ages came fixed instruments much larger and capable of grander and more varied sound. Germans later added pedals to extend the range and power of the instrument. The **clavichord** is a small household keyboard instrument in which keys are connected to brass nubs which strike the string, causing it to vibrate. The *harpsichord* also has keys, but these are connected to a quill which plucks the string. The harpsichord has a much bolder sound and grew to have two and even three keyboards. It became one of the two most important keyboard instruments in music of the Baroque period, the other being the organ.

What were these instruments playing? As noted, they were added to vocal music to round out and fill in the sound. In time they acquired independent music of their own, with no relation to or reliance upon a composition intended for vocal production. It is important to note that instrumental music was increasingly viewed as independent from vocal music.

While some instrumental music was arranged from pre-existing vocal music, other forms of instrumental music include settings of existing melodies such as chorale melodies of the churches, songs, and dance music. The first instrumental works that had no connection to earlier vocal music appeared at this time. These instrumental works established in the Renaissance include the *prelude, fantasia, toccata, ricercar, canzona, sonata,* and *variation. Variation* form was invented in the sixteenth century. It reflected a practice in existence where the musician would vary the music that was presented to him or her in written form. A basic theme could be enhanced by changing the harmony, adding upper or lower notes, using flourishes and runs, and including other devices that inspired the composer or performer.

Venice now emerges as a principal area of for the arts. Venice was a major urban center in the sixteenth century – a conflux of trade routes, international society, and wealthy patronage. All aspects of society were affected by the immense wealth that predominated. Churches were ornate; the best sculptors, painters, and architects abounded, and musicians were no less affected. St. Mark's Basilica is a prime example of these displays of artistic endeavor.

Figure 2.17 St. Mark's Basilica, Venice. This is the view from the museum towards the altar.

Lavishly ornate, with an altar of gold, huge Byzantine domes, and decoration of every known variety and ornament, St. Mark's also boasted numerous balconies and spacious acoustics. Performance in this place attained spectacular effects in the music of *Giovanni Gabrieli* (ca. 1555-1612). For example, <u>Jubilate Deo</u> (Rejoice in the Lord), composed for eight voices, shows several techniques that Gabrieli brought to perfection:

- the use of two vocal choirs of four voices each

- alternating effects of the two choirs

- high voices juxtaposed by low voices

- imitation throughout

- interspersed sections of full choral texture

On a recording there is no way to capture the complete effect of two choirs, sitting across from each other in the vast space of St. Mark's, singing into the space underneath the resonant main dome of the church. These techniques are not unique to Gabrieli, but he brought them to high achievement.

The Renaissance was a period of re-birthing ancient philosophies (and ancient music) into current life and practices, and of enhancing faith in God and the authority of the Church with faith in human reason and capability. From the organum of Leoninus and Perotinus came the multi-voiced motet and complete settings for the Mass. From the practices of troubadours, trouveres, and minnesingers came the Italian madrigal. From accompanying voices and filling in parts in vocal compositions came the independence of instrumental forms. The stage was now set for the birth of opera, the standardization of the Baroque orchestra, the rewriting of rules of composition to reflect major and minor tonality rather than use of modes, and the creation of forms out of older models.

Closing

In this chapter we have seen Western Art Music progress in two distinct areas: sacred and secular. Very broadly speaking, during this period music moved from one-voice monophony to many-voiced polyphony. Monophony began moving toward polyphony with the use of drones and organum. Instituting the use of parallel fifths rather than simply single-line chanting started the process of independent voices moving away from the original monophonic chants. Later all voices moved independently, with none being based on a chant. At first only sacred texts were used for all vocal music; eventually texts came to reflect other themes. This gave rise to new forms of music including the motet. In secular music, instruments were used merely to double voice parts at first, and in time, music was written for instruments alone. The time period of these developments is approximately 1400-1600, and the areas involved are principally in what is referred to in the modern-day as Europe.

The Transformative Power of Music

This week, watch the video "The Transformative Power of Music," part of the Annenberg Learner video series we will be viewing throughout the text.

Guiding Questions:

Identify, describe, and provide examples of various types of early music.

1. How did music move from one-line monophony to many-voiced polyphony?

2. How did instruments come to be independent of vocal music?

3. What societal developments influenced the composing and writing down of music?

4. What were the texts used for these independent voices?

5. What forms developed that set the stage for the birth of opera, oratorio, and independent musical forms of the Baroque period?

Self-Check Exercises

Complete the following self-check exercises to verify your mastery of key music terms presented in this chapter.

1. **What is one-line (one-voice) music called?**
   a. Monophony
   b. Heterophony
   c. Polyphony
   d. Stereophony

2. **What cathedral and what 2 composers working there are associated with major progress toward many-voiced music?**
   a. Chartres - Leonin/Perotin
   b. Bordeaux - Hildegard/Bernart de Ventadorn
   c. Notre Dame - Leonin/Perotin
   d. Orleans - Adam de la Halle/Philippe de Vitry

3. **How were instruments used in vocal music from the Renaissance and earlier?**
   a. They filled in for missing human voices.
   b. They played vocal music when there were no human voices.
   c. They played when all human voices were present.
   d. All of the above.

4. **Of the following, which contain sacred and secular forms of music from this time?**
   a. Sonata, Symphony, Gregorian Chant, Lieder
   b. Gregorian Chant, Chanson, Mass, Organum, Madrigal, Round
   c. Concerto, Suite, Organum, Madrigal
   d. Variations, Rondo, Mass, Frottola

If you would like additional information about these terms, please review before proceeding.

After you have read the questions above, check your answers at the bottom of this page.

Self-check quiz answers:
1. a. 2. c. 3. d. 4. b.

Works Consulted

Ball, David. *Troubadour. Wikimedia Commons*. Wikipedia Foundation, 28 Feb. 2007. Web. 15 Feb. 2012. <http://commons.wikimedia.org/wiki/File:Troubadour-2003.jpg>.

Byrd, William, composer. "William Byrd - Fantasia #2 - Viol Consort." YouTube, 2 Sep. 2008. Web. 18 Feb. 2012. <http://youtu.be/w-qS7ms5apQ>.

Construction tools sign, used with permission from Microsoft. "Images." *Office*. Web. 4 Sept. 2012. <http://office.microsoft.com/en-us/images/results.aspx?ex=2&qu=tools#ai:MC900432556|mt:0|>.

Couperin, François, composer. "Harpsichord - Bridget Cunningham plays Les Baricades MisterieusesCouperin." Perf. Bridget Cunningham. YouTube, 14 Feb. 2009. Web. 28 July 2012. <http://youtu.be/Z-LV4_mem6Q>.

De Lassus, Orlande, composer. "Orlando di Lasso – Eco." Perf. Czech Philharmonic Orchestra Choir. YouTube, 22 March 2010. Web. 18 Feb. 2012. <http://youtu.be/-foB75466zY>.

De Vitry, Philippe, composer. "Medieval music - Vos qui admiramini by Philippe de Vitry." Perf. Lumina Vocal Ensemble. YouTube, 14 May 2011. Web. 17 Feb. 2012. <http://youtu.be/4Qatw5B3vc4>.

Dies Irae. 13th C. Benedikt Emmanuel Unger. *Wikimedia Commons*. Wikipedia Foundation, 25 June 2006. Web. 7 Aug. 2012. <http://commons.wikimedia.org/wiki/File:Dies_irae.gif>.

Dies Irae. 13th C. Pabix. *Wikimedia Commons*. Wikipedia Foundation, 2 Dec. 2007. Web. 26 July 2012. <http://commons.wikimedia.org/wiki/File:Dies_Irae.svg>.

Gabrieli, Giovanni, composer. "Giovanni Gabrieli - Jubilate Deo. Perf. Dresdner Kreuzchor. YouTube, 15 April 2009. Web. 18 Feb. 2012. <http://youtu.be/NCRm2t2tpB0>.

Gregorian Chant Mass. Internet Archive, 10 March 2001. Web. 26 July 2012. <http://archive.org/details/GregorianChantMass>.

Hall, Barry, perf. *Medieval Fiddle (Vielle) Music*. YouTube, 5 Oct. 2008. Web. 15 Feb. 2012. <http://youtu.be/jPKhBkLgFLk>.

Hildegard von Bingen, composer. *Columba Aspexit*. Perf. Gothic Voices. Last.fm., 4 July 2012. Web. 28 July 2012. <http://www.last.fm/music/Hildegard+von+Bingen/_/Columba+Aspexit>.

Hildegard von Bingen. *Text and Translation of Plainchant Sequence Columba Aspexit by Hildegard von Bingen*. New York University School of Continuing and Professional Studies. N.d., Web. 7 Aug. 2012. <http://www.kitbraz.com/tchr/hist/med/hildegardtxt.columba.html>.

Iowa State University Musica Antiqua. *Pipe and Tabor*. Iowa State University. N.d., Web. 27 July 2012. <http://www.music.iastate.edu/antiqua/pipetabr.htm>.

—. *The Bladder Pipe*. Iowa State University. N.d., Web. 28 July 2012. <http://www.music.iastate.edu/antiqua/bladpipe.htm>.

—. *The Hurdy-Gurdy*. Iowa State University. N.d., Web. 27 July 2012. <http://www.music.iastate.edu/antiqua/hurdy.htm>.

—. *The Lizard*. Iowa State University. N.d., Web. 28 July 2012. <http://www.music.iastate.edu/antiqua/lizard.htm>.

—. *The Lute*. Iowa State University, N.d. Web. 28 July 2012. <http://www.music.iastate.edu/antiqua/lute.htm>.

—. *The Psaltery*. Iowa State University. N.d., Web. 27 July 2012. <http://www.music.iastate.edu/antiqua/psaltery.htm>.

—. *The Recorder*. Iowa State University. N.d., Web. 27 July 2012. <http://www.music.iastate.edu/antiqua/r_record.htm>.

—. *The Renaissance Shawm*. Iowa State University. N.d., Web. 8 Aug. 2012. <http://www.music.iastate.edu/antiqua/renshawm.htm>.

—. *The Serpent*. Iowa State University. N.d., Web. 28 July 2012. <http://www.music.iastate.edu/antiqua/serpent.htm>.

—. *The Transverse Flute*. Iowa State University. N.d., Web. 16 Feb. 2012. <http://www.music.iastate.edu/antiqua/tr_flute.htm>.

Memoryboy. *Contrary Motion*. *Wikimedia Commons*. Wikipedia Foundation, 9 June 2008. Web. 16 Feb. 2012. <http://commons.wikimedia.org/wiki/File:ContraryMotion.png>.

—. *Oblique*. *Wikimedia Commons*. Wikipedia Foundation, 9 June 2008. Web. 16 Feb. 2012. <http://commons.wikimedia.org/wiki/File:Oblique.png>.

Merulo, Claudio, composer. "Claudio Merulo (1533-1604) - Toccata quarta del sesto tono (M. Raschietti - Organ)." Perf. M. Raschietti. YouTube, 10 Nov. 2009. Web. 9 Aug. 2012. <http://youtu.be/VUR6kW-GfhO>.

"mode". *Encyclopædia Britannica*. *Encyclopædia Britannica Online*. Encyclopædia Britannica Inc., 2012. Web. 12 Feb. 2012 <http://www.britannica.com/EBchecked/topic/386980/mode>.

Morn. *St. Mark's Basilica, View from the museum balcony*. *Wikimedia Commons*. Wikipedia Foundation, 17 May 2011. Web. 28 July 2012. <http://commons.wikimedia.org/wiki/File:St._Mark%27s_Basilica,_View_from_the_museum_balcony.jpg>.

Neitram. *Streichpsalter-Spielerin*. *Wikimedia Commons*. Wikipedia Foundation, 4 Aug. 2007. Web. 27 July 2012. <http://commons.wikimedia.org/wiki/File:Streichpsalter-spielerin.jpg>.

OboeCrack. *Three double reed instruments. Wikimedia Commons.* Wikipedia Foundation, 11 Sept. 2008. Web. 28 July 2012. <http://commons.wikimedia.org/wiki/File:Cu_oboe.jpg>.

Da Palestrina, Giovanni Pierluigi, composer. "Gloria - Missa Papae Marcelli - Palestrina." Perf. Oxford Camerata. YouTube, 13 Jan. 2012. Web. 10 Apr.. 2014. <http://youtu.be/5k3bfqQ1SpU>.

Pérotin, composer. "Pérotin – Viderunt Omnes, Sheet Music + Audio." Perf. The Hilliard Ensemble. YouTube, 19 Aug. 2010. Web. 16 Feb. 2012. <http://youtu.be/aySwfcRaOZM>.

—. *Viderunt Omnes.* Circa 1200 CE. Manuscript. Bibliotheca Mediceo Laurenziana. *Wikimedia Commons.* Wikipedia Foundation,1 Jan. 2010. Web. 8 Aug. 2012. <http://commons.wikimedia.org/wiki/File:P%C3%A9rotin_-_Viderunt_omnes.jpg>.

Phintias . *Music Lesson.* 510 BCE. Bibi Saint-Pol. *Wikimedia Commons.* Wikipedia Foundation,10 Sep. 2007. Web. 6 Aug. 2012. <http://commons.wikimedia.org/wiki/File:Music_lesson_Staatliche_Antikensammlungen_2421.jpg>.

Pollini. *Trovadores. Wikimedia Commons.* Wikipedia Foundation, 6 Sep. 2008. Web. 26 July 2012. <http://commons.wikimedia.org/wiki/File:Trovadores.png>.

Praetorius, Michael. *Renaissance recorder flutes.* 3 Sept. 2005. *Wikimedia Commons.* Wikipedia Foundation, 5 March 2012. Web. 7/29/12. <http://commons.wikimedia.org/wiki/File:Barocke_Blockfl%C3%B6ten.png>.

Sadler, Joseph Ignatz. *Saint Gregory the Great.* 18th C. David Hrabálek. *Wikimedia Commons.* Wikipedia Foundation, 19 Aug. 2008. Web. 10 Feb. 2012. <http://commons.wikimedia.org/wiki/File:Kostel_Nejsv%C4%9Bt%C4%9Bj%C5%A1%C3%AD_Trojice_(Fulnek)_%E2%80%93_frs-009.jpg>.

Song of Seikilos. Perf. Atrium Musicae de Madrid. YouTube. 6 Sep. 2008. Web. 15 Feb. 2012. <http://youtu.be/9RjBePQV4xE>.

Sumer Is Icumen In. Blahedo. *Wikimedia Commons.* Wikipedia Foundation, 21 Dec. 2005. Web. 16 Feb. 2012. <http://commons.wikimedia.org/wiki/File:Sumer_is_icumen_in.png>.

"Sumer Is Icumen In." Perf. The Hilliard Ensemble. YouTube, 18 Apr. 2011. Web. 10 Apr. 2014. <http://youtu.be/BVdA9t-AOfU>.

Verdi, José. *Medieval Fiddle or Vielle. Wikimedia Commons.* Wikipedia Foundation, 2 Dec. 2011. Web. 27 July 2012. <http://commons.wikimedia.org/wiki/File:Fidulaconfrascos.JPG>.

"Viderunt Omnes (Christmas, Gradual)." Perf. Choir of the Monks of the Benedictine Abbey of St. Martin, Beuron. Youtube, 10 April 2011. Web. 28 July 2012. <http://youtu.be/EN73kO2_PZA>.

Zuffe. *Notre Dame de Paris*. *Wikimedia Commons*. Wikipedia Foundation, 28 April 2009.
    Web. 28 July 2012.
        <http://commons.wikimedia.org/wiki/File:Notre_Dame_dalla_Senna.jpg>.

Chapter 3

The Baroque Era

By David Whitehouse

The term ***baroque*** is an arbitrary term used for stylistic practices existing from 1600 to 1750. It may derive from the word *barroco* in Portuguese meaning "irregular shape." Originally used in a derogatory fashion to describe artistic trends of this time period, baroque has come to broadly refer to the century and a half beginning in 1600. This time period, known as the Baroque era, saw the rise of scientific thinking in the work of discoverers such as Galileo Galilei, Johannes Kepler, William Gilbert, Robert Boyle, Robert Hooke, and Isaac Newton. Changes in the arts were ushered in by painters such as Rembrandt van Rijn, Johannes Vermeer, Peter Paul Rubens, Andrea Pozzo, and el Greco. Architecture underwent fascinating changes, including boldness of size, curving lines

Figure 3.1 Baroque art and music exhibited drama, underlying structure, grandiose dimensions, synthesis of religion and secularism, and florid ornamentation. This picture shows a Baroque organ case made of Danish oak in Notre Dame Cathedral, St. Omer, France.

suggesting motion, and ornate decoration. These trends are represented in the works of

Gian Lorenzo Bernini, a leading sculptor and prominent architect in Rome.

Figure 3.2 This view of St. Peter's Square in Rome shows Bernini's famous columns, four rows deep and curving, as if they were massive arms enveloping the faithful. Figure 3.3 Francesco Mochi, *St. Veronica*, 1580. This sculpture by Mochi, who lived from 1580 to1654, shows the drama of movement carved in marble.

Sculptors, too, took a turn toward the dramatic and ornate in their works. The marble

statue of St. Veronica by Francesco Mochi shows trends toward vivid motion, dramatic

action, and a play to the emotions, including religious fervor.

All of Baroque art, including music, has a tendency to be dramatic. Drama in music

was displayed most obviously in opera but extended to sacred, secular, vocal, and

instrumental music. In music for solo instruments—solo voice, orchestra, and orchestra with

chorus—the use of musical devices enhanced musical forms and techniques of the previous

era. These devices included increasingly daring use of dissonance (harsh sound),

chromaticism (half-step motion) and the use of altered notes, counterpoint that was driven

by harmony where horizontal musical lines suggested vertical chords, regularity of rhythm

with the universal use of bar lines, and ornamentation of melodic line.

In addition, there was free use of improvisatory skill using the device known as **_basso continuo,_** the use of harpsichord and cello playing from musical shorthand. In this practice, the composer wrote down the desired bass notes along with the melody line. Above or below the bass line the composer wrote numbers to indicate what notes were to go along—the so-called **_figured bass_** (figure signifies the number above the bass line). The exact way the performer played these suggestions, however, was left up to his or her skill and taste. Instead

Figure 3.4 Rembrandt van Rijn, *The Music Party,* 1626. This work by Dutch painter Rembrandt (1606-1669) shows dramatic use of light, gesture, facial expression, and color.

of just playing clusters of chords underneath the melodic line, the performer could include passing notes, trills, suspensions, ornaments, flourishes, and other devices to add interest to the music.

Figure 3.1 This excerpt from Henry Purcell's opera *Dido and Aeneas* shows figured bass. Solitary flat and natural signs refer to the third of the chord. Ctrl+click on image to listen to this excerpt.

As the seventeenth century progressed, the tendency of all music was toward *major* and *minor tonality*, arrangements of notes in scales that are still use today, which was in direct contrast to the use of late-medieval modes through the end of the sixteenth century, especially in church music (see the example from Giovanni Pierluigi da Palestrina in Chapter 2). Theorists reflected this tendency in new rule books written to instruct those intending to become composers. Johann Joseph Fux wrote a treatise on counterpoint called *Gradus ad Parnassum* (Steps to Parnassus) in 1725. Jean-Phillippe Rameau (1683-1764), who was influenced by the writings of René Descartes and Newton, wrote *Traité de l'harmonie* (Treatise on Harmony) in 1722. Both of these works were used and revered for the next two-hundred years. Today, Rameau's ideas, though revolutionary at the time, are learned by every student of harmony as the foundation of the foundation of musical learning.

Opera

The dramatic and expressive capabilities shown in the Renaissance madrigal, especially in Italy, paved the way for the birth of *opera*, stage works that are entirely sung. Through their interest in how Greek and Roman civilizations presented dramatic works and how music was used to enhance those productions, composers in seventeenth-century Italy sought to incorporate ideas from ancient sources into their own creations. In the works of two notable Italian composers, true opera was born. Jacopo Peri (1561-1633) and Giulio Caccini (1551-1618) are generally credited with giving opera its unique style in two respects: *recitative* and *aria*, two techniques to convey dramatic action and feeling in the course of a sung play. **Please note that for this chapter, transcripts of song and music lyrics are not necessary to gain an understanding of the material.**

Recitative (narrative song) was developed to convey dialogue and *aria* (meaning "air" or expressive melody) was designed to convey intensity of emotion in the characters using aspects of melody derived from the madrigal. These techniques made opera distinct from earlier plays that used music to a greater or lesser extent. In addition to developing these two types of vocal declamation, Peri and Caccini were convinced that ancient Greek plays were sung throughout, with no spoken dialogue, and sought to emulate this technique in their new genre. Thus, everything was set to music meant to convey the emotions of the characters. The combination of these techniques in one package gave birth to the new form of music called opera.

As with all types of art and new advances in technique, the first practitioners of that art merely hinted at the possibilities inherent in new design and practice. Claudio

Figure 3.2 Portrait of Claudio Monteverdi, after Bernardo Strozzi. Monteverdi was the first master of opera to uncover and point the way to the rich possibilities of the genre.

Monteverdi (1567-1643) was the first master of opera to uncover and point the way to the rich possibilities inherent in the genre. In his early career, Monteverdi published madrigals in the older style of Renaissance polyphony. In 1605 and thereafter, his published books of madrigals also contained songs in homophonic style, a break from the past. *Homophony* is music that has a melody with chordal accompaniment. All contemporary popular songs, for instance, are homophonic. Bringing one melody to the fore allowed composers to convey the meaning of words in clearly defined ways. Doing so was not possible, they felt, with older techniques of polyphony, which laid equal emphasis on each melodic line and often had differing texts for each line of music. Monteverdi's *L'Orfeo* was the first opera of significance utilizing the new techniques of aria and recitative. Listen to Arnalta's aria, "Oblivion Soave," from Act II of Monteverdi's final opera, *L'incoronazione di Poppea (The Coronation of Poppea).*

As Poppea is overcome by fatigue, her old nurse and confidante, Arnalta, sings her a gentle lullaby. The aria is full of deep emotion, tenderness, and sadness. This display of emotion is evident in the new style of opera and can be considered a general tendency of the Baroque period called the *doctrine of affections*. This theory showed itself in music by a close association of the meaning of the words with musical devices used. Thus, for example, words such as *running* or texts conveying activity would be reflected in quick passages of sixteenth notes, while words of sadness would be reflected in a slow tempo.

This excerpt shows a modern staging of the beginning of L'Orfeo. The opening instrumental sets a serious tone. Dark emotions are in the foreground. Orpheus makes his entrance and sings to establish place. After the first shepherd sings his response, a group of shepherds make their assertions about the character of their work, followed by a chorus of nymphs and shepherds. The mood of the music is one of jubilation, of seriousness of intent, and of reflecting the meaning of the words in the context of relation to each other.

Monteverdi's Italian opera continued to develop. The principle centers of growth and experimentation were Venice, Milan, and Florence, but use of operatic elements in other dramatic situations continued in these places and elsewhere in Italian society. Vocal chamber music, on a smaller scale than the opulent productions of opera, nonetheless reflected the developments in dramatic expressiveness, recitative text declamation, and especially in the composition of arias. In the church, composers continued to use the old polyphonic contrapuntal style but increasingly incorporated the use of basso continuo, recitative, and aria.

Instrumental Music

In instrumental music in the second half of the seventeenth century, Italians retained their preeminence as they did in opera. Great violin makers such as Nicoló Amati (1596-1684), Antonio Stradivari (Stradivarius, 1644-1737), and Bartolomeo Giuseppe Guarneri (1698-1744) made instruments of unrivaled expressive capability and technical reliability.

Figure 3.3 This image shows a pair of Baroque trumpets. Notice the elongated bodies and lack of valves. Figure 3.4 This image shows a Stradivarius violin circa 1687.

These instruments went hand in hand with the development of the ***sonata*** (a work for solo instrument with keyboard accompaniment) and the instrumental concerto (a work for solo instrument with orchestral accompaniment). Composers such as Archangelo Corelli (1653-1713) composed works called ***sonata da camera*** (chamber sonata) and ***sonata da chiesa*** (church sonata), which were set in a form that came to be known as the ***trio sonata*** because they most often were for three players, a harpsichord, and a violin, with a cello reinforcing the bass line of the harpsichord. Set in groups of movements, these sonatas featured contrasting styles between movements, florid melodies, ornamentation, double stops, and flourishes that displayed virtuosity and wealth of invention. The music was increasingly marked by a tonal center emphasizing the major and minor tonalities over the older use of modes.

The ***instrumental concerto*** also achieved growing use in Italy and spread to other countries throughout this period. The ***concerto grosso***, written for a larger ensemble known as the Baroque orchestra, contained music for a small group within the larger ensemble, thus providing for dialogue effects and shifts in dynamics that continued to be exploited

throughout the eighteenth century in Italy and other countries. This shift in dynamics was

not gradual; it was made in an instant between the larger and smaller ensembles and gave

rise to the technique of **terraced dynamics** (levels of loudness). In addition, the concerto

grosso was set in a form that is termed **ritornello** (return), which meant a return to the full

orchestra from flights, called episodes, of the smaller ensemble, often with the same music

upon each return. Ritornello form was developed by Antonio Vivaldi (1678-1741).

The **Baroque suite** is a collection of dances of Renaissance origin that developed in

the Baroque era to reflect general musical tendencies. These tendencies were regularly

recurring rhythmic patterns (meter), gravitation to major and minor tonalities (moving away

from the use of Renaissance modes), and firming up of binary (AB) and ternary (ABA) forms

(A signifies an opening section of music, B is a departure to a second section of music, and

A is a return to the opening).

Keyboard music holds a place in the canon of Baroque instrumental music. Keyboard

instruments include the clavichord, the harpsichord, and the pipe organ. The harpsichord

became the predominant keyboard instrument of orchestras and chamber music, and the

organ became the principle accompaniment instrument of church services, with solo works

of increasing complexity being written for both throughout the seventeenth and eighteenth

centuries. Two principle genres of keyboard music during this era were the Baroque suite

and the **fugue** (an imitative, polyphonic composition). It is important to remember that

composers used these two forms in other music as well, including instrumental music, but

these forms predominated in keyboard music.

The fugue is an extended piece of polyphonic writing for instruments in which a theme is treated in various ways depending on the composer's skill and ingenuity. Beginning with a subject (theme), a second statement of the subject is made in another voice, with the first voice accompanying it with a new melody called a countersubject. As voices enter, they play the subject while other voices supply accompanying material, including the countersubject. Various keys are explored via modulation (change of key), and other devices are used to show compositional skill and inspiration, including augmentation, diminution, inversion, and stretto (overlapping of subject). The exposition is the first part of the fugue where all voices make their entrance. Episodes occur between statements of the theme, and pedal point occurs when one note is held (usually in the bass) for a long period, building suspense and usually leading to the close.

In all genres of the Baroque era—opera, solo song, sonata, concerto, church cantata, oratorio, suite, and fugue—the music provided the performers with vehicles to show off their abilities. The emphasis on the solo singer in arias of opera and the instrumental soloist in concertos and sonatas paved the way for the development of the virtuoso player/composer and the operatic diva in the Classical era as well as the exploitations of virtuosos in the nineteenth century.

Cantata and Oratorio

The eighteenth century saw the rise of two types of compositions for chorus, soloists, and orchestra. The ***cantata*** is a vocal piece in several movements usually based on a single melody. It typically begins with an opening piece for full chorus and orchestra then continues with alternating solos, duets, small ensembles, and other choruses, ending with a statement of the melody. Cantatas are classified as either secular or sacred depending on the text used. Antonio Vivaldi, George Frideric Handel, Jean-Philippe Rameau, Domenico Scarlatti, Johann Sebastian Bach, and others composed cantatas during the Baroque era.

The *oratorio* is also a vocal work of music, written in movements with soloists, chorus, and orchestra. The texts used are taken from Biblical scripture or are based on sacred themes. Oratorios incorporate the operatic devices of recitative, aria, and chorus to convey the action contained in the text. Though they are sacred in nature, they are not necessarily performed in church nor are they designed to be included in liturgy like cantatas sometimes are. Italian and German oratorios predominated with Handel in England synthesizing elements of various styles in his unique blend. Perhaps the most famous of all oratorios is Handel's *Messiah*. Other oratorio composers include Marc-Antoine Charpentier, Heinrich Schütz, and J. S. Bach.

Listening Goals

1. In Baroque opera and oratorio, listen for the fluid sound of an aria. How does it differ from the declamatory (i.e., reciting speech set to music) style of recitative?

2. In the Baroque concerto for orchestra, listen for terraced dynamics. When is the full ensemble playing and when is the smaller ensemble playing?

3. Terraced dynamics can be heard in solo organ and harpsichord music from the Baroque era. Echo effects were popular. *Solo* means these instruments were playing alone with no other instrument playing. Listen to solo organ and solo harpsichord music from the Baroque era. The effects that are achieved include echo, terraced dynamics, and textures that vary from thick to thin.

4. While listening to Baroque sonatas, take note of how many movements are there. What are the tempos of the movements? Can you hear when musical material repeats? Can you hear the use of terraced dynamics?

Key Music Terms

 Instrumentation Five basic classes of instruments—strings, woodwinds, brass, percussion, and keyboard—were used during the Baroque era. The viol family of stringed instruments gradually gave way to the violin family. *Family* in this context means soprano, alto, tenor and bass, which cover the full range of sounds from low to high. Renaissance brass instruments developed into the modern trumpet, trombone, and tuba. Hunting horns with no valves developed into the French horn with valves. Woodwind instruments included flutes, oboes, and bassoons. Percussion instruments included kettle drums and little else. Keyboard instruments included clavichord, harpsichord, and organ. In addition, solo singing and singing in chorus led to the use of the human voice as an instrument during the Baroque era.

Timbre or Tone Quality What did instruments and human voices sound like in the years 1600 to 1750? When answering that question, think of how we listen to music today and how people listened to music then. Also think about instruments as solo, part of small ensemble, and part of a full ensemble. A group of violins, violas, cellos, and double basses playing together sound different than a solo string playing alone. The same is true of each family of instruments. Each section of the Baroque orchestra—strings, woodwinds, brass, percussion, and keyboard—has its own group sound. Combining all groups or combinations of groups produces other effects. A composer thinks about his/her tonal resources when deciding what will convey the musical ideas.

Texture Texture has to do with how many instruments are playing and how many lines of music are playing at the same time. You can have a hundred musicians playing the same melody in unison, and the sound will have a different texture than those same musicians all playing different melodies. Which example do you think would be thicker sounding? Baroque orchestras were not as large as Romantic-era orchestras. The instruments did not have as fully developed overtones, so their sound was less full.

 Harmony Harmony grew into distinct patterns during the Baroque era. The Western tonal system was finalized when Johann Sebastian Bach equalized the tuning of the twelve notes of the chromatic scale. Each interval of a fourth above and a fifth below was tuned exactly the same amount, leaving them all slightly but bearably out of tune. All twelve major and minor modes became usable. Harmonic progression could move freely from a starting point to any other point and back again. Composers and theorists such as Johann Joseph Fux and Jean-Philippe Rameau set down strict rules about which harmonies went with other harmonies and how they moved in and out of each other. Forms were based on accepted patterns of harmonic progression. Claudio Monteverdi's operatic compositions, George Frideric Handel's oratorios, and other composers' choral and orchestral compositions advanced the art of homophony. Johann Sebastian Bach brought to perfection the art of Baroque counterpoint, independent musical lines relating to each other.

 Tempo Tempos increased in the Baroque era. The basic pulse of music in the Renaissance era was a modern whole note with swift-moving passages in quarter and eighth notes for human voices. The tempo was even faster for instrumental voices. By the Baroque era, the basic pulse became the modern quarter note with sixteenth notes common for both human and instrumental voices.

Dynamics Dynamics in the Baroque era were classified into levels called terraced dynamics. The sound of a full ensemble was contrasted with a smaller ensemble. Harpsichords and organs that had more than one keyboard could instantly jump from one of those keyboards to the other. Both techniques produced terraced dynamics, loud and soft. As a general rule, there were no gradual crescendos or diminuendos, as, for instance, in opera and oratorio a human singing solo or a chorus singing together could gradually increase or decrease the sound gradually. The human voice, however, was treated in the same way as instrumental voices. Gradual changes in sound level were not the norm.

Form While musical forms have been in constant development throughout history, several formal designs were finalized in the Baroque era. These forms include the concerto, ritornello, sonata, fugue, toccata, prelude, chorale, theme and variations, opera, oratorio, aria, and recitative. The designation *finalized* means only for a time, as the enduring aspects of some of the forms underwent further development in ensuing eras. Some forms, such as the fugue and ritornello, were exploited to their fullest potential by the end of the Baroque era. Others, such as the concerto and sonata, were developed further after the Baroque era.

The Eighteenth Century

The eighteenth century saw the culmination of Baroque practices and the beginning of the Classical period. Musicians cultivated new genres such as opera buffa, ballad opera, keyboard concerto, symphony, and concerto. Composers birthed new forms, like the rondo, and developed others, like the sonata, and thought in terms of tonality (key centers) in all compositions, replacing church modes almost entirely. Endless arguments regarding musical taste took place in newly invented newspapers, in composers' journals, in musical treatises, in coffee houses, and in the homes of the populace.

It is important to mention at this point that the tonal system used in the Middle Ages and Renaissance is different from the one used today. The tonal system used during the Middle Ages is called just intonation, which is based on natural harmonics, or the way sound resonates in nature. The major/minor system used today is called equal temperament, which began to be utilized in the Baroque era. Equal temperament is a system of tonality in which all of the notes are distanced equally apart. Technically it is slightly out of tune in relation to how sound resonates in nature. Some cultures, such as the Chinese, have resisted the change to equal temperament, believing that it creates disharmony in the environment. See Chapter 8 to learn more about music in other cultures.

Vivaldi, Handel, and Bach

Antonio Vivaldi, George Frideric Handel, and Johann Sebastian Bach are three composers who represent culminations of styles and practices in full bloom in the mid-1700s, when instrumental forms such as the concerto, opera, oratorio, cantata, dance suites, and fugue were developed to their highest potential using homophonic, polyphonic, and contrapuntal techniques.

Antonio Vivaldi and the Concerto

Antonio Vivaldi (1678-1741) was born in Venice, Italy, spending a great deal of his life there. He was ordained as a priest in the Catholic Church and spent the greater part of his career as a teacher, composer, conductor, and superintendent of musical instruments at the Pio Ospedale della Pietà. There were four such so-called hospitals in Venice where poor,

Figure 3.5 Pier Leone Ghezzi, *The Red Priest,* **1723. Ghezzi created this caricature of Antonio Vivaldi using pen and ink on paper.**

illegitimate, and orphaned boys and girls were given housing and schooling. All of the students at the Pietà, however, were girls who provided the talent for performing groups, including duos, trios, quartets, and full orchestras. While employed at the Pietà, Vivaldi composed numerous works, including operas, cantatas, sacred music, and concertos, for which he is known today. Vivaldi composed more than four hundred concertos during his lifetime.

The following example is the first movement of the first of Vivaldi's four concertos called *The Four Seasons*. Each concerto has three movements and each is dedicated to one of the four seasons of the year. The first movement, "Spring," is an example of ritornello form, which is a flexible approach to concerto writing. A small group of players is contrasted with the larger ensemble, with musical motives returning in varied guises as the two groups alternate. Sometimes the material returns with exact repetition, sometimes it's abbreviated, and sometimes it varies with slight alterations of melodic curve and harmonization. The music is entirely for strings, with a smaller ensemble integrated throughout that admirably demonstrates terraced dynamics. The ensemble is led by a violinist who is joined by other players from the large ensemble to create special effects when contrasting with the entire ensemble. A harpsichord provides the continuo, violins are divided into first and second, and there are violas, and cellos to complete the ensemble. In Vivaldi's time there were bass viols in this ensemble as well. This collection of instruments became the standard ensemble of concertos throughout Vivaldi's writings, but he also wrote solo concertos for various wind instruments and used them in his ensemble writing.

Vivaldi was held in high esteem all over Europe. His trios, solo sonatas, and cantatas reflected earlier masters, showing the propensity for Baroque composers to synthesize and develop existing forms. His concertos developed mainstream tendencies, including three movements (fast, slow, fast), terraced dynamics, and ritornello form. His concerto writing and the broad fame of his concertos helped solidify the concerto form. Vivaldi brought rhythmic vitality and thematic invention to his operas while continuing with advances made by earlier Italian composers. He carried operatic style over to his sacred music. But it is in his varied and prodigious output of concertos in ritornello form that he had the greatest influence.

Johann Sebastian Bach

One of those Vivaldi most influenced was Johann Sebastian Bach. Bach's musical output represents the culmination of many contrapuntal forms in use during the Baroque era. In his instrumental—including solo keyboard—works, writing for chorus and orchestra, cantatas, passions (church works depicting the life of Christ), and settings of chorales he infused a wealth of technical, melodic, and harmonic richness and variety with a depth of formal organization. His works for solo instruments, especially his keyboard pieces for harpsichord and organ, brought forms such as the toccata (virtuoso keyboard piece), prelude (keyboard piece preceding another), chorale variation (Lutheran church hymn with altering), Baroque sonata, and fugue to perfection. He wrote monumental works for chorus, soloists, and orchestra in the form of two passions, the *St. Matthew Passion* and the *St. John Passion*, and a large-scale setting of the mass, the Mass in B minor, for the same

Figure 3.6 Elias Gottlob Haussmann, *Portrait of Johann Sebastian Bach,* **1748.**

instrumental groupings as the passions. Bach worked his entire career for towns and churches, and his positions did not require him to compose any operas. He was a pious Lutheran, heading all of his compositions with the mark S.D.G. (*Soli deo gloria*) meaning "To God alone be glory."

Bach spent his entire career in Germany. He traveled when he could, getting into trouble several times with his employers for being away from his employment too long. On one occasion he walked two hundred miles from Arnstadt to Lübeck to hear the famous organist and composer Dietrich Buxtehude. He arranged several of Vivaldi's concertos while adding to and strengthening the counterpoint, filling out the melodic contours, and reinforcing the basic harmonic schemes. He was familiar with trends in French Baroque music, including the flair for the dramatic, exquisite use of dissonance and suspension, and vagaries of counterpoint as practiced there. As he sought to educate himself in all styles and to keep abreast of current developments, Bach was a master synthesizer of styles. Bach never imitated other composers; he synthesized stylistic trends and harmonic advances and brought forms to levels of expression unheard of and unmatched since.

The following are three examples of Bach's enormous output. In "Wachet auf, ruft uns die Stimme" BWV 140 (BWV stands for Bach-Werke-Verzeichnis, the numbering system used to identify Bach's works), several arrangements of this chorale are heard. The chorale is set in sparse style, with only three lines of music playing: the chorale melody in the tenor voices, and the bass and soprano lines taken by instruments. One can hear the opening melodic motive in the instruments throughout the piece as the chorale soars in long notes on harmonic patterns underpinned by the bass line. This piece is one section of a longer composition, the cantata, mentioned previously. In all of his cantatas, including "Wachet auf," Bach used conventions of the time, including choral sections both a capella and with accompaniment, arias, orchestral introductions and interludes, and a final setting of the chorale for chorus or chorus with orchestra as the closing of the cantata.

The second example of Bach's work is from his orchestral music. He wrote six concerti grossi (plural of concerto grosso) for the margrave (ruler) of Brandenburg, a small state near Berlin. Listen to the first movement of the Brandenburg Concerto no. 4 in G major, BWV 1049. Follow along with the PDF music score at Stanford University's Center for Computer Assisted Research in the Humanities. The piece is scored for a string orchestra consisting of violins I and II, violas, violoncello, violone (contrabass), and continuo. This ensemble is called the **ripieno,** or full orchestra. In addition, Bach used a violin and two flutes as a smaller ensemble (called solo but actually with three players) to contrast with the ripieno. In thinking of the orchestra in this way, Bach and others in the Baroque era devised ways of contrasting the timbres and dynamics of the music they were writing.

Two principles are evident from hearing the second example above. The first principle is terraced dynamics, clearly heard when the solo (violin and two flutes), and the full orchestra play. There is an immediate decrease in sound when the smaller group plays and a return to a full sound when the full orchestra plays. No crescendos or diminuendos are heard, thus the designation terraced dynamics. The second principle is ritornello form, which was favored by Baroque composers of concertos. In the case of concertos, ritornello is a return to the music of the opening, much as in popular music of today when a refrain is sung between verses. Each solo section has contrasting music with a division of the sections following a typical pattern: tutti, solo, tutti, solo, tutti, solo (***tutti*** means "full," i.e., the ripieno). While that alternating between ripieno and tutti was a typical pattern, composers found flexibility in ritornello form and would often use material from each solo part to enrich the tutti or in combination with other solo sections. The entire piece would be written with Baroque counterpoint, major and minor tonal centers, and rhythmic regularity. These characteristics form the basis of Baroque-era developments of Renaissance ideas or techniques.

Figure 3.7 This image shows the opening of the toccata from Bach's Toccata and Fugue in D minor for organ solo. Notice the ornamentation (squiggly lines above some of the eighth notes), the fast-running passages, and the thick chordal texture of the final notes in the example.

The third example from Bach is his Toccata and Fugue in D minor, BWV 565. A ***toccata***

(touch) is a keyboard work that shows the dexterity of the player. Composers wrote toccatas

from the second half of the sixteenth century through the end of the Baroque era. Using fast-

running passages, intricate ornamentation, chromatic harmonies, and thick textures,

toccatas were meant to show the resources of the instrument they were written for and the

abilities of the keyboard player. These things are thoroughly explored in Bach's toccata from the Toccata and Fugue in D minor, which is written and played on the pipe organ. A clear subject, countersubject, and stretto are evident in Bach's fugue, which has one of the most recognizable themes of fugal writing in the entire repertoire of classical music. The piece ends with a dazzling display of virtuosity that recalls the toccata and leaves the subject behind.

Figure 3.8 Shown is Bach's portrait by Haussmann brought up to date with a six-string bass. Listen to a power metal version of Bach's Toccata and Fugue in D minor.

George Frideric Handel

George Frideric Handel (sometimes spelled Georg Friedrich Händel, among other ways)

(1685-1759) was born the same year as Domenico Scarlatti and Bach. He was born in the

town of Halle in Saxony. His mother nurtured his musical gifts, but his father hoped that he

would study law. The attraction of music was greater than law for Handel and he traveled to

Hamburg when he was eighteen, playing in the orchestra there and teaching violin. In 1706,

Figure 3.9 Thomas Hudson, *Georg Friedrich Händel*, 1748-49.

Handel traveled to cities in Italy, including Florence, Rome, Naples, and Venice. He studied the Italian styles in vogue at the time, including concertos and opera. He made acquaintances of some of the leading figures in music, including Antonio Lotti, Domenico Scarlatti, and Alessandro Scarlatti. Handel studied with the most renowned Italian composer of the period, Archangelo Corelli, whose compositions for string orchestra solidified the Baroque concerto grosso form. During his youthful three-year stay in Italy, Handel absorbed Italian vocal and instrumental compositional styles, including a flair for the dramatic.

In 1709, Handel became the *Kapellmeister* (master of music) for the elector of Hanover but soon after moved to England. There he stayed for the rest of his life, with only brief returns to his native Germany, even though he had obligations as the elector's music director. This fact proved embarrassing to Handel, as the elector became King George I of Great Britain in 1714. Handel was reunited with his patron when he composed the *Water Music* suites after a mediator begged them to reconcile. The work was played on a barge on the river Thames for an evening festival thrown by the king, who had it repeated twice because he loved it so much.

Though Handel was a composer of Italian opera in London during this time, he also forayed into the realm of oratorio. Composing more than forty operas in the Italian style, he eventually stopped composing opera altogether as tastes changed. He then turned exclusively to oratorio. His last opera, *Deidamia,* was produced in 1741, but Handel had been composing in English as well as Italian since 1733. As he wrote opera he increasingly wrote choruses for oratorios, improving his technique with more chorus work in each succeeding oratorio; double choruses, which are his signature; and balance of chorus movements with solo arias and orchestral preludes and interludes. This experience in writing oratorios led Handel in 1742 to compose his famous *Messiah,* which premiered on April 13, 1742, in Dublin, Ireland. For the next ten years, Handel composed one oratorio per year on average. His sight began to fail as early as 1750, with complete loss by 1752. Handel spent his final years supervising performances of his works, writing new material for some of them, and rewriting parts of others. He is buried in Westminster Abbey in London.

The following are two examples of Handel's prodigious output, which fills one hundred volumes and is almost equal to that of both Bach and Ludwig van Beethoven, both prolific composers, put together. The first example is Suite No. 2, HWV 349, from the famous *Water Music* suites. The example is called "Alla Hornpipe" and is the second movement of the suite. In it the ABA form can be heard. The A section is a lively dance, with solos for two trumpets and two horns alternating with each other and with the full strings and ending with all instruments playing a cadence. The B section is in a related minor key,

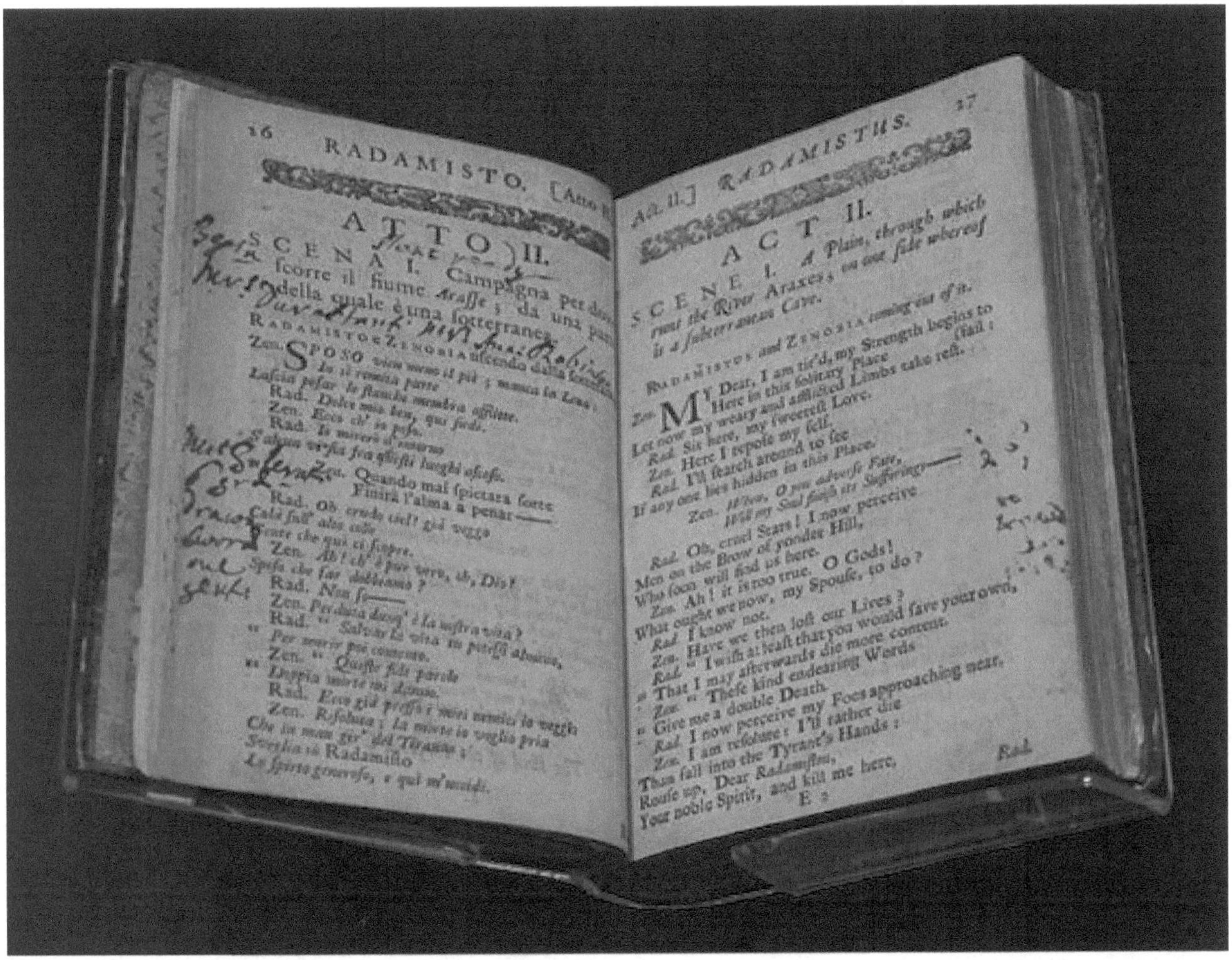

Figure 3.14 Shown is the libretto (with Italian on the left and English on the right) from a prompt book from Handel's opera *Radamisto*. Throughout this book, notes were made by the stage hands responsible for things such as lighting, sound effects, and curtain draws. Copies also were available (without notes) for the audiences to read as the opera progressed. Lighting was kept on in the theaters during performances around this time in England. Take an interactive look at this prompt book.

with only the strings playing throughout. The A section returns note for note with no **cadenza** (ending music incorporated after the main section is played).

The second selection from Handel is from *Messiah,* an oratorio that is known worldwide. The "Hallelujah" chorus is the culmination of the second section of the three-section work. It is scored for Baroque orchestra and four-part chorus: soprano, alto, tenor, and bass. The words are taken from the Bible. Handel composed the music for *Messiah* in a heat of inspiration which was much faster than his normal phenomenally quick rate of composing. It took him less than four weeks to complete the entire score in August and September of 1741. In Handel's oratorios, operatic show of solo voices generally predominate, with the chorus adding portions here and there. In *Messiah,* however, the chorus work gives impetus to the dramatic response of human beings to the message of divine intervention in the affairs of humans and has much more of an even status with the arias of the soloists. Of all the choruses in the work, the "Hallelujah" chorus remains a favorite, with amateur choirs all over the world attempting to render the piece at Christmas and Easter. And there is no reason to wonder why, as the wedding of text and music has never been more consummate in any other choral work ever written. The words are a jubilant expression of joy to the savior. The music is exuberant, reflecting the intense emotions of an awakening realization of the importance of what the divine has done. Rhythmic punctuations are enhanced with running passages of strings, marching bass lines, and trumpet calls that ring clearly over all, summoning the faithful to a more intense awareness. The ending climaxes on a rhythmic elongation of the word *hallelujah,* which is repeated throughout.

Closing

In Europe around 1600, developments taking place in society were reflected in music. Specific trends included dramatic declamation, formal organization, and the use of standard metrical patterns grouped into measures. These trends also included increasing dissonance, chromatic notes, counterpoint based on harmonic schemes, rhythms that were regulated by bar lines, and melodic lines that were increasingly ornamented. Composer-performer combinations increasingly gave way to performers coming into their own as separate entities. The Baroque orchestra developed a standard size. Music publishing

developed so that dissemination of styles improved. The design, manufacture, and

affordability of instruments improved, and increasingly reliable instruments led to the

development of more complex music where forms were explored with new compositional

devices. Opera, ritornello, concerto, sonata, fugue, and other forms continued to be

exploited by composers, resulting in near exhaustion of their possibilities. By 1750, this

exhaustion was leading to a new era of musical history: the Classical period.

Music and Memory

This week, watch the video "Music and Memory," part of the Annenberg Learner video series

we will be viewing throughout the text.

Guiding Questions

1. What years are designated as the Baroque era?

2. Who were major composers of the Baroque era?

3. What forms were used in the Baroque era? List at least five.

4. What instruments were used? List instrument families.

5. What development allowed all twelve major and minor keys to be used? Who

   finalized this development?

Self-Check Exercises

Complete the following self-check exercises to verify your mastery of key music terms presented in this chapter. After you have read the questions above, check your answers at the bottom of this page.

1. **Developments in music during the Baroque era include what?**
   a. Opera, the suite, and fugue
   b. Ornamentation of the melodic line, regularity of rhythm
   c. Increasing use of dissonance, use of chromaticism, and regular use of bar lines
   d. All of the above

2. **Opera was birthed with two major characteristics. What are they?**
   a. Aria and chorale
   b. Aria and recitative
   c. Recitative and brevita
   d. Drama and declamare

3. **The tonal system in the Middle Ages and Renaissance went from being based on modes and using just intonation to what system?**
   a. The Romantic-era system of chromaticism
   b. The Classical-era system of easy conformality
   c. The Baroque-era system of equal temperament, or major/minor tonality
   d. The modern system of atonality

4. **Which set of composers are ALL from the Baroque era?**
   a. Vivaldi, Handel, Bach
   b. Vivaldi, Handel, Schumann
   c. Handel, Bach, Gaga
   d. Vivaldi, Handel, Mozart

Self-check exercise answers:
1. D, 2. B, 3. C, 4. A.

Works Consulted

Bach, Johann Sebastian. *Brandenburg Concerto no. 4 in G major*. Circa 1721. Center for Computer Assisted Research in the Humanities, Stanford University, 2004. Web. 29 July 2012. <http://scores.ccarh.org/bach/brandenburg/bwv1049/bwv1049.pdf>.

—. *Brandenburg Concerto no. 4 in G major*. Circa 1721. *Wikimedia Commons*. Wikipedia Foundation, 15 Apr. 2011. Web. 29 July 2012. <http://commons.wikimedia.org/wiki/File:Brandenburg_No4-1_BWV1049.ogg>.

—. *Toccata and Fugue in D minor*. Circa 1708-10. Perf. Ian Tracey. June 1989. *Music Online: Classical Music Library*. Alexander Street Press. Web. 21 Oct. 2014. <http://ezproxy.apus.edu/login?url=http://search.alexanderstreet.com/view/work/928413>.

—. *Toccata and Fugue in D minor*. Circa 1708-10. *Wikimedia Commons*. Wikipedia Foundation, 27 Feb. 2012. Web. 29 July 2012. <http://commons.wikimedia.org/wiki/File:BachToccataAndFugueInDMinorOpening.GIF>.

—. "Bach - Cantata 140: Wachet auf, ruft uns die Stimme, BWV 140 (1731)." 1731. Cond. Nikolaus Harnoncourt. Perf. Concentus Musicus Wien. *Youtube*. 23 Jan. 2011. Web. 29 15 Apr. 2014. <http://youtu.be/3sj-NKqROtw>.

Buxtehude, Dietrich. *Jubilate Domino:* No. 2 aria. Perf. Columbia Baroque Soloists. *Early Music America*. 21 Dec. 2011. Web. 24 Feb. 2012. <http://www.earlymusic.org/audio/jubilate-domino-no-2-aria>.

Construction tools sign, used with permission from Microsoft. "Images." *Office*. Web. 4 Sept. 2012. <http://office.microsoft.com/en-us/images/results.aspx?ex=2&qu=tools#ai:MC900432556|mt:0|>.

Ghezzi, Pier Leone. *The Red Priest*. 1723. Codex Ottoboni, Vatican Library, Rome. *Wikimedia Commons*. Wikipedia Foundation, 13 Aug. 2012. Web. 29 July 2012. <http://commons.wikimedia.org/wiki/File:Vivaldi_caricature.png>.

Grossman, Dave. *Updated Portrait of Johann Sebastian Bach*. 10 July 1999. *Johann Sebastian Bach. (*unpronounceable) Productions, 18 Sep. 2007. Web. 29 July, 2012. <http://www.jsbach.net/bass/>.

Haas, Johann Wilhelm. *Baroque trumpets*. Photo by BenP. 12 Jan. 2006. *Wikimedia Commons*. Wikipedia Foundation, 16 Apr. 2012. Web. 29 July 2012. <http://commons.wikimedia.org/wiki/File:Trompettes_baroques.jpg>.

Handel, George Frideric. "Alla Hornpipe." *Water Music*. 1717. Cond. Rimma Sushanskaya. Perf. Berlin Sinfonietta. Berlin Philharmonic Hall, Berlin. 25 Dec. 2008. *YouTube*. 11 March 2009. Web. 29 July 2012. <http://youtu.be/TRNmXwNnB9w>.

—. "Hallelujah." *Messiah*. 1741. Cond. Stephen Simon. Perf. Handel Festival Orchestra of Washington, D.C., and Howard University Choir. 1985. *Music Online: Classical Music*

Library. Alexander Street Press. Web. 21 Oct. 2014.
        <http://ezproxy.apus.edu/login?url=http://search.alexanderstreet.com/view/work/1
        78837>.

Haussmann, Elias Gottlob. *Portrait of Johann Sebastian Bach.* 1748. Collection of Dr.
        William H. Scheide, Princeton, New Jersey. *Wikimedia Commons.* Wikipedia
        Foundation, 10 Dec. 2011. Web. 29 July 2012.
        <http://commons.wikimedia.org/wiki/File:Johann_Sebastian_Bach.jpg>.

Hudson, Thomas. *Georg Friedrich Händel.* 1748-49. Hamburg State and University Library,
        Hamburg, Germany. *Wikimedia Commons.* Wikipedia Foundation, 11 March 2012.
        Web. 29 July 2012.
        <http://commons.wikimedia.org/wiki/File:Georg_Friedrich_H%C3%A4ndel.jpg>.

Lully, Jean-Baptiste. "Enfin il est en ma puissance." *Armide. Wikimedia Commons.* Wikipedia
        Foundation, 5 Mar. 2012. Web. 13 Mar. 2012.
        <http://commons.wikimedia.org/wiki/File:Armide_Enfin.ogg>.

Mochi, Francesco. *St. Veronica.* 1629. St. Peter's Basilica, Rome. *Wikimedia Commons.*
        Wikipedia Foundation, 18 April 2012. Web. 21 Feb. 2012.
        <http://commons.wikimedia.org/wiki/File:Francesco_Mochi_Santa_Ver%C3%B3nica
        _1629-32_Vaticano.jpg>.

Monteverdi, Claudio. "L'Orfeo." 1607. *YouTube.* 10 Jan. 2009. Web. 29 July 2012.
        <http://youtu.be/jb2TURdBeEQ>.

—. "Oblivion Soave." *L'incoronazione di Poppea.* 1642. Perf. Karim Sulayman. *Guy Barzilay
        Artists.* Web. 29 July 2012.
        <http://guybarzilayartists.com/upload/audio_Sulayman2.mp3>.

"Music and Memory." *Exploring the World of Music.* Prod. Pacific Street Films and the
        Educational Film Center, 1999. *Annenberg Learner.* Web. 31 July 2012.
        <http://www.learner.org/vod/vod_window.html?pid=1239>.

Plamondon, Taran. "Bach Rock." *YouTube.* 23 Dec. 2010. Web. 29 July 2012.
        <http://youtu.be/I6pwtZsYuG4>.

Portrait of Monteverdi, after Bernardo Strozzi. N.d. *Wikimedia Commons.* Wikipedia
        Foundation, 13 June 2012. Web. 29 July 2012.
        <http://commons.wikimedia.org/wiki/File:Claudio_Monteverdi.jpg>.

Praefcke, Andreas. *Prompt book for Radamisto 1720 VA.* June 2011. *Wikimedia Commons.*
        Wikipedia Foundation, 1 July 2011. Web. 29 July 2012.
        <http://commons.wikimedia.org/wiki/File:Prompt_book_for_Radamisto_1720_VA.jp
        g>.

"Prompt book for *Radamisto* by George Friedrich Handel." 1720. *Victoria and Albert
        Museum,* London. Web. 29 July 2012.
        <http://www.vam.ac.uk/content/articles/p/prompt-book-for-radamisto-by-george-
        friedrich-handel/>.

Purcell, Henry. "Purcell diatonic chromaticism." 14 Jan. 2011. *Wikimedia Commons.*
    Wikipedia Foundation, 12 Mar. 2012. Web. 21 Feb. 2012.
    <http://commons.wikimedia.org/wiki/File:Purcell_diatonic_chromaticism.png>.

—. "Henry Purcell - Dido and Aeneas - Dido's lament 1688. Perf. Xenia Meijer. *YouTube.* 11
    June 2010. Web. 60 Apr. 2014. <http://youtu.be/ivlUMWUJ-1w>.

Stradivari, Antonio. *Spanish II violin.* 1689. Palacio Real de Madrid, Spain. Photo by Hakan
    Svensson. 23 July 2003. *Wikimedia Commons.* Wikipedia Foundation, 21 April 2010.
    Web. 28 July 2012.
    <http://commons.wikimedia.org/wiki/File:PalacioReal_Stradivarius1.jpg>.

Reinholdbehringer. *Baroque Organ, Cathedral of St. Omer.* 30 Dec. 2011. *Wikimedia
    Commons.* Wikipedia Foundation, 11 Jan. 2012. Web. 21 Feb. 2012.
    <http://commons.wikimedia.org/wiki/File:Baroque_Organ,_Cathedral_of_St.Omer.JP
    G>.

Valyag. *Saint Peter's Square from the Dome.* 26 May 2005. *Wikimedia Commons.* Wikipedia
    Foundation, 5 July 2010. Web. 21 Feb. 2012.
    <http://commons.wikimedia.org/wiki/File:Saint_Peter%27s_Square_from_the_dome
    _v2.jpg>.

van Rijn, Rembrandt. *The Music Party.* 1626. Rijksmuseum, Amsterdam. *Wikimedia
    Commons.* Wikipedia Foundation, 16 May 2012. Web. 26 Feb. 2012.
    <http://commons.wikimedia.org/wiki/File:Rembrandt_concert.jpg>.

Vivaldi, Antonio. "La Primavera (Spring)." *The Four Seasons.* 1723. Perf. John Harrison and
    Wichita State University Chamber Players. Cond. Robert Turizziani. Wiedemann
    Recital Hall, Wichita State University. 6 Feb. 2000. *Wikimedia Commons.* Wikipedia
    Foundation, 13 April 2012. Web. 29 July 2012.
    <http://commons.wikimedia.org/wiki/File:01_-_Vivaldi_Spring_mvt_1_Allegro_-
    _John_Harrison_violin.ogg>.

Chapter 4

The Classical Era (1750-1820)

By Bethanie L. Hansen

Figure 4.1 Saverio Della Rosa, *Wolfgang at Verona*, 1770.

The Classical period was known as the Enlightenment, or the Age of Reason. The era spanned about seventy years (1750-1820), but in its short duration, musical practices began that have influenced music in the nearly two hundred years since. Classical period music is by far the most common Western music known today. During this period, public concerts became prominent, instrumental music was further developed, secular music became more prevalent than church music, and opera took a new role as a more important form of vocal entertainment and musical drama. Wolfgang Amadeus Mozart and Franz Joseph Haydn each found a place in the music world and produced music as expression, art, and entertainment.

Relevant Historical Events

The Western world of the mid-1700s transformed through intellectual and industrial revolutions. Early in the Enlightenment period, René Descartes and Sir Francis Bacon streamlined the scientific method, leading to Isaac Newton's physics discoveries. People began to experiment and explore ideas like never before, which resulted in developments and inventions. The Industrial Revolution brought agricultural changes, mechanized textile manufacturing, and new power sources like the steam engine. On assembly lines, workers began to specialize in the monotonous creation of only one small part rather than an entire product. In the home, families that had created homespun wool could no longer earn wages by making and selling hand-woven materials. Changes in the structure of work and community paved the way for salon gatherings and public concerts.

Learn more about developments of the Industrial Revolution through this <u>YouTube video</u> (<u>transcript available</u>).

Figure 4.2 Jean-Marc Nattier, Portrait of Princess Ekaterina Dmitrievna Golitsyna, 1757.

Political Influences

The period of 1600 through 1750, known as the Age of Absolutism, focused on the divine right of kings and other monarchs as chosen by God. During the Enlightenment, however, this philosophy began to change. European countries were regularly at war with each other. Britain declared war on France; France and Austria entered into an agreement against Prussia called the first treaty of Versailles; Frederick II invaded Saxony and began the Seven Years' War; and France and Austria entered into the second treaty of Versailles with a plan to split up Prussia. For several years, political leadership came from royalty who had inherited their thrones and courts. Despite invasions and wars throughout Europe, a few leaders tried to improve the conditions of their people. These monarchs, commonly known as enlightened despots, implemented reforms like religious toleration and economic development. Joseph II, a leader in the Habsburg Empire that included Austria and Hungary, set peasants free, suppressed church authority, and promoted education, music, literature, and a free press. This positive atmosphere lured artists from outside areas to Vienna, where they could create freely. Mozart, from Salzburg, Haydn, from Rohrau, Austria, and Ludwig van Beethoven, from Bonn, are a sampling of the artists who flocked to Vienna.

At the beginning of the Enlightenment era, courts and noblemen ruled Europe, and European powers governed the American colonies. By then end of the era, though, the United States had fought in the Revolutionary War, created the Declaration of Independence, and adopted the Bill of Rights. Government by the people became a theme of the period. Exploration and freedom in the United States allowed creativity and inventiveness to develop.

Social Influences

The Enlightenment was a movement of intellectual and social ideals. Writers and philosophers examined social theories. The phrase "life, liberty, and the pursuit of happiness" was based on the ideas that English philosopher John Locke (1632-1704) held about human beings having the right to freedom and autonomy. Locke believed that people gained wisdom and knowledge from personal experience. The Swiss philosopher Jean-Jacques Rousseau (1712-78) declared that the shared creation of laws could help people obtain happiness and build a better society. The ideals of these and other philosophers of the era led to societal and governmental changes that placed power in the hands of citizens. General theories of identity shifted from an emphasis on estates, ranks, and nobility to the perception of the individual as the basic unit in society. It was this kind of thinking that led Mozart to rebel against tradition and common practice by pursuing independent music sales and commissions rather than serving a court for his livelihood.

Cultural Influences

As European society gradually changed from agrarian to working class and an emphasis was placed on enjoying beauty and pleasure, public concerts became important, and the arts were widely developed. In 1748, the first concert hall was built in Oxford, England, and it is still being used today. People regularly attended concerts and operas for entertainment as music became available to the lower classes. This trend allowed for a gradual shift from the patronage system, where musicians worked for royal courts, to the free enterprise system, where they earned money through commissions, ticket sales, and other performance-related income.

Figure 4.3 Ny Björn, *The Holywell Music Room*, 2008. The Holywell Music Room in Oxford, England, built in 1748, was the first European concert hall and is still used today.

Figure 4.4 Anicet-Charles-Gabriel Lemonnier, In the Salon of Madame Geoffrin in 1755,1812. The painting shows people dressed in 1700s clothing meeting and discussing ideas.

Amateur musicians became common, with women in particular pursuing music studies. Music involvement was a social activity. Printed music was sold publicly for pianoforte (an instrument much like today's piano), voice, and small ensembles. Just as learning to play one's own music became widespread, literacy across Europe increased, and the availability of printed materials also increased. Coffee houses grew to become microcosms of academic life and hubs of public information. Debate clubs emerged, meeting in salons and other gathering spots to discuss political matters, philosophy, and other intellectual issues.

In the visual arts of the period, religious influences were still prominent in addition to formal portraits of royalty, nature scenes, and sculpted busts, masks, and statues. Some paintings depicted the ideal physical form like that of the Greek Classical period. In the painting *Joseph and his Brothers,* brothers presented in the lower left and right corners of the image possess sculpted muscles from hard labor, emphasizing their physique. In contrast, Joseph stands calmly, bathed with light, portraying an image of power, prosperity, and authority through his clothing and demeanor.

Defining Characteristics of Classicism in Music

Figure 4.5 Franz Anton Maulbertsch, Joseph and his Brothers, 1745-50.

Although Baroque music was evenly divided between vocal and instrumental music genres and secular and sacred music, composers began to move toward specific trends in the Classical period that followed. Instrumental music grew in popularity during the Classical period because instruments, tonal systems, and orchestral writing in the Baroque period had become more standardized. The harpsichord declined in popularity as the pianoforte became prominent. Composers concentrated on creating new music with larger forms, including sonatas, symphonies, and string quartets, that allowed audiences to be continually entertained over a longer period of time. Vocal music also continued to develop in the Classical period, taking opera to a new level where composers integrated recitative and aria forms to move the drama of opera forward.

In contrast to the ornamentation and decoration of the Baroque period, Classical music was focused on clarity, precision, and formal structure. The melody in a musical work was the most important component. An emphasis on melody meant that the harmony in most works was homophonic. Instead of several competing melodies, as was the case in the polyphonic textures of the Renaissance and Baroque eras, background materials supported the main melody as much as possible. Tonality and tonal centers were very clearly defined, with chord progressions helping to define major sections of the music.

Figure 4.6 Clip art image of a man wearing headphones and seated in front of a computer, used with permission from Microsoft.

Critical Listening

Several significant works are presented in this chapter, though they are only a small part of the many great works created during the Classical period. As you listen to Classical music, use the key music terms presented in Chapter 1 as tools to describe what you hear. Apply your new skills to the listening examples throughout the course and other music you listen to for pleasure.

Listening Goals

1. Identify any Classical period traits in the music.

2. Listen for instruments and timbres, identify the type of ensemble you hear and who is performing, and note whether a harpsichord is present.

3. Observe patterns, rhythms, melodies, and motives that occur within the form.

4. Listen for dynamic and tempo changes, including sudden or gradual changes in both dynamics and tempo.

5. Practice describing these observed concepts using the music terms instrumentation, timbre, texture, tempo, dynamics, and form.

Key Music Terms

 Instrumentation became more standardized during the Classical period. For example, the symphony orchestra was organized into a format with specific instruments and sections, as we recognize orchestras today. During

Figure 4.7 Derek Gleeson, Dublin Philharmonic Orchestra in Performance, Tchaikovsky 4th Symphony, 2011.

the Classical period, the harpsichord was no longer a prominent instrument, but the pianoforte—a forerunner of the modern piano—became very popular.

 Timbre, or tone quality, describes the quality of a musical sound. Timbre is generally discussed using adjectives, like *bright, dark, buzzy, airy, thin,* and *smooth*. Many different adjectives can be effectively used to describe timbre, based on your perceptions and opinions about what you hear in the sound. Classical composers used instruments for their traditional sounds. Performers sometimes became virtuosos, extremely skilled at demonstrating advanced performing abilities.

 Texture is a term that describes what is going on in the music at any moment. Musical texture is the way that melody, harmony, and rhythm combine. Texture can be described in musical terms like *monophonic, homophonic,* and *polyphonic* or with adjectives like *thin, thick,* and *rich.* A lot of Classical period music was homophonic and revolved around melody or melodic statements. Some Classical music included the fugue, which was polyphonic.

 Harmony is created when at least two voices perform together. Two different types of textures exist in music that may create harmony: homophony and polyphony. One additional musical texture, monophony, does not include any harmony. Monophony was not as common during the Classical period as it was in earlier years.

When considering musical texture, ask yourself these questions:

- *What instruments or voices am I hearing?*
- *Do I hear one melody, or more than one?*
- *Are the extra voices or instruments changing together or at different times?*
- *Is it difficult to identify the melody, perhaps because there are several melodies happening at once?*

 Tempo is the speed of the music. Tempo may also be called *time.* Tempo can change during a piece to add expression or emotional communication. One example of tempo change is *rubato,* which means to slow the tempo. Speeding up the tempo is called an *accelerando,* and slowing down gradually is called *ritardando.* Classical period music began to explore tempo changes.

Rhythm became an important area of focus in Classical music. Although during the Baroque period rhythms were constant and repetitive, Classical music rebelled against this uniformity. Rhythm was used as a tool to drive audience interest during the late 1700s and became flexible. Rhythm became one of several ways composers provided variety in their works while still maintaining enough cohesiveness to keep listeners interested.

Dynamics are changing volume levels of musical sounds. Dynamics can range from softer than *piano* (soft or quiet) to above *forte* (loud). Dynamics can also change, getting louder (*crescendo*) and getting softer (*diminuendo*). Dynamics and changing dynamics give the music expression, make it interesting, and add variety.

Form is the organization and structure of a musical selection. In the Classical period, new and precise forms were created to help composers produce large quantities of quality music on demand. Some of these forms included the sonata, rondo, theme and variations, and minuet and trio. The multimovement symphony was developed to provide extended performances that entertained audiences for greater lengths of time, as concert halls were built and concert attendance became a public pastime.

Instrumental Music Forms

Instrumental music from this period mostly fit into the multimovement format. Movements are complete sections of a work with their own form, often a binary (aab) or ternary (aba) form. In ***binary form***, the music consists of two distinct sections without a return of the first section as in the minuet and trio form. In ***ternary form***, the first section presents the theme or main ideas, the next section develops in a new key using other musical ideas, and the final section returns to the familiar material from the first section either in part or whole.

A typical four-movement work was organized in the following manner:

1. A fast movement in sonata (aba) form
2. A slower movement in theme and variation form or some kind of ternary (aba) form
3. A dance movement, often a minuet and trio (aab) or scherzo and trio
4. A fast movement, often a rondo (abacada) or sonata (aba) form

When a musical work consisted of only three movements, the third dance movement was left out—a choice commonly made by Mozart.

The term ***sonata*** refers to both a piece of music performed by a single instrument—usually the piano—or a small group and also to the first movement in a large, multimovement work. Listen to Mozart's <u>Piano Sonata no. 11 in A Major, Rondo Alla Turca, K. 331</u>. This particular Mozart sonata includes a first movement in theme and variations form, a second movement in minuet and trio form, and a final movement in rondo form. Mozart left out the typical first-movement sonata form altogether.

Composers

The two most significant composers of the Classical era were Wolfgang Amadeus Mozart (1756-1791) and Franz Joseph Haydn (1732-1809). Both men were Austrians, and both continue to gain popularity among today's audiences through public orchestra

Figure 4.8 Joseph Lange, Mozart at the Pianoforte, 1782-83.

performances of their works and thousands of recordings available through the Alexander Street online library and other sources.

Mozart

Mozart (1756-1791) was born in January 1756, in Salzburg, Austria. At the time of his birth, several European countries were fighting over territory, entering treaties, and declaring war. Despite the politically turbulent events of his time, Mozart flourished as a young musician. He learned his first scherzo on pianoforte at age five and performed twice as a singer that year—once in a play and once as part of a children's group in Munich. His father, Leopold, taught him to play piano as well as academic subjects and languages. Listen to part of Mozart's Piano Concerto no. 21.

Early in his childhood, Mozart showed musical genius, dedication, and creativity. At age five, he composed six keyboard works, including Andante in C Major, Allegro in F Major, three different minuets in F, and Allegro in B-flat Major, all of which were dedicated to his father. In his childhood, Wolfgang showed early musical genius, dedication, and creativity. Mozart's father recognized his son's unusual musical talents, and he subsequently invested all of his time and energy into training and promoting his son. He took Mozart and his sister, Maria Anna, also a musician, on an extensive performance tour across Europe to perform for political leaders and dignitaries. During this tour, which took place from 1763 to 1766, France, Spain, and Great Britain signed the Treaty of Paris (1763) and Prussia and Austria signed the Peace of Hubertusburg treaty (1763), ending the Seven Years' War. All of Mozart's family members became ill during the tour, and he himself had scarlet fever and several unnamed illnesses during the trip. Despite the hardship, Mozart composed more than fifteen varied musical works and performed in many royal courts and public venues while traveling.

Figure 4.9 Louis Carmontelle, Leopold Mozart and His Children, Wolfgang and Maria Ana, 1763 or 1764.

When he turned twelve, Mozart's father took him back to Vienna to build his musical career. By this time, his second symphony had already been completed. In Vienna, he was commissioned to write an entire opera buffa (an Italian comic opera), which was completed but not performed in Vienna. Mozart and his father returned to Salzburg, where the opera buffa was performed. After two performance tours in Italy, which yielded commissions to write operas and other works but no offers of employment, Mozart was eventually hired as the Salzburg *Konzertmeister* (conductor) and given a salary at age sixteen. Mozart was an energetic and brilliant but arrogant teen who thought he could find better opportunities for more pay. He and his mother traveled to Paris in 1778 hoping that he would find more desirable employment. Unfortunately, no offers appeared, and his mother became ill and died during the trip.

Mozart settled in Vienna and married at age twenty-six. He and his bride moved constantly, and they had six children, though four died as infants. Mozart was constantly unemployed and poor, wielding an arrogance and impulsivity that angered potential employers. Those who knew him well described him as intensely focused about his music while manic much of the rest of the time. Mozart carried out practical jokes, wrote dramatic and occasionally obscene letters, and appreciated scatological humor.

Mozart was influenced by George Frideric Handel and Johann Sebastian Bach, whose fugues he imitated in some of his later opera works. He also influenced many composers, including Johann Nepomuk Hummel, Beethoven, Frédéric Chopin, and Pyotr IlyichTchaikovsky, for hundreds of years. Mozart composed more than six hundred works, including many symphonies, operas, and concertos. His opera *The Magic Flute (Die Zauberflöte*, K. 620) premiered shortly before his death. Listen to "Der Hölle Rache" from act 2 of *The Magic Flute.* Mozart died at thirty-five from rheumatic fever in 1791.

For additional information about Mozart, visit the following websites:

- The Mozart Project: http://www.mozartproject.org/

- Salzburg Tourism: http://www.salzburg.info/en/art_culture/mozart

- Digital Mozart Edition: http://dme.mozarteum.at/DME/main/index.php?l=2

Haydn

Franz Joseph Haydn (1732-1809), was born in Rohrau, Austria. He was called Joseph rather than Franz by those who knew him and had been born into a large, musical family of twelve children. His father was a master wheelwright (a person who builds wagon wheels) and a magistrate who played the harp well but did not read music. Haydn's mother worked in Harrach castle (an estate in Rohrau) as a cook prior to marrying and was an excellent singer. As a child, Haydn was invited

Figure 4.10 Ludwig Guttenbrunn, *Portrait of Joseph Haydn,* **circa 1770.**

to live with a cousin in Hainburg who was a church choir director and school principal. While there, Haydn learned to read and write, sing, and play string, wind, and percussion instruments. When he was seven years old, he became a choirboy in Vienna, singing soprano for the next ten years. At age seventeen, once his voice had broken and he was not able to sing the high pitches of a soprano any longer, Haydn was forced to leave the choir.

Haydn spent the first part of his career working for the prince of Esterházy in Austria, which he continued to do for thirty years until the prince died. As part of his service to the prince, Haydn wrote a variety of music for every occasion and had an in-house orchestra and opera company. His most famous works are string quartets, sonatas, and symphonies. Listen to Haydn's String Quartet no. 62 in C Major, known as "Emperor" (1796-1797). Haydn became an independent musician and composer after the prince's death, selling his music privately. He was a tough businessman who negotiated dishonestly at times, but he also shared his wealth freely with those he cared about. Over the course of his life, Haydn was an interesting example of the cultural change from the patronage system in which composers served courtly nobles to the free enterprise system in which composers created music to "sell" through public performances and other means.

Figure 4.11 Thomas Hardy, *Joseph Haydn*, 1791.

Throughout his life, Haydn was affectionately called Papa Haydn. He was a conservative man who cared for others. The term *Papa* referred both to his concerns for others and to his contributions to the music discipline. Haydn lived to be seventy-seven years old. He taught younger students and directed performers with a patient manner, and he possessed virtue and character. At the same time, Haydn was proud of his own works and let others know it.

Haydn had a good sense of humor and enjoyed creating musical "jokes," such as something unexpected within a piece. For example, in his *Surprise* symphony, the joke is presented as a suddenly loud note in the middle of the opening melody, after which the music immediately returns to a very quiet dynamic. Listen to part of the four-movement Symphony no. 94 in G Major (1791). Haydn's music focused on single themes that developed throughout a piece rather than including a secondary theme as other composers often did. A reviewer who attended one of his concerts described the music as "simple, profound, and sublime" (Robbins Landon, 1976). Haydn composed polite, dignified music that pleased audiences immensely.

Haydn contributed much to music during the Classical era. He composed just fewer than 300 works, including 104 symphonies, 35 concertos, 60 piano sonatas, 82 string quartets, two oratorios, and several masses. Listen to Haydn's Trumpet Concerto in E-flat Major (1796). During early musical periods like the Classical era, trumpets in several different keys were used because instruments had not been standardized. The Haydn Trumpet Concerto was performed on an E-flat trumpet, which musicians still use today to perform the work, rather than the B-flat trumpet commonly used.

For more information about Franz Joseph Haydn, visit Encyclopaedia Britannica's page on the composer.

Closing

In the years commonly recognized as the Classical era, the aristocratic conditions of Austria produced two of the world's most significant composers—Haydn and Mozart. During their lives, both men experienced the decline of the patronage system and the growth of free enterprise, commissions, concerts, and personal music sales. Throughout Europe, the middle class became more influential, and the Industrial Revolution began. With this revolution, the musical world also experienced a revolution of sorts. A new musical style emerged that produced hundreds of great works, including string quartets, symphonies, concertos, and operas along with several new forms such as the sonata and rondo forms.

Form

This week, watch the video "Form: The Shape of Music," part of the Annenberg Learner

video series we will be viewing throughout the text.

Guiding Questions:

1. What are some characteristics of Classical-era music?

2. What new developments were noteworthy during the Classical era?

3. How did forms change during the mid-eighteenth century from the previous period?

4. Who were some of the significant composers during the period of 1750 to 1820?

5. What noteworthy pieces were composed during this period?

Self-Check Exercises

Complete the following self-check exercises to verify your mastery of key music terms presented in this chapter. Check answers at the bottom of page.

1. **Which of the following traits could describe music of the Classical era?**
    a. Extreme emotion
    b. Dissonance
    c. Supernatural or macabre themes
    d. Simplicity and pleasing variety

2. **Which composer became prominent during the Classical era?**
    a. Mahler
    b. Mozart
    c. Stravinsky
    d. Ventadorn

3. **What type of music is performed in more than one movement and involves instrumental performers?**
    a. Bel Canto
    b. Symphony
    c. Opera
    d. Lieder

4. **Which type of music did Haydn compose?**
    a. Concertos
    b. Symphonies
    c. Sonatas
    d. All of the above

Self-check quiz answers:
1. d. 2. b. 3. b. 4. d.

Additional Resources

Complete the following activities and consult the included resources.

1. As part of the Chapter 4 assignments, please visit <u>SFO Instrument Garden</u>. Explore the instruments in the instrument library. Here you can play a scale on each instrument and feel how the instrument is played.

2. Visit the following websites:

   a. <u>The Orchestra</u>

   b. <u>Radio Mozart</u>

Optional Enrichment

These examples are provided for additional enrichment for interested students, not as required viewing.

- Performance of <u>Mozart's opera *The Marriage of Figaro* from the Alexander Street Press.</u>

- A clip explaining <u>the plot of Mozart's *The Marriage of Figaro*</u> from the Alexander Street Press.

- "<u>The Pursuit of Happiness</u>," a personal view by Kenneth Clark. This video depicts art and music of the late Baroque and early Enlightenment eras.

Transcript: "Industrial Revolution"

What does it take to move a mountain?

During the Industrial Revolution, technological and socioeconomic mountains were not only moved but transformed, and the sweeping changes initiated in Britain eventually affected countries all over the world.

In the eighteenth century, domestic peace, economic health, and the availability of critical iron and coal resources in Britain set the stage for change. Ingenuity turned the spinning wheel, a simple craftsperson's tool for hundreds of years, into a time- and labor-saving device. It wasn't long before textile and loom factories essentially replaced home spinning and weaving. With the textile industry leading the way, the shift in manufacturing created unprecedented demand for new machines, mechanical components, processed materials, and skilled labor. Transportation systems expanded to keep up with the escalating flow of goods. Cities grew. Work became increasingly specialized, mechanized, and urbanized. An agriculture-based economy evolved into an industrial one.

The marriage of science and industry produced great changes both at home and abroad. Eli Whitney's cotton gin, 1763. Charles Babbage's mechanical computer, 1834. The first steam carriage, steam ship, and steam locomotive—all these inventions emerged within a very fertile eighty-year span. And even today, many of the world's mountains are still being moved as the products and processes born of the Industrial Revolution continue to shape and transform our modern lives.

Works Consulted

Arnold, Denis and Julian Rushton. "Mozart." *The Oxford Companion to Music*. Ed. Alison
　　　Latham. Oxford: Oxford University Press, 2011. *Oxford Music Online*. Web. 5 May
　　　2012.

Björn, Ny. *Holywell Music Room*. 18 Sept. 2008. *Wikimedia Commons*. Wikipedia
　　　Foundation, 6 Jan. 2012. Web. 5 May 2012.
　　　<http://commons.wikimedia.org/wiki/File:Holywell_Music_Room.jpg>.

Boerner, Steve. *The Mozart Project*. 24 Sept. 2011. Web. 15 Apr. 2014.
　　　<http://www.mozartproject.org/>.

Carmontelle, Louis. *Leopold Mozart and his Children, Wolfgang and Maria Anna*. 1763 or
　　　1764. Carnavalet Museum, Paris. *Wikimedia Commons*. Wikipedia Foundation, 21
　　　Dec. 2011. Web. 15 Apr. 2012.
　　　<http://commons.wikimedia.org/wiki/File:Wolfgang_Leopold_Nannerl.jpg>.

Clark, Caryl. "Haydn, Joseph." *The Oxford Companion to Music*. Ed. Alison Latham. Oxford:
　　　Oxford University Press, 2011. *Oxford Music Online*. 20 Apr. 2012.

"Classical period." *Encyclopaedia Britannica Online Academic Edition*. Encyclopaedia
　　　Britannica Inc. 2012. Web. 17 Aug. 2012.

Construction tools sign, used with permission from Microsoft. "Images." *Office*. Web. 4 Sept.
　　　2012. <http://office.microsoft.com/en-
　　　us/images/results.aspx?ex=2&qu=tools#ai:MC900432556|mt:0|>.

Della Rosa, Saverio. *Wolfgang at Verona*. 1770. Collection of Alfred Cortot, Lausanne.
　　　Wikimedia Commons. Wikimedia Foundation, 5 July 2006. Web. 2 May 2012.
　　　<http://commons.wikimedia.org/wiki/File:Mozart_at_Melk09.jpg>.

Eisen, Cliff, et al. "Mozart." *Oxford Music Online*. *Grove Music Online*. Web. 2 May 2012.

"Form: The Shape of Music." *Exploring the World of Music*. Prod. Pacific Street Films and the
　　　Educational Film Center, 1999. *Annenberg Learner*. Web. 31 July 2012.
　　　<http://www.learner.org/resources/series105.html>.

Gleeson, Derek. *Dublin Philharmonic Orchestra in performance, Tchaikovsky 4th Symphony*.
　　　24 June 2011. *Wikimedia Commons*. Wikipedia Foundation, 29 Mar. 2012. Web. 7
　　　May 2012. <http://commons.wikimedia.org/wiki/File:Tch_In_Charlotte.JPG>.

Guttenbrunn, Ludwig. *Portrait of Joseph Haydn*. Circa 1770. *Wikimedia Commons*. Wikipedia
　　　Foundation, 6 Apr. 2012. Web. 5 May 2012.
　　　<http://commons.wikimedia.org/wiki/File:Haydnportrait.jpg>.

Hardy, Thomas. *Joseph Haydn. 1791*. Royal College of Music, London. *Wikimedia Commons*.
　　　Wikipedia Foundation. 7 May 2012. Web. 23 Aug. 2012.
　　　<http://commons.wikimedia.org/wiki/File:Haydn_portrait_by_Thomas_Hardy_(small)
　　　.jpg>.

"Haydn, Franz Joseph." *The Oxford Dictionary of Music*, 2nd edition revised. Eds. Michael Kennedy and Joyce Bourne. *Oxford Music Online*. Web. 1 May 2012.

Haydn, Joseph. *String Quartet no. 62 in C Major*. Perf. Carpe Diem Quartet of HSPVA. *YouTube*. 23 Mar. 2012. Web. 22 Aug. 2012. <http://youtu.be/QKVFDAQ2KAs>.

—. *"Surprise," Symphony No. 94 in G major*. 1791. Perf. Barry Wordsworth. *YouTube*. 10 Dec. 2008. Web. 23 Aug. 2012. <http://youtu.be/OgF-Wzp8Ni8>.

—. *Trumpet Concerto in E-flat Major*. 1796. Perf. Peter Skvor, Capella Istropolitana, and Miroslav Kejmar. *YouTube*. 21 Mar. 2010. Web. 23 Aug. 2012. <http://youtu.be/Xz_4jrhwliQ>.

"Joseph Haydn." *Encyclopaedia Britannica Online Academic Edition*. Encyclopaedia Britannica Inc. 2012. Web. 17 Aug. 2012.

Lange, Joseph. *Mozart at the Pianoforte*. 1782-3. Stiftung Mozarteum, Salzburg, Austria. *Wikimedia Commons*. Wikipedia Foundation, 2 Dec. 2010. Web. 7 Apr. 2012. <http://commons.wikimedia.org/wiki/File:Mozart_Lange.png>.

"Le Nozze di Figaro: Bonus Material." Mozart, Wolfgang Amadeus. *Le Nozze di Figaro (The Marriage of Figaro)*. 1786. Dir. David McVicar. Cond. Antonio Pappano. Perf. Chorus of the Royal Opera House and Covent Garden & Orchestra of the Royal Opera House. Covent Garden, London. 17 Feb. 2006. *Music Online: Classical Music Library*. Alexander Street Press. Web. 23 Aug. 2012. <http://ezproxy.apus.edu/login?url=http://vasc.alexanderstreet.com/view/603662/play/true/>.

Lemonnier, Anicet-Charles-Gabriel. *In the Salon of Madame Geoffrin in 1755*. 1812. Malmaison Castle Museum, Rueil-Malmaison, France. *Wikimedia Commons*. Wikimedia Foundation, 3 Feb. 2012. Web. 5 May 2012. <http://commons.wikimedia.org/wiki/File:A_Reading_in_the_Salon_of_Mme_Geoffrin,_1755_Small.jpg>.

Little, Meredith Ellis. "Minuet." *Oxford Music Online*. *Grove Music Online*. Web. 17 May 2012.

Man wearing headphones and seated in front of a computer, used with permission from Microsoft. "Images." *Office*. Web. 4 Sept. 2012. <http://office.microsoft.com/en-us/images/results.aspx?qu=listening%20to%20headphones&ctt=1#ai:MP900422541|mt:2|>.

Maulbertsch, Franz Anton. *Joseph and his Brothers*. 1745-50. Museum of Fine Arts, Budapest, Hungary. *Wikimedia Commons*. Wikipedia Foundation, 5 Jan. 2012. Web.12 May 2012 <http://commons.wikimedia.org/wiki/File:Franz_Anton_Maulbertsch_-_Joseph_and_his_Brothers_-_WGA14678.jpg>.

Mozart, Wolfgang Amadeus. "Der Hölle Rache." *Die Zauberflöte* .1791. Dir. David McVicar. Cond. Colin Davis. Royal Opera House, Covent Garden, London. *YouTube.* 21 July 2006. Web. 22 Aug. 2012. <http://youtu.be/DvuKxL4LOqc>.

—. *Le Nozze di Figaro (The Marriage of Figaro).* 1786. Dir. David McVicar. Cond. Antonio Pappano. Perf. Chorus of the Royal Opera House and Covent Garden & Orchestra of the Royal Opera House. Covent Garden, London. 17 Feb. 2006. *Music Online: Classical Music Library.* Alexander Street Press. Web. 23 Aug. 2012. <http://ezproxy.apus.edu/login?url=http://vasc.alexanderstreet.com/view/578411/play/true/>.

—. *Piano Concerto no. 21, Andante.* 1785. Perf. Netherlands Chamber Orchestra. *YouTube.* 14 Jan. 2008. Web. 21 Aug. 2012. <http://youtu.be/df-eLzao63l>.

—. *Piano Sonata no. 11 in A Major, K 331.* 1783. Perf. Lili Kraus. 1 Jan. 2004 *Music Online: Classical Music Library.* Alexander Street Press. Web. 21 Oct. 2014. <http://ezproxy.apus.edu/login?url=http://search.alexanderstreet.com/view/work/2488544>.

Nattier, Jean-Marc. *Portrait of Princess Ekaterina Golitsyna.* 1757. Pushkin State Museum of Fine Arts, Moscow. *Wikimedia Commons.* Wikipedia Foundation, 10 Jan. 2012. Web. 5 May 2012. <http://commons.wikimedia.org/wiki/File:Jean-Marc_Nattier,_Portrait_de_la_princesse_Ekaterina_Dmitrievna_Golitsyna_(1757).jpg>.

"Peace of Hubertusburg." *Encyclopaedia Britannica Online Academic Edition.* Encyclopaedia Britannica Inc. 2012. Web. 15 Apr. 2012.

Radio Mozart. 4 Jan. 2010. Web. 21 Oct. 2014. <http://www.radiomozart.net/Pages/default.aspx>.

Robbins Landon, H. C. *Haydn: Chronicle and Works, Vol. III: Haydn in England, 1791-1795.* Bloomington: Indiana University Press, 1976. Print.

San Francisco Symphony. *Instrument Garden.* SFSKids. N.d. Web. 15 Apr. 2014. <http://www.sfskids.org/index.html?f=perform>.

"Seven Years' War." *Encyclopaedia Britannica Online Academic Edition.* Encyclopaedia Britannica Inc. 2012. Web. 2 Apr 2012

Sisman, Elaine. "Variations." *Oxford Music Online. Grove Music Online.* 5 May 2012.

"The Orchestra." *Classics for Kids.* Cincinnati Public Radio. Web. 21 Oct. 2014. <http://www.classicsforkids.com/music/orchestra.asp>.

"The Pursuit of Happiness." Dir. Peter Montagnon. British Broadcasting Corporation. 1996. *Music Online: Classical Music Library.* Alexander Street Press. Web. 23 Aug. 2012. <http://ezproxy.apus.edu/login?url=http://vasc.alexanderstreet.com/view/883240/play/true/>.

Webster, James and Georg Feder. "Haydn, Joseph." *Oxford Music Online. Grove Music Online*. 11 May 2012.

"Wolfgang Amadeus Mozart." *Encyclopaedia Britannica Online Academic Edition*. Encyclopaedia Britannica Inc. 2012. Web. 17 Aug. 2012.

Chapter 5

The Romantic Period

By Bethanie L. Hansens

"Opera is when a guy gets stabbed in the back and, instead of bleeding, he sings."
    – Ed Gardner as Archie, Duffy's Tavern

Romanticism was a period in the arts and literature that emphasized passion and intuition over reason and logic. The Romantic Period (about 1820-

Figure 5.1 Joseph Karl Stieler, Beethoven with the Manuscript of the Missa Solemnis, 1820.

1910) was a time of rebellion against structure, traditional expectations, and rationalism. Use of the term *Romanticism* began in literature; authors used the term to describe nineteenth-century expressive literature, like short stories and novels. Composers too embraced this term to describe their music written during this era. Although music of the Romantic era was generally innovative and emotionally intense, this period produced composers who were highly individualistic and widely known for their own special approaches to composing.

The Romantic era began with Beethoven and also included Chopin, Wagner, Schubert, Schumann, Brahms, Verdi, Mahler, Strauss, Liszt, Berlioz, Mussorgsky, and Tchaikovsky, among others. We know many exceptional composers from this period because much of what was produced survives and is commonly performed today. Composers of the Romantic era sought to communicate emotion and expression over the use of form, fueled by the societal and political changes taking place around them. While the Classical period thrived on formulaic music that pleased courtly audiences, Romantic period music gained momentum through the growing popularity of public performances and composers' using musical tools in new ways.

Relevant Historical Events

After the Renaissance and Reformation, Western Europe began to experience social, political and economic revolution. The Catholic Church that had dominated previous centuries no longer ruled society, as its influence had diminished from the sixteenth century onward. Protestants believed more in performing good works as signs of mortality, which created a Protestant work ethic and emphasis on humanism. For the first time, people focused on the moral worth or value of individuals during their earthly lives. People began to think about having "good" character and enjoying a high quality of life. This change contrasted the "afterlife" emphasis of previous centuries.

People worked to learn and develop themselves, and medical and scientific innovation blossomed. An unprecedented sudden population boom occurred in Europe that doubled the population to four hundred million. This population boom was mostly the result of increased knowledge of anatomy, disease prevention, and basic health care. Louis Pasteur (1822-95), a French scientist, discovered new theories about germs and bacteria. Pasteur invented the rabies vaccine, developed a method to stop milk and wine from souring (now referred to as pasteurization), and solidified theories about germs. Pasteur and other scientists developed the fields of microbiology and chemistry in beneficial ways.

In America, the early 1800s were years of expansion and migration west. In 1803, the United States purchased a piece of land from France known as the *Louisiana Purchase*, which doubled the size of the United States. Lewis and Clark traveled west in 1804 to discover and document the countryside all the way to the Pacific Ocean, through what we now know as Idaho and Washington. The California Gold Rush began in 1848. The first transcontinental railroad was completed in 1869, making it possible for people to travel

Figure 5.2 Felix Nadar, *Louis Pasteur*, 1978. Black and white photograph of French biologist Louis Pasteur (1822-95).

America freely to pursue their ambitions and take command of their own destinies. The first national park, Yellowstone, was established in 1872; in 1893, Frederick Jackson Turner declared that there was no longer an "American Frontier."

Significant inventions and developments took place during the nineteenth century that modernized Western civilization. The

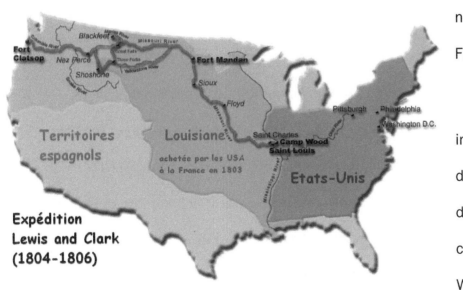

Figure 5.3 Urban, *Expédition Lewis and* Clark, 2005. This is an image depicting the Lewis and Clark Expedition route to explore uncharted areas of the western United

Second Industrial Revolution began in 1871, while twenty-six million people in India and thirteen million people in China died from famine. There was a significant disparity between the West and the rest of the world. During these years, wealth and prosperity in the United States expanded to create the "Gilded Age" (circa 1870-96). Westerners "discovered" and explored large land masses worldwide and developed many new modes of transportation. Automobiles with steam and electric engines were created during this century, leading to early gas-powered cars at the end of the 1800s.

Political Influences

The world political climate in the early 1800s affected the arts and human expression significantly. Jean-Jacques Rousseau (1712-78), the French philosopher, taught theories of social reform and opposed political tyranny. These ideas became the theme of common people in many places and influenced liberal and revolutionary events of the late eighteenth and early nineteenth centuries.

Figure 5.4 Jacques-Louis David, Portrait of Napoleon in his study at the Tuileries, 1812. This painting depicts Napoleon in the uniform of the Imperial Guard horse hunters.

The American Revolutionary War (1775-83) shifted the focus from a ruling monarchy to empowered civilians. The French Revolution (1789-99) began a period of political upheaval throughout much of Europe that lasted for many years. Features of this revolution included the pursuit of empowerment of the common individual, struggles over territory and power, and the leadership of Napoleon Bonaparte; Napoleon worked his way up French military ranks to eventually crown himself as Emperor of the French in 1804. In many countries, the idea that common people had a "voice" and could challenge governments took hold, resulting in turbulence between tradition, idealism, and revolution. Beethoven's music categorized as his "middle" period was composed during this time and was heavily influenced by the tubulence and revolutionary ideas around him.

The influence of political changes on the arts is evident in the type of music Beethoven composed beginning with the *Eroica Symphony* (Symphony No. 3, 1804). The *Eroica* was a large-scale dramatic piece Beethoven composed and dedicated to revolutionary ideas. The symphony had first been dedicated to Napoleon and called "Buonaparte," until the leader declared himself to be the Emperor. At this news, Beethoven feared that Bonaparte would simply become another political tyrant, and he changed the title to *Eroica*, or "Heroic." The piece followed Classical period structure but introduced more grandiose musical ideas on a large scale in four smaller parts, or ***movements***. The *Eroica* was the beginning of musical change for Beethoven and other composers. This work was so significant that it is frequently considered the piece that changed Beethoven's focus and began Romanticism in music.

- Click to view a performance of the first movement from the *Eroica*, performed by the Wiener Philharmoniker Orchestra, conducted by Leonard Bernstein.

- Click to view the BBC 2003 production of *Eroica*, based on Beethoven's composing of the symphony and its political context. (Viewing of this film is optional, and not necessary for class completion.)

Political developments in America and France introduced new governmental ideas based on constitutions and democracy. The French aristocrat Alexis de Tocqueville wrote two significant works discussing government based on the will of the people, *Democracy in America* (1835), and *The Old Regime and the Revolution* (1856). The American and French revolutions set a precedent for future political ideals throughout the modern world.

Social Influences

While the masses were empowered by political changes, industrial development began to change the way people interacted, where they lived, and how they worked. The Industrial Revolution, which began in Great Britain, swept through cities and towns, bringing manufacturing industries with smokestacks and large machinery. Industrialized society included a focus on the individual rather than the group, as well as the espousing of intellectually-determined "rights" by people or groups rather than dominance by divinely-appointed authorities. A large percentage of agricultural workers moved from farms into cities. Machines were used to increase productivity beyond what had been obtained through manual and animal-assisted work.

Many people in both Europe and America began to feel helpless or hopeless due to oppressive and inhumane working conditions. Children commonly worked in factories. Additionally, people began to spend their time in designated ways, such as "at work," and in leisure pursuits. Work time became separate from family and socialization. Previously, families had been cooperative groups who worked together and benefitted together. Industrialization took the collective family economy and created consumers who either owned businesses or depended on them.

Cultural Influences

Figure 5.5 Francisco Goya, The 2nd of May 1808 in Madrid: the charge of the Mamelukes, 1814.

Artistic professions emerged in the nineteenth century out of necessity, because music and other arts were no longer solely supported by the patronage system. As composers created more challenging works, extremely skilled professional performers were needed. Artists began to depict scenes of loneliness, isolation, and discontent, as well as extreme emotions like fear and insanity later in the century. The chaos and terror of war was illustrated by visual artists like Francisco Goya of Spain (see figure 5.5). In war-related art, dismal grey colors portrayed the mood of battle, and brighter colors depected characteristics such as lost innocence, death, and strife.

Artistic expression reflected the conditions of the times. In the latter half of the Romantic period, Carnegie Hall (1891) was built in New York. Modern transportation allowed musicians and audiences to travel, bringing magnificent performers to remote areas.

Literature developed, including Gothic novels, such as *Frankenstein* by Mary Shelley (1818); fiction, like the Grimm brothers' *Fairy Tales*; and the poetry of Goethe, Keats, Whitman, Wordsworth, and Edgar Allan Poe. Automation of the printing press between 1812 and 1818, due to the new steam-powered press of Friedrich Koenig, led to rapid printing on both sides of a page simultaneously (Bolza).

Printing technology continued to progress, as the rotary press of 1843 increased speed and efficiency. New presses produced printed pages ten times faster than hand presses, which advanced the creation of mass-produced newspapers and books. Widely available printed materials increased literacy throughout the century.

Figure 5.6 Stanhope hand-powered printing press, late 1770's.

Figure 5.7 N. Orr, Hoe 6-Cylinder Motored Rotary Printing Press, 1864.

Figure 5.8 Ford Maddox Brown. Romeo and Juliet, 1870. This oil on canvas painting portrays Romeo and Juliet meeting at the balcony of Juliet's home, kissing.

Composers were heavily influenced by literature, and many included themes and stories in their works. Examples of this connection include Tchaikovsky's *Romeo and Juliet* (1870), based on Shakespeare's play, and "Der Erlkönig" (1813) by Franz Schubert, based on a poem by Goethe. "Der Erlkönig" is a frantic piece about a father rushing his ill child to help while speeding along on a horse, which ends in the child's death by supernatural means. This piece exemplified the extreme emotions of terror, insanity, and hysteria popular in the Romantic Era.

Defining Characteristics of Romanticism in Music

Music during the Romantic period became wildly expressive and emotional. Composers experimented with new chords, unusual chord progressions, dissonance (notes that are close together and seem to create tension), and smaller motifs for thematic development. Music began to include creative and innovative harmonies. Symphonies and operas were still the mainstay of performance music, but smaller works that used to be confined to private performances also began taking the stage—such as sonatas, lieder

(German songs), and other works. Instrumental program music (music that tells a story without words) mimicked opera by portraying scenes and stories through non-vocal music.

Composers of the Classical period produced music that often sounded similar, like Mozart and Haydn, but composers in the Romantic period distinguished themselves by developing unique personal styles, practices, and modes of expression. For the first time, rather than characterizing an era by a set of practices and trends, this period began to present composers as individuals. Common themes during this period included intense emotions, nationalism, extreme perceptions of nature, exoticism (focus on faraway places such as Asia), and the supernatural or macabre. *Symphonie Fantastique* (1830), by Berlioz, is an example of many common Romantic themes. The symphony lasts forty-five minutes and portrays the story of a young artist who envisions unrequited love, jubilant dancing at a ball, a pastoral nature scene, anger and murder, an execution, a burial, and a "Witches' Sabbath." Click to listen to the fifth track and final movement,

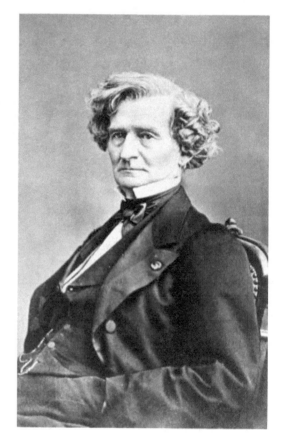

Figure 5.9 Franck, Hector Berlioz (1803-69), ca. 1855.

"Songe d'une nuit du Sabbat" or "Dreams of a Witches' Sabbath."

Critical Listening

"If a composer could say what he had to say in words he would not bother trying to say it in music."

– Gustav Mahler (Blaukopf 171)

Only a brief sampling of Romantic music is presented in this chapter, although hundreds of diverse works were composed during this era. As you listen to Romantic music, use the key music terms as tools to describe what you hear. Continue practicing to remember concepts, become more comfortable identifying traits in the music, and become able to apply your skills to new pieces that are not covered in this course. Keep in mind the general traits of Romantic music previously discussed, including intense emotions, nationalism, extreme perceptions of nature, exoticism, and the supernatural or macabre. Listen for these traits as you explore music of the four composers highlighted in this chapter: Beethoven, Wagner, Liszt, and Verdi.

Listening Objectives

Your listening objectives during this unit will be to:

Microsoft clipart image of man sitting at a computer, wearing headphones. Used with permission from Microsoft.

1. Identify any Romantic period traits in the music.

2. Listen for instrumentation and timbres, including voices or instruments that are performing.

3. Observe small motifs in music and listen for their repetition, manipulation, change, and overall presentation throughout a piece, including the return of familiar musical sounds and/or melodies that could signal a repeated section in the larger form of the work.

4. Listen for dynamic and tempo changes, incluncding sudden loud or soft passages, and sudden faster or slower sections.

5. Practice describing these observed concepts using the music terms instrumentation, timbre, texture, tempo, dynamics, and form.

Key Music Terms

 Instrumentation describes what kind of instrument or voice produced the music. During the Romantic period, the piano continued to become a prominent instrument. Other instruments became standardized, such as the saxophone (which was patented in 1846), the Boehm flute, and the Moritz tuba. Instruments were expected to produce sound in their extreme upper and lower ranges as needed. Specific instruments were used to communicate ideas to represent story characters or returning themes in program pieces like Berlioz's *Symphonie Fantastique.*

***Timbre, or tone quality*,** describes the quality of a musical sound. Timbre is generally discussed using adjectives, like *"bright," "dark," "buzzy," "airy," "thin,"* and *"smooth."* Many different adjectives can be effectively used to describe timbre, based on your perceptions and opinions about what is heard in the sound. Romantic composers often explored varying timbres to create specific moods and emotions—such as the terror communicated by shrill, high-pitched, dissonant tones. Timbre at times seemed edgy, rough, or shrill. At other times, timbres were warm and very lush as in Tchaikovsky's *Romeo and Juliet.*

Texture is a term that describes what is going on in the music at any moment. Musical ***texture*** is the way that melody, harmony, and rhythm combine. Texture can be described in musical terms, like *monophonic, homophonic,* and *polyphonic*—or with adjectives, like *"thin," "thick,"* and *"rich."* Much Romantic period music was homophonic and revolved around melody or melodic statements.

Melody is a recognizable line of music that includes different notes, or pitches, and rhythms in an organized way. A melody may be simple or complex, and it may be comprised of smaller pieces called "motifs." Beethoven's 5th Symphony, for example, includes a melody based on repeated motifs. Listen to an example of Beethoven's 5th Symphony, and take notice of the motif first heard in the first four notes of the piece, as you hear it pass by. After several statements of this smaller motif, the smaller motivic pieces begin to form a more recognizable melody. The melody stands out from the background musical material because it is stronger, louder, and more aggressively played.

Harmony is created when at least two voices perform together. Two different types of harmony generally exist in music—homophony, and polyphony. One additional musical texture, monophony, does not include any harmony.

When considering musical texture, ask yourself these questions:

- *What instruments or voices am I hearing?*

- *Is there a clear melody, with supporting harmony (homophony)? Or do I hear smaller segments of a melody, broken up and difficult to follow?*

- *Are the voices or instruments used in traditional, predictable ways, or do I hear unusual/extreme sounds?*

Tempo is the speed of the music. Tempo may also be called *"time."* Tempo can change during a piece to add expression, such as a *rubato* (slowing of the tempo). Speeding up the tempo is called an *accelerando,* and slowing down gradually is called a *ritardando.* Romantic period music explored the extremes of tempo fluctuation, often changing tempos throughout a piece to communicate emotion.

Dynamics are changing volume levels of musical sounds. Dynamics can range from softer than *piano* (soft or quiet) to above *forte* (loud). Dynamics can also change, getting louder (*crescendo*) and getting softer (*diminuendo*). Dynamics and changing dynamics give the music expression, make it interesting, and add variety. Dynamics are another tool exploited by Romantic period composers to create expression and emotional communication. Sudden dynamic extremes were commonly used.

Form is the organization and structure of a musical selection. The form of a work may include repeating large sections, repeating a theme or motif, or non-repeating sections. Large parts within a musical form are usually labeled with capital letters like "A" and "B." Within these larger sections, smaller parts may be labeled with lower-case letters like "a" and "b" to further designate repeated and non-repeated sections. In the Romantic period, forms became both larger and smaller than those of previous periods. The multi-movement symphony continued to develop, along with variations on existing ideas—such as the creation of an overture without any connection to an opera—and symphonic poems that expressed ideas without lyrics or an underlying story line. Forms were much more flexible during this period, with the expression or story sometimes more important than following a specific form.

Composers

"...music is a higher revelation than all wisdom and philosophy, the wine which inspires one to new generative processes, and I am the Bacchus who presses out this glorious wine for mankind and makes them spiritually drunken."

– Ludwig van Beethoven (Thayer 494)

Beethoven

Beethoven was generally considered the first Romantic composer. Ludwig van Beethoven (1770-1827) began his music career as a German court composer and musician

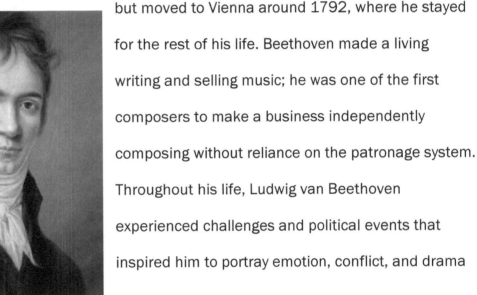

Figure 5.10 Christian Hornemann, Portrait of Ludwig van Beethoven, 1803.

but moved to Vienna around 1792, where he stayed for the rest of his life. Beethoven made a living writing and selling music; he was one of the first composers to make a business independently composing without reliance on the patronage system. Throughout his life, Ludwig van Beethoven experienced challenges and political events that inspired him to portray emotion, conflict, and drama in his music. Beethoven's father was a failed musician with little professional success who became an alcoholic. It is believed that he forced Ludwig to emulate Mozart's skills; Mozart was only fourteen years older than Beethoven. Ludwig's mother died in his youth, leaving him to help raise his siblings due to his father's incapacitation.

When Ludwig traveled to Vienna at age twenty-two, he studied with Haydn and several other composers. He was taught counterpoint—a specific method of composing common to the Classical period—and various functional composing techniques. Although

Haydn and others recognized Ludwig's obvious talent and exceptionally powerful piano performance abilities, they all struggled to teach Beethoven. He was a difficult student who disregarded rules and authority figures. To complicate matters, he began to gradually lose his hearing in 1796, at the age of twenty-six.

To develop ideas and work at composing throughout the day, Beethoven always carried a music notebook. He kept many notebooks throughout his life, several of which survive and are housed in the Berlin State Library. In his notes, Beethoven often began with a single musical motif or idea and worked with it until he developed the idea in detail and worked it into an entire piece of music. In all, Beethoven composed nine symphonies, thirty-two piano sonatas, nine piano trios, five piano concertos, one opera, two large choral works, and several other pieces.

Beethoven's music can be divided into three distinct periods within his composing career. Early Beethoven music (to 1802) generally fit under Classical period techniques and traditions and was influenced by Mozart and Haydn. Piano Sonata No. 14 in C sharp minor, "Moonlight," Op. 27 _Moonlight Sonata (1801)_ is one example from this period. Listeners may have heard the first movement in popular films or television programs (*Adagio Sostenuto*). Middle period music (1802-14) broadened to more expressive style and included more significant works. Some examples from this period include _"Allegro Con Brio," from Symphony No. 5, Op. 67_ (1808), and _String Quartet No. 11 in F Minor "Serioso", Op. 95_ (1810). Late Beethoven pieces (1815-27) were more serious and personal, likely due to Beethoven's deafness late in his life. In his late period, Beethoven retreated to more intellectual composing techniques, such as the use of Bach-like fugues, likely due to his total deafness and reclusive nature.

A comparison between Beethoven's Symphony No. 5 and Haydn's *Symphony No. 94 "Surprise"* illustrates the extreme impact Beethoven had on the music world in his day. The *Fifth Symphony* is intense, dramatic and edgy when compared to the "proper," polite and dignified Haydn piece. Audiences of the time would have been shocked by the extremes of Beethoven's music. Rather than expressing musical restraint, Beethoven opened the flood gates of emotion and communicated stronger ideas than had ever taken the stage previously.

As you listen to the *Allegro con Brio* from Symphony No. 5, exercise your developing music analysis skills. Describe the instrumentation by naming instruments that you hear. There are a lot of stringed instruments in this piece, but at times, you will hear the higher violins or the lower cellos and basses, and you will also hear timpani drums. Listen particularly for extreme ranges—very high and very low pitches. Observe the texture of the work, as melodies first enter in monophony, or unison, then play back and forth with a bit of polyphony (from about 0:07 to 0:16) leading into homophony. The influence of Bach's fugue-style, which Beethoven learned as a young organ student, can be heard early in this piece through the brief polyphony. Throughout the piece, listen for extreme dynamic changes, involving either the entire ensemble or just a few instruments. Notice tempo changes as the music seems to speed up, slow down, or stop altogether. Beethoven's *Symphony No. 5* is an excellent example of Romanticism and expression that flies in the face of traditional order and restraint.

For additional information about Beethoven, visit the following websites:

- Encyclopedia Brittanica:

  http://www.britannica.com/EBchecked/topic/58473/Ludwig-van-Beethoven

- Raptus Association for Music Appreciation: http://raptusassociation.org/index.html

- Ludwig van Beethoven Site: http://www.lvbeethoven.com/index_En.html

Wagner

Richard Wagner (1813-83) was a composer who wrote large opera-style works. He was born in the Jewish Quarter of Leipzig, a city known for its great German musicians and writers like Bach and Goethe. Wagner's father died six months after he was born. He was then raised by his mother and stepfather, actor and play-write Ludwig Geyer, who died when Richard was eight. Before his death, Geyer brought Richard into the theater industry. Richard later pursued music lessons in order to set his own plays to music. Richard had a natural gift of playing music

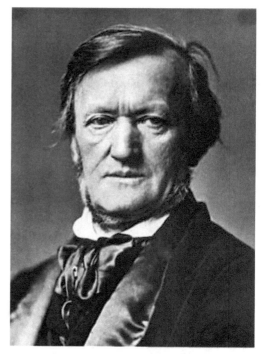

Figure 5.11 Franz Seraph Hanfstaengl,. Richard Wagner (1813-1883), 1871.

"by ear," which means to play without written music. In just a few years, Richard transcribed others' complicated pieces of music and began composing his own works. He was inspired by Beethoven and composed a symphony similar to Beethoven's 9th after only five years of music lessons and one year of university studies.

Wagner's career was a turbulent one. His first performed opera, *Das Liebesverbot,* was a failure and even bankrupted the production company which sponsored it. He struggled financially and married an actress, with whom he experienced a torrid relationship. Wagner moved from city to city trying to promote his operas, fleeing with his wife to Paris at one point just to avoid debt collectors. It was several years before anyone accepted his musical works for production, but Wagner persevered with the determination that he would eventually succeed.

When success finally came, Wagner moved back to Germany to produce his operas and was able to pay back old debts and take a leadership position in local music activities. He could not resist becoming a political activist, and he wrote anti-aristocratic articles for the local radical newspaper. He also physically participated in leftist rebellion activities and fled Germany a second time, to avoid arrest. During his exile, Wagner continued composing operas, including *Lohengrin*, and writing literary works, including *Art and the Revolution*. The *Lohengrin* opera was sent back to Dresden where it was performed in Wagner's absence and thrilled audiences. As a result of gaining King Ludwig II of Bavaria as a patron of his operas, Wagner was eventually pardoned and allowed to return.

Figure 5.12 Wallmüller, Die Meistersinger von Nürnberg by Richard Wagner, opera performance, 1960.

Music by Richard Wagner was extremely dramatic. Many of his works are also very long. *Die Meistersinger Overture, WWV 96* (1862) opens an opera that has three acts and lasts five hours. The *Die Meistersinger von Nürnberg* (The Mastersingers of Nuremberg) opera is commonly performed and popular today. In his large works, Wagner developed a type of melody he called the "leitmotif." Leitmotifs were themes associated with places, characters, or ideas in his dramas. This tool gave audience members something familiar to identify when watching his performed works. Wagner also named his tendency to write very large and dramatic operas, calling them *"Gesamtkunstwerk,"* or total works of art. He wrote both the libretto (the storyline and lyrics) and the music for all of his staged works, which was different than most other composers who hired others to write their libretti. As illustrated in the photograph in this section, Wagner's operas also involved constructed sets and large choruses.

As you listen to the *Die Walküre; Walkürenritt (The Ride of the Valkyries)* (1854) by Wagner, continue exercising your skills by analyzing the music. First, listen to a few minutes of the piece for your overall first impression. Determine whether the music has a steady or changing tempo. Throughout the piece, listen for extreme dynamic changes, involving either the entire ensemble or just a few instruments. Describe the instrumentation and/or voices by naming instruments and vocal parts that you hear. High-range female singers are sopranos, mid-range female singers are mezzo-sopranos or altos, mid-range males are tenors or baritones, and low-range males are basses. There are a lot of stringed instruments in this piece, but at times, you will hear other instruments. Listen particularly for extreme ranges—very high and very low pitches. Observe the texture of the work. Wagner typically composed thick, rich harmonies underneath the melody that sounds driven or heroic. Determine whether you hear an influence from Beethoven in this music. Wagner's opera changed the philosophy of opera and presented key Romantic traits but profited from the inspiration of other composers during his lifetime.

Liszt

Franz Liszt (1811-86) was a Hungarian pianist and composer. His father worked for Prince Esterhazy and was a skilled cellist. As a resident in the palace, Franz observed court concerts and impressive musicians. At five, he began taking piano lessons from his father, and at eight, he began composing his own music. He performed a public concert at age nine, which inspired local dignitaries to pay for his education. Franz studied in Vienna with Czerny, one of Beethoven's former students, and Salieri, the Viennese Court music director.

Liszt also studied in Paris, afterward touring Europe to perform for dignitaries at age thirteen. When he was only fourteen years old, Liszt's first and only opera was performed. His father accompanied him during his performance tours and died of typhoid fever during a trip to Italy.

Franz Liszt was a European traveler with diverse interests and extreme abilities, which at times presented challenges for him. Franz suffered from anxiety and depression that impacted his life significantly. In 1828, at age seventeen or eighteen, his depression after a failed romance caused him such intense illness that others thought he was going to die. An obituary was

Figure 5.13 W. & D. Downey, Photographers, Franz Liszt, ca. 1880.

prematurely printed in the local newspaper. He stopped playing the piano completely for an entire year and longed to become a priest. As he recovered, his interest in political matters piqued, and he composed a symphony in honor of the 1830 revolution in France. He met Hector Berlioz after attending a performance of *Symphonie Fantastique* and was inspired to transcribe that and many of Berlioz's works for piano. Liszt met and worked with many other composers, including Chopin, Schubert, and Mahler. He toured Europe again, performing for several years in many countries, lived in Germany for a time, and also lived in Italy.

Liszt was both an exceptional pianist and an outstanding composer. He was the first performer to give long piano concerts and featured the works of many other composers. His role in the Romantic era came from pushing the limits of piano compositions, adding to the harmonic language of the era, introducing **chromaticism** (the use of twelve pitches from the chromatic scale rather than eight pitches from a major or minor scale within a piece), developing the orchestral symphonic poem, and using musical themes in unique ways. Liszt's use of themes led to Wagner's "leitmotif" techniques, and his chromaticism led to the tonal changes that occurred in twentieth-century music. Liszt was a friend to other musicians and a teacher to many.

As you listen to *Hungarian Rhapsody No. 2, in C minor, S. 244* (1847) by Liszt, think about your music analysis tools. Begin by listening for tempo, dynamics, and style of the work. This piece is heavily influenced by Liszt's interest in Hungarian Romani melodies (commonly referred to in Liszt's time as "gypsy" melodies), which seem both haunting and exciting in the arrangement. Consider the form of this piece and listen for repeated melodies or motives. After you have listened to and described the *Hungarian Rhapsody No. 2*, listen to two other pieces by Liszt to compare their musical traits. The first, *Appassionata, etude for piano in F major (Transcendental etude No. 10),* (1851) is a technique study for pianists to improve skills. The second, *Piano Concerto No. 3 in E Flat Major* (1839), is a piano solo accompanied by an orchestra, designed to show off the pianist's abilities. These two pieces have opposing purposes (study vs. performance), but they both demonstrate Liszt's strong composing skills.

For another interpretation of Liszt's Hungarian Rhapsody, *visit the following link:*

- *Liszt's Hungarian Rhapsody, performed by Lang Lang*

Verdi

Giuseppe Verdi (1813-1901) was an Italian composer born near Parma, Italy in the same year as Richard Wagner. His father was an innkeeper and owned a farm, and the valley where his family resided was impoverished. Despite their hardships, the Verdi family provided piano lessons to Giuseppe from age four, bought him a spinet piano, and ensured that he attended the village school. He occasionally accompanied congregations on the organ for his church at age nine. Verdi was denied admission to the Milan conservatory

Figure 5.14 Giovanni Boldini, Portrait of Giuseppe Verdi, 1886.

because he played the piano poorly and was too old to attend, so he studied with Vincenzo Lavigna, a composer at the La Scala opera house. Verdi remembered his humble beginnings and called himself the least formally educated of all composers.

Verdi produced his first opera *Oberto, Conte di San Bonifacio* at age twenty-six (1839). Its success sent the production on a small performance tour to two other cities and provided a contract to write three more operas. After he experienced the loss of two children in their infancy and his wife also, Verdi's second opera (1840) was a failure. His third opera, *Nabucco* (1841), inspired by the biblical Nebuchadnezzer, was a fantastic success and toured all over Europe, Russia, and even Argentina. A theme from this opera, "Va,pensiero" became an unofficial anthem for Italy. In all, Verdi composed twenty-seven operas during his lifetime.

Personally, Verdi possessed great determination and a solid work ethic. He forced himself to compose two complete operas each year for a period, which involved finding the libretto (lyrics), editing, composing the music, locating suitable singers, conducting rehearsals, and publishing. His intensity and willingness to work paid off, and he eventually became a celebrity. In his later years, he composed operas for Paris that demanded different structures and the inclusion of a ballet. After he believed he had officially retired in 1873, Verdi wrote several works based on Shakespeare's dramas. A few of these works were his only compositions that appeared to have any musical influence from Wagner, and much of Verdi's work portrayed his own unique style.

Figure 5,15 Gran Teatro La Fenice. *Rigoletto* Opera Premiere Poster, 1851.

As you listen to Verdi's <u>"La donna è mobile" from the opera Rigoletto</u> (1851), notice the interesting and "singable" melody of this piece. Verdi possessed the capacity to write memorable singing parts throughout his operas, many of which are commonly used in pop culture today for television commercials, programs, and movies. Right away, the texture of this piece is obvious. The singer's part is easy to hear, and the background instruments support it fully. "La donna è mobile" has homophonic texture. The instrumentation is a solo voice, accompanied by a full orchestra. Throughout the piece, listen for extreme dynamic changes, involving either the entire ensemble or just a few instruments. Describe the instrumentation and/or voices by naming instruments and vocal parts that you hear. The music itself uses an older form, a strophic pattern (verses that musically repeat with new lyrics each time, like in modern songs) with an orchestra ritornello (repeated section), which originated in the Baroque era. The impact of this selection comes from its text, which conveys the Romantic traits of extreme emotion (love and passion) and drama (trust vs. dishonesty).

Italian Text	English Translation of "La donna è mobile"
La donna è mobile	Woman is flighty
Qual piùma al vento,	Like a feather in the wind,
Muta d'accento — e di pensiero.	She changes her voice — and her mind.
Sempre un amabile,	Always sweet,
Leggiadro viso,	Pretty face,
In pianto o in riso, — è menzognero.	In tears or in laughter, — she is always lying.

È sempre misero	Always miserable
Chi a lei s'affida,	Is he who trusts her,
Chi le confida — mal cauto il cuore!	Who confides in her — his unwary heart!
Pur mai non sentesi	Yet one never feels
Felice appieno	Fully happy
Chi su quel seno — non liba amore!	Who on that bosom, does not drink love!

Table 5.1 "La donna è mobile," Italian text and English translation

Summary of the Romantic Era

The Romantic era was a "coming of age" in the arts. As the world changed and tradition was challenged or abolished, artists changed or broke traditional barriers as well. The Western world changed dramatically, as America became widely settled, the Second Industrial Revolution developed, mass communications and transportation modes were created, and governments were revolutionized. Musical extremes in instrumental ranges, dynamics, tempo, and texture were employed to express an equal set of extremes in emotional states. Composers crafted highly individualized works that sometimes mirrored their own lives and often reflected the world around them. Art and literature focused on intense beauty, morbidity, characterizations of nature, the supernatural and the exotic, and extreme emotion.

Harmony

This week, watch the video "Harmony," part of the Annenberg Learner video series we will be

viewing throughout the text.

Guiding Questions

Identify, describe, and provide examples of various pieces of music from the Romantic

period.

1. What are some characteristics of early Romantic music?

2. What purposes/subject matters are represented in early Romantic music?

3. How did forms change during the early nineteenth century?

4. Who were some of the significant composers during the 1800s?

5. What were some of the noteworthy pieces that were composed during this period?

Self-Check Exercises

Complete the following self-check exercises to verify your mastery of key music terms presented in this chapter.

e. Which of the following traits could describe music of the Romantic era?
a. Expressed extreme emotion
b. Expressed nationalism
c. Presented supernatural or macabre themes
d. All of the above

f. Which composer became prominent during the rise of Napoleon Bonaparte?
a. Mozart
b. Beethoven
c. Ventadorn
d. Haydn

g. What type of music is known as a "total work of art," including both libretto (text) and music all written by the composer?
a. Bel Canto
b. Gesamtkunstwerk
c. Opera
d. Symphony

h. What type of music did Verdi compose?
a. Operas
b. Symphonies
c. Sonatas
d. Concertos

If you would like additional information about these terms, please review before proceeding. After you have read the questions above, check your answers at the bottom of this page.

Self-check quiz answers:
1. d. 2. b. 3. b. 4. a.

Additional Listening Examples

Opera

"Overture" from *Die Fledermaus,* by Johann Strauss II (1874)

Ballet

"Miniature Overture"(track 5) from *The Nutcracker*, Opus 71, by Tchaikovsky (1892)

Vocal Music, Song

"Nun will die Sonn' so hell aufgeh'n" from *Kindertotenlieder*, by Gustav Mahler (1901)

Instrumental Music (small group)

"Papillons" and *"Pierrot,"* from Carnaval, *Op. 9,* piano solo, by Robert Schumann (1835)

Instrumental Music (large group)

"Promenade" from *Pictures at an Exhibition,* by Modest Mussorgsky (1874)

"Scherzo (Lebhaft)" from *Symphony No. 4, Op 120*, for orchestra, by Robert Schumann (1841)

Additional Resources

1. Perfect Pitch Related to Language –podcast link. A 2009 study found that speakers of tonal languages (languages where the meaning of sounds can be differentiated by both shape and pitch) such as Cantonese are more likely to have perfect pitch than speakers of non-tonal languages like English. The link contains a transcript of the podcast.

2. Minnesota Public Radio – Streaming radio link. Take a few minutes to listen live to Minnesota Public Radio. After you have clicked on the site link, then click on **Listen**, which is located in the upper right-hand side of the page under the Classical heading.

As you are listening, see if you can identify the instruments and the style of music you hear. Listening to classical music radio is a wonderful way to gain a greater understanding of the Western music tradition!

Figure 5.16 Alexy Tyranov, Girl with Tambourine, 1836.

Works Consulted

Arnold, Denis and Barry Cooper. "Beethoven, Ludwig van." *The Oxford Companion to Music.* Ed. Alison Latham. *Oxford Music Online.* Web. 24 Apr. 2012.

Barry Millington, et al. "Wagner." *The New Grove Dictionary of Opera.* Ed. Stanley Sadie. *Grove Music Online. Oxford Music Online.* Web. 24 Apr. 2012.

Beethoven, Ludwig van. *Piano Sonata No. 14 in C Sharp Minor "Moonlight."* 1801. Perf. André Watts. 1999. *Music Online: Classical Music Library.* Alexander Street Press. Web. 27 Aug. 2012. <http://ezproxy.apus.edu/login?url=http://search.alexanderstreet.com/music-performing-arts/view/work/1478062>.

—. *String Quartet No. 11 in F Minor "Serioso", Op. 95, No.11.* 1810. Perf. The New Russian Quartet. *YouTube.* 4 Dec. 2009. Web. 24 Apr. 2012. <http://youtu.be/qsbMjPztW6U>.

—. *Symphony No.3 in E flat major, "Eroica."* 1804. Cond. Leonard Bernstein. *YouTube.* 26 June 2011. Web. 1 Apr. 2012. <http://youtu.be/W-uEjxxYtHo>.

—. *Symphony No. 5 in C Minor.* 1808. Cond. Riccardo Muti. Perf. The Philadelphia Orchestra. 1997. *Music Online: Classical Music Library.* Alexander Street Press. Web. 27 Aug. 2012. <http://ezproxy.apus.edu/login?url=http://search.alexanderstreet.com/view/work/1532772>.

"Beethoven, Ludwig van." *The Oxford Dictionary of Music*, 2nd ed. rev. Ed. Michael Kennedy. *Oxford Music Online.* Web. 24 Apr. 2012.

Berlioz, Hector. "Songe d'une nuit du Sabbat." *Symphonie Fantastique.* 1830. Cond. Yehudi Menuhin. Perf. Royal Philharmonic Orchestra. *Music Online: Classical Music Library.* Alexander Street Press. Web . 11 Apr. 2014. <http://ezproxy.apus.edu/login?url=http://search.alexanderstreet.com/view/work/961102>.

Blaukopf, Herta, ed. *Gustav Mahler: Briefe.* 2nd ed. Vienna: Zsolnay, 1996. Print.

Boldini, Giovanni. *Portrait of Giuseppe Verdi.* 1886. National Gallery of Modern Art, Rome. *Wikimedia Commons.* Wikipedia Foundation, 9 Aug. 2010. Web. 28 Aug. 2012. <http://commons.wikimedia.org/wiki/File:Verdi.jpg>.

Bolza, Hans. "Friedrich Koenig und die Erfindung der Druckmaschine." *Technikgeschichte* 34.1 (1967): 79-89. Print.

Brown, Ford Maddox. *Romeo and Juliet.*1870. Oil on canvas. Delaware Art Museum. *Wikimedia Commons.* Wikipedia Foundation, 30 Dec. 2008. Web. 24 Apr. 2012. <http://commons.wikimedia.org/wiki/File:20070205000653!Romeo_and_juliet_brown.jpg>.

Bubo bubo. *Erste Druckpresse (Stanhope Press) der Zeitung.* 1 May 2008. *Wikimedia Commons.* Wikipedia Foundation, 28 Aug. 2009. Web. 24 Apr. 2012. <http://commons.wikimedia.org/wiki/File:Iserlohn-Druckpresse1-Bubo.JPG>.

"chamber music." *Encyclopaedia Britannica. Encyclopaedia Britannica Online Academic Edition.* Encyclopaedia Britannica Inc., 2012. Web. 24 Apr. 2012. <http://www.britannica.com/EBchecked/topic/104861/chamber-music>.

Chou, Peter Y., ed. *Beethoven's Eroica Symphony: Symphony #3 in E flat Major, Opus #55. WisdomPortal.com.* 22 Sept. 2006. Web. 24 Apr. 2012. <http://www.wisdomportal.com/EroicaSymphony.html>.

Construction tools sign, used with permission from Microsoft. "Images." *Office.* Web. 4 Sept. 2012. <http://office.microsoft.com/en-us/images/results.aspx?ex=2&qu=tools#ai:MC900432556|mt:0|>.

"concerto." *Encyclopaedia Britannica. Encyclopaedia Britannica Online Academic Edition.* Encyclopaedia Britannica Inc., 2012. Web. 24 Apr. 2012. <http://www.britannica.com/EBchecked/topic/131077/concerto>.

David, Jacques-Louis. *Portrait of Napoleon in his study at the Tuileries.* 1812. National Gallery of Art. *Wikimedia Commons.* Wikipedia Foundation, 26 Feb. 2011. Web. 11 Apr. 2012. <http://commons.wikimedia.org/wiki/File:Napoleon_Bonaparte.jpg>.

Daverio, John and Eric Sams. "Schumann, Robert." *Grove Music Online. Oxford Music Online.* Web. 24 Apr. 2012.

De Goya, Francisco y Lucientes. *The 2nd of May 1808 in Madrid: the charge of the Mamelukes.* 1814. Prado Museum. *Wikimedia Commons.* Wikipedia Foundation, 24 May 2007. Web. 24 Apr. 2012. <http://commons.wikimedia.org/wiki/File:Francisco_de_Goya_y_Lucientes_026.jpg>.

Duffy's Tavern 118 Eps. Internet Archive. Internet Archive, n.d. Web. 27 Aug. 2012. <http://archive.org/details/DuffysTavern_524>.

Eroica. Dir. Simon Cellan Jones. Prod. Liza Marshall. BBC, 2003. *YouTube.* 2 Feb. 2011. Web. 28 Apr. 2012. <http://youtu.be/M3PzPKD5ACA>.

Franck (De Villecholle, François-Marie-Louis-Alexandre Gobinet). *Hector Berlioz.* Ca.1855. *Wikimedia Commons.* Wikipedia Foundation, 11 Aug. 2011. Web. 24 Apr. 2012. <http://commons.wikimedia.org/wiki/File:151_Franck_Hector_Berlioz.JPG>.

Franklin, Peter. "Mahler, Gustav." *Grove Music Online. Oxford Music Online.* Web. 27 Apr. 2012.

"Franz Liszt." *Encyclopaedia Britannica. Encyclopaedia Britannica Online Academic Edition.* Encyclopaedia Britannica Inc., 2012. Web. 27 Apr. 2012. <http://www.britannica.com/EBchecked/topic/343394/Franz-Liszt>.

Frolova-Walker, Marina. "Mussorgsky, Modest Petrovich." *The Oxford Companion to Music.*
Ed. Alison Latham. *Oxford Music Online.* Web. 28 Apr. 2012.

"Giuseppe Verdi." *Encyclopaedia Britannica. Encyclopaedia Britannica Online.*
Encyclopaedia Britannica Inc., 2012. Web. 29 Apr. 2012.
<http://www.britannica.com/EBchecked/topic/625922/Giuseppe-Verdi/215474/Late-years>.

Gran Teatro La Fenice. *Rigoletto.* 1851. Poster. *Wikimedia Commons.* Wikipedia Foundation,
21 Apr. 2012. Web. 28 Aug. 2012.
<http://commons.wikimedia.org/wiki/File:Rigoletto_premiere_poster.jpg>.

Hamilton, Kenneth. "Liszt, Franz." *The Oxford Companion to Music.* Ed. Alison Latham.
Oxford Music Online. Web. 21 Apr. 2012.

Hanfstaengl, Franz Seraph. *Richard Wagner, Munich.* 1871. Photograph. *Wikimedia
Commons.* Wikipedia Foundation, 7 Feb. 2005. Web. 27 Aug. 2012.
<http://commons.wikimedia.org/wiki/File:RichardWagner.jpg>.

"harmony." *Encyclopaedia Britannica. Encyclopaedia Britannica Online Academic Edition.*
Encyclopaedia Britannica Inc., 2012. Web. 20 Apr. 2012.
<http://www.britannica.com/EBchecked/topic/255575/harmony>.

"Harmony." *Exploring the World of Music.* Prod. Pacific Street Films and the Educational Film
Center, 1999. *Annenberg Learner.* Web. 29 Aug. 2012.
<http://www.learner.org/resources/series105.html>.

Haydn, Joseph. *Symphony No. 94 in G major "Surprise."* 1791. Cond. Neeme Järvi. Perf.
Accademia Nazionale di Santa Cecilia. *YouTube.* 11 Sept. 2011. Web. 24 Apr. 2012.
<http://youtu.be/Cbf6lns3i2E>.

Hornemann, Christian. *Portrait of Ludwig van Beethoven.* 1803. Beethoven-Haus, Bonn.
Wikimedia Commons. Wikipedia Foundation, 3 Nov. 2007. Web. 27 Aug. 2012.
<http://commons.wikimedia.org/wiki/File:Beethoven_Hornemann.jpg>.

Kennedy, Michael. "Mahler, Gustav." *The Oxford Companion to Music.* Ed. Alison Latham.
Oxford Music Online. Web. 24 Apr. 2012.

Kerman, Joseph, et al. "Beethoven, Ludwig van." *Grove Music Online. Oxford Music Online.*
Web. 24 Apr. 2012.

Liszt, Franz. *Appassionata, Etude for Piano in F Minor (Transcendental Etude No. 10), S.
139/10.* 1851. Perf. splico17. *YouTube.* 5 Apr. 2008. Web. 28 Aug. 2012.
<http://youtu.be/82XpOXElKmQ>.

—. *Hungarian Rhapsody No. 2 in C minor, S. 244.* 1847. Perf. Alexander Paley. 1999. *Music
Online: Classical Music Library.* Alexander Street Press. Web. 28 Aug. 2012.
<http://ezproxy.apus.edu/login?url=http://search.alexanderstreet.com/music-performing-arts/view/work/1665195>.

—. *Hungarian Rhapsody No. 2 in C minor, S. 244.* 1847. Perf. Lang Lang. *YouTube.* 21 Aug. 2008. Web. 28 Aug. 2012. <http://youtu.be/R-EGKpblBuw>.

—. *Piano Concerto No. 3 in E Flat Major.* 1839. Perf. Stephen Mayer and the London Symphony Orchestra. Cond. Tamàs Vàsàry. *YouTube.* 14 Jan. 2011. Web. 28 Aug. 2011. <http://youtu.be/yHoVOetOs74>.

"Ludwig van Beethoven." *Encyclopaedia Britannica. Encyclopaedia Britannica Online Academic Edition.* Encyclopaedia Britannica Inc., 2012. Web. 24 Apr. 2012. <http://www.britannica.com/EBchecked/topic/58473/Ludwig-van-Beethoven>.

Mahler, Gustav. "Nun will die Sonn' so hell aufgeh'n." *Kindertotenlieder.* 1901. Perf. Dietrich Fischer-Dieskau and Berliner Philharmoniker. Cond. Karl Böhm. 1964. *YouTube.* 27 Jan. 2012. Web. 29 Aug. 2012. <http://youtu.be/6O8Jn-Uk56k>.

"Mahler, Gustav." *The Oxford Dictionary of Music,* 2nd ed. rev. Ed. Michael Kennedy. *Oxford Music Online.* Web. 24 Apr. 2012.

Man wearing headphones and seated in front of a computer, used with permission from Microsoft. "Images." *Office.* Web. 4 Sept. 2012. <http://office.microsoft.com/en-us/images/results.aspx?qu=listening%20to%20headphones&ctt=1#ai:MP900422541|mt:2|>.

Minnesota Public Radio. "Classical Music Playlist: Program Highlights." *Classical Minnesota Public Radio.* Minnesota Public Radio, 2012. Web. 28 Aug. 2012. <http://minnesota.publicradio.org/radio/services/cms/pieces_played/>.

Mirsky, Steve. "Perfect Pitch Related to Language." *Scientific American.* 21 May 2009. Web. 25 Apr. 2012. <http://www.scientificamerican.com/podcast/episode.cfm?id=perfect-pitch-related-to-language-09-05-21>.

Mussorgsky, Modest. "Promenade." *Pictures at an Exhibition.* 1874. Cond. Simon Denis Rattle. Perf. Berliner Philharmoniker. 2008. *Music Online: Classical Music Library.* Alexander Street Press. Web. 28 Aug. 2012. <http://ezproxy.apus.edu/login?url=http://search.alexanderstreet.com/music-performing-arts/view/work/1533068>.

"Mussorgsky, Modest." *The Oxford Dictionary of Music,* 2nd ed. rev. Ed. Michael Kennedy. *Oxford Music Online.* Web. 24 Apr. 2012.

Nadar, Felix. *Louis Pasteur.* 1878. *Wikimedia Commons.* Wikipedia Foundation, 10 Oct. 2010. Web. 24 Apr. 2012. <http://commons.wikimedia.org/wiki/File:Louis_Pasteur.jpg>.

Norris, Geoffrey and Marina Frolova-Walker . "Tchaikovsky [Chaykovsky], Pyotr Il'yich." *The Oxford Companion to Music.* Ed. Alison Latham. *Oxford Music Online.* Web. 24 Apr. 2012.

Orr, N. "Richard March Hoe's Printing Press—Six Cylinder Design." 1864. *History of the Processes of Manufacture. Wikimedia Commons.* Wikipedia Foundation, 23 Sept. 2007. Web. 24 Apr. 2012. <http://commons.wikimedia.org/wiki/File:Hoe%27s_six-cylinder_press.png>.

Parker, Roger. "Verdi, Giuseppe." *Grove Music Online. Oxford Music Online.* Web. 20 Apr. 2012.

—. "Verdi, Giuseppe (Fortunino Francesco)." *The Oxford Companion to Music.* Ed. Alison Latham. *Oxford Music Online.* Web. 22 Apr. 2012.

Prevot, Dominique. *Ludwig van Beethoven's Website.* Dominique Prevot, 2012. Web. 27 Aug. 2012. <http://www.lvbeethoven.com/index.html>.

Raptus Association for Music Appreciation. *Ludwig van Beethoven: the Magnificent Master.* Raptus Association for Music Appreciation, 2011. Web. 27 Aug. 2012. <http://raptusassociation.org/index.html>.

"Richard Wagner." *Encyclopaedia Britannica. Encyclopaedia Britannica Online Academic Edition.* Encyclopaedia Britannica Inc., 2012. Web. 20 Apr. 2012. <http://www.britannica.com/EBchecked/topic/633925/Richard-Wagner>.

"Romantic(ism)." *The Oxford Dictionary of Music,* 2nd ed. rev. Ed. Michael Kennedy. *Oxford Music Online.* Web. 24 Apr. 2012.

Roland John Wiley. "Tchaikovsky, Pyotr Il'yich." *Grove Music Online. Oxford Music Online.* Web. 24 Apr. 2012.

Samson, Jim. "Romanticism." *Grove Music Online. Oxford Music Online.* Web. 29 Apr. 2012.

Schubert, Franz. "Der Erlkönig." 1815. Perf. Daniel Washington. *YouTube.* 30 Aug. 2010. Web. 1 Apr. 2012. <http://youtu.be/oLpsF4uwEVg>.

Schumann, Robert. "Papillons" and "Pierrot." *Carnaval, Op. 9.* 1835. Perf. Yuri Egorov. 2001. *Music Online: Classical Music Library.* Alexander Street Press. Web. 28 Aug. 2012. <http://ezproxy.apus.edu/login?url=http://search.alexanderstreet.com/music-performing-arts/view/work/956408>.

—. "Scherzo (Lebhaft)." *Symphony No. 4, Op 120.* 1841. Cond. Marek Janowski. Perf. Royal Liverpool Philharmonic Orchestra. 1993. *Music Online: Classical Music Library.* Alexander Street Press. Web. 28 Aug. 2012. <http://ezproxy.apus.edu/login?url=http://search.alexanderstreet.com/music-performing-arts/view/work/179728>.

Stieler, Joseph Karl. *Beethoven with the Manuscript of the* Missa Solemnis. 1820. Beethoven-Haus, Bonn. *Wikimedia Commons.* Wikipedia Foundation, 15 Dec. 2010. Web. 11 Apr. 2012. <http://en.wikipedia.org/wiki/File:Beethoven.jpg>.

Strauss, Johann II. "Overture." *Die Fledermaus.* 1874. Cond. Kurt Redel. Perf. Luxembourg Radio Symphony Orchestra. 2009. *Music Online: Classical Music Library.* Alexander Street Press. Web. 21 Oct. 2014.

<http://ezproxy.apus.edu/login?url=http://search.alexanderstreet.com/view/work/2
    000083>.

Taruskin, Richard. "Nationalism." *Grove Music Online. Oxford Music Online.* Web. 20 Apr.
    2012.

Tchaikovsky, Pyotr. "Miniature Overture." *The Nutcracker.* 1892. Cond. André Previn. Perf.
    London Symphony Orchestra. 2007. *Music Online: Classical Music Library.*
    Alexander Street Press. Web. 21 Oct. 2014.
    <http://ezproxy.apus.edu/login?url=http://search.alexanderstreet.com/view/work/1
    705500>.

"Tchaikovsky, Pyotr." *The Oxford Dictionary of Music,* 2nd ed. rev. Ed. Michael Kennedy.
    Oxford Music Online. Web. 24 Apr. 2012.

Thayer, A.W. *Thayer's Life of Beethoven.* Ed. Elliot Forbes. Rev. ed. 2 vols. Princeton:

Tyranov, Alexey. *Girl with Tambourine.* 1836. Oil on canvas. *Wikimedia Commons.* Wikipedia
    Foundation, 1 Mar. 2011. Web. 28 Aug. 2012.
    <http://commons.wikimedia.org/wiki/File:Alexey_Tyranov_-
    _Girl_with_tambourine.jpg>.

Urban. "Expédition Lewis and Clark." 31 Dec. 2005. *Wikimedia Commons.* Wikipedia
    Foundation, 21 Aug. 2009. Web. 24 Apr. 2012.
    <http://commons.wikimedia.org/wiki/File:Carte_Lewis-Clark_Expedition.png>.

Verdi, Giuseppi. "La donna è mobile." *Rigoletto.* 1851. Perf. Luciano Pavarotti. Dir. Jean-
    Pierre Ponnelle. *YouTube.* 11 Apr. 2006. Web. 28 Aug. 2012.
    <http://youtu.be/8A3zetSuYRg>.

—. "La donna è mobile, the Duke's aria from Rigoletto." *The Aria Database.* Trans. Randy
    Garrou. Ed. Robert Glaubitz. 2010. Web. 28 Aug. 2012. <http://www.aria-
    database.com/translations/rig15_donna.txt>.

"Verdi, Giuseppe." *The Oxford Dictionary of Music,* 2nd ed. rev. Ed. Michael Kennedy. *Oxford
    Music Online.* Web. 29 Apr. 2012.

Verdi, Giuseppe. "Va, pensiero." *Nabucco.* 1842. *YouTube.* 19 Sept. 2009. Web. 28 Aug.
    2012. <http://youtu.be/D6JNOI7A_mE>.

W. & D. Downey, Photographers. *Franz Liszt.* Ca. 1880. Photograph. *Wikimedia Commons.*
    Wikipedia Foundation, 23 Apr. 2012. Web. 27 Aug. 2012.
    <http://commons.wikimedia.org/wiki/File:Franz_Liszt_1880s.jpg>.

Wagner, Richard. *Die Meistersinger Overture, WWV 96.* 1862. Cond. Herbert von Karajan.
    Perf. Berliner Philharmoniker. 2004. *Music Online: Classical Music Library.* Alexander
    Street Press. Web. 27 Aug. 2012.
    <http://ezproxy.apus.edu/login?url=http://search.alexanderstreet.com/music-
    performing-arts/view/work/1475142>.

"Wagner, Richard." *The Oxford Dictionary of Music*, 2nd ed. rev. Ed. Michael Kennedy. *Oxford Music Online*. Web. 22 Apr. 2012.

Wagner, Richard. *Walkürenritt (The Ride of the Valkyries), Act 3. Die Walküre.* 1854. Cond. Pierre Boulez. Dir. Patrice Chéreau. *YouTube*. 20 July 2007. Web. 1 Apr. 2012. <http://youtu.be/1aKAH_tOaXA>.

Walker, Alan, et al. "Liszt, Franz." *Grove Music Online*. *Oxford Music Online*. Web. 29 Apr. 2012.

Wallmüller. *Leipzig Apernhaus, Aufführung der 'Meistersinger.'* 1960. Photograph. German Federal Archives. *Wikimedia Commons*. Wikipedia Foundation, 4 Dec. 2008. Web. 27 Apr. 2012. <http://commons.wikimedia.org/wiki/File:Bundesarchiv_Bild_183-76973-0002,_Leipzig,_Opernhaus,_Auff%C3%BChrung_der_%22Meistersinger%22.jpg>.

Warrack, John. "Romanticism." *The Oxford Companion to Music*. Ed. Alison Latham. *Oxford Music Online*. Web. 22 Apr. 2012.

Chapter 6

Twentieth-Century Music

By Bethanie L. Hansen

". . . . a song has a few rights, the same as other ordinary citizens. . . . If it happens to feel like trying to fly where humans cannot fly, . . . to scale mountains that are not, who shall stop it?"

- Charles Ives (1874-1954)

Figure 6.1 Ray Man, Portraitfoto von Arnold Schonberg, 1927.

As the nineteenth century ended, common musical rules were questioned, bent, reinvented, altered, and sometimes thrown away completely. Beginning in the Romantic era, music began to diverge into many genres and styles. It would be difficult to present music of the twentieth century (1910 to present) clearly as a unified style because many new and unusual trends developed and continue to develop today. Composers both returned to tradition and moved farther from it during the twentieth century. This chapter will give a brief overview of artistic developments that led to significant twentieth-century styles, the historical context of the twentieth century, and detailed introductions to specific schools of thought and genres of the modern age.

The term **twentieth-century music** generally refers to formal concert music of the 1900s, rather than rock, pop, jazz, or world music (Burkholder). Twentieth-century composers embraced this term to name their musical era because it seemed modern and exciting and the various styles of music could not be combined together under one stylistically descriptive term. Twentieth-century music was preceded by several late Romantic era developments, including *impressionism* and *neoclassicism*. In the 1900s, ***expressionism, serialism, modernism, electronic music, minimalism, experimental music,*** and ***chance music*** emerged and became intellectually based musical styles. While music was distinguished by form and instrumentation in the Classical period and by composer and nationality in the Romantic period, music of the twentieth century seems to fit into trends and movements tied closely to visual arts.

Relevant Historical Events

By the early 1900s, the Western world had experienced the second industrial revolution and welcomed the age of the automobile. A major earthquake hit San Francisco early in the century, devastating residents and destroying their property. The aviation industry was developed by creative and courageous pioneers who conducted early flights and combined the internal combustion engine with the winged glider to produce an airplane. Just as a general feeling of prosperity settled on people of the twentieth century, the luxurious cruise ship *Titanic* sank and World War I began.

Figure 6.2 Wright Aeroplane, 1908.

Political Influences

The early twentieth century brought wars and major political changes throughout the world. World War I (1914-18) involved what were commonly referred to as the *great powers*. This term refers to major nations that participated in the war and sat on either the Allies side or the Central Powers side. This war involved more than seventy million servicemen and women, more than nine million of whom died. The impact of World War I was widespread and led to political changes in various nations, including the former German, Ottoman, Russian, and Austro-Hungarian empires—all of which dissolved. A second major war followed only twenty-one years after the first one ended. World War II (1939-45) was a global war even larger in scope and significance than the first. More than one-hundred million people served in militaries throughout the war. This time, though, countries joined either the Allies or the Axis' side. Both military and civilian deaths occurred, including many casualties from the atomic bomb explosion and the Holocaust. It has been estimated that between thirty-five and sixty million people died in World War II ("World War II").

Social Influences

The women's suffrage movement began in the 1800s. It was first formalized in 1848 at the convention in Seneca Falls, New York. This movement aimed to reform voting rights to allow women to vote and run for political offices. Women gained the right to vote in 1920 after WWI had ended.

Figure 6.3 Rose Sanderson, Bain News Service, 1913. Women suffragists demonstrate in February 1913. The triangular pennants read "Votes for Women."

During the 1920s, Igor Stravinsky (1882-1971) began to compose neoclassical works that involved composing techniques from the Classical period (beginning with the ballet *Pulcinella*), and Arnold Schoenberg (1874-1951) shifted from writing a massive opera to creating twelve-tone serialism. Both of these composers are presented later in this chapter.

A few years later, between WWI and WWII, countries throughout the world experienced economic hardship as they entered a period known as the Great Depression. In the United States, unemployment soared and stock prices declined by 89 percent. Between 1929 and 1954, stock prices were volatile, and unemployment hit 24.9 percent at one point (Taylor). Franklin D. Roosevelt was inaugurated as president in 1933 and resolved to help the nation regain its strength and stability. The president introduced his New Deal, which reformed banking, stabilized agricultural production, created public works programs, built dams and power plants, and brought relief to the downhearted (Beschloss and Sidey).

President Roosevelt presented encouraging fireside chats over the radio to hearten

Americans. The Depression was difficult for people to endure, and after having been at war

for several years during WWI, society struggled to feel hopeful.

Cultural Influences

Recorded sound was developed in the late nineteenth century, and movies and

television were invented during the 1900s. The first films with sound were music-only

presentations. Eventually, voices, music, and sound effects were combined and used to

present films, such as *The Jazz Singer* for Warner Brothers in 1927, called talkies ("Motion

Picture"). Paris and the rest of Europe were behind the United States in developing this

revolutionary and impressive art. *The Jazz Singer* was shown in London in 1928, and before

long studios in both Europe and the United States had moved to using recorded sound in

films. The first feature-length European talkie was the British film *Blackmail* (1929), directed

by Alfred Hitchcock (Thompson and Bordwell 3-4).

The development of recorded sound and video affected music production in the

1900s in two ways. First, musical works became available to an even wider audience, as

early films used Western concert music as accompaniment. Second, an unfortunate

negative effect was that musicians who used to sing and play instruments in communities

for enjoyment began to compare themselves to trained instrumental and vocal stars, and

over time, the general population produced fewer and fewer musicians.

Defining Characteristics of Modernism in Music

In the late nineteenth and early twentieth centuries, certain composers wrote pieces that left the realm of tonality and entered the world of abstract musical sounds. Claude Debussy paved the way for unique approaches to tonality by writing impressionist music, where the key or tonal center was de-emphasized or hidden. He worked with new scales, like the whole-tone scale. In 1913, Stravinsky's ballet *The Rite of Spring* changed performance music dramatically with its aggressive music. Some composers' works were called neoclassical because they clung to older tonalities and rules of composing and created music inspired by the Classical period with modern flair. More remote and innovative composers, such as John Adams, György Ligeti, John Cage, and others, created experimental, chance, and minimalist works.

Specific Modern Genres

Modernism is a term used to describe a period of change and progress. As a musical term, modernism describes the period beginning in the late nineteenth century when new techniques, sounds, and forms were created. Stravinsky's music can be described as modernist, as can Schoenberg's. Some musical styles within the modernist movement were impressionism, serialism, minimalism, electronic music, experimental music, and chance music. Composers from this period who created innovative and nontraditional works were called *avant-garde*, meaning they radically departed from the traditional methods of composing and performing music (Samson). Notable avant-garde composers, other than Schoenberg and Stravinsky, were Anton Webern, Charles Ives, John Cage, Milton Babbitt, Karlheinz Stockhausen, and György Ligeti. Listen to Ligeti's piece "Artikulation."

French Impressionism

Impressionism originated in France as a reaction against the emotional music of the Romantic era. During the late Romantic period, impressionism produced the work of French composer Claude Debussy ("Impressionism"), whose work consisted of special <u>whole-tone</u> and <u>pentatonic</u> scales. The goal of impressionist music was to produce a mood or sense of something without boldly presenting it. Impressionist music is delicate, sensuous, and calm.

In visual arts, the impressionist movement included such well-known artists as Edgar Degas, Claude Monet, Édouard Manet, Paul Cézanne, and Pierre-Auguste Renoir. Painters converged on Paris as the place to develop impressionist art focusing on light and movement. To learn more about impressionist art, visit the <u>Musée d'Orsay website</u>.

Figure 6.4 Edgar Degas, Ballet Rehearsal on Stage. 1874.

Claude Debussy (1862-1918) was the primary composer of impressionism. He worked to communicate images, feelings, and moods through his music rather than by portraying literal descriptions common to program music. Debussy can be considered the bridge between the Romantic period and the twentieth century, similar to Beethoven being considered the transitional composer between the Classical and Romantic periods. Some of Debussy's popular piano and orchestral works include *Prelude to the Afternoon of a Faun* (1894), *Nocturnes* (1899), *La Mer* (1905), and "Claire de Lune" (1905) a simple melody included in any concert band method book on the market today. Debussy's impressionist compositions were instrumental works for both piano and orchestra.

The rich texture of Debussy's music is lush and sensual. The tonality is vague and difficult to pin down, as there is no clear tonal center. The basis of a whole-tone scale is that all notes are equally separated, and there are no patterns of whole and half steps. Instead, all pitches in a whole-tone scale are a whole step apart. Using this and other new scales, Debussy invented unusual harmonies in his music that kept listeners on edge as they waited for the music to settle somewhere.

To learn more about impressionism in music, watch Yale University's Open Yale Courses lecture "Musical Impressionism and Exoticism: Debussy, Ravel and Monet," presented by Professor Craig Wright. Viewing this lecture content is not required in the APUS MUSI200 Music Appreciation course and is for additional information only.

Expressionism

Pioneered by Schoenberg and his students Anton Webern and Alban Berg, *expressionism* was a style of atonal music that later led to the development of serialism. Together Schoenberg, Webern, and Berg were known as the Second Viennese School (1903-25) because they developed revolutionary musical ideas in Vienna—the same city where Mozart, Haydn, and Beethoven (the First Viennese School) composed and performed during the seventeenth and eighteenth centuries. Schoenberg was a traditional and conservative music composition teacher, but his spirit of ingenuity and creativity drove the expressionist movement.

One of Schoenberg's first expressionist works was the Five Pieces for Orchestra, Op. 16 (1909), which was written in an attempt to avoid any kind of structure or form. This goal was a direct rebellion against the structure and form valued in the Classical and Romantic periods. Schoenberg was influenced by the philosophies of the subconscious mind published by Austrian neurologist Sigmund Freud (1856-1939). As a result Schoenberg attempted to create music that flowed freely of its own will, like subconscious thought (Carpenter). While this method of composing was interesting, it was difficult to regulate and eventually led to the creation of *serialism*, which, in contrast, was ruled by strict order, form, and method. For a detailed explanation of atonalism and the twelve-tone row system, watch "Atonal Music Explained in a Nutshell" (transcript available).

Serialism

Serialism naturally developed out of the expressionist music of Schoenberg, Berg, and Webern, though Schoenberg himself is credited with having created it. The twelve notes of an octave are used in whatever order the composer decides (all of the black and white keys of the piano between one note and its same named note above or below it) (Whittall). The first twelve-note set is called the "prime." The prime set can be played backward, upside down, and upside down and backwards (see illustration, below). Then, the note sets can be chunked into smaller motifs, paired with other notes and rhythms, passed from one instrument to another in an ensemble, and repeated, unless the composer using serialism is a purist. Then, the entire twelve-note phrase must be played out before a new one can be started. In addition to its own stylistic rules, serialism was further supported through

harmony and music concepts from earlier periods. To see serialism explained visually, watch

the video "12 Tone Serialism" on YouTube.

Figure 6.5 Image courtesy of Hyacinth at en.wikipedia, "Prime, retrograde, (bottom-left) inverse, and retrograde-inverse," 2011. This image shows an example of the twelve notes used in serialism. P signifies "prime," or the original melody; R signifies "retrograde," or the original melody played exactly backward; I signifies "inversion," or the original melody flipped upside down; RI signifies "retrograde inversion," or the original melody flipped upside down and backward.

Figure 6.6 Arnold Schoenberg, "Bar 1-5 from Schönbergs Opus 24, 1." 1920-23. This image illustrates twelve-tone writing.

Serialism was not a style for instrumental music alone; many vocal and orchestral

pieces also were composed in this style. One Schoenberg piece, *Pierrot Lunaire*, includes a

combination of dramatic singing and speechlike sounds called *Sprechstimme*. Listen to

Schoenberg discuss his art during an interview. All elements of a piece, including the

dynamics, could be serialized. The dynamics would then cycle through changes in a controlled manner. Listen to "Nacht" from *Pierrot Lunaire* and try to identify a melody or pieces of a melody. Finding a melody will be a nearly impossible task, as twelve-tone music is calculated and not composed with an idea of recognizable melody. Furthermore, Schoenberg in particular seems to have aimed for wide melodic leaps, serialized rhythms as well as notes, and even timbres organized in a serial pattern. Some people struggle to find the musical value in serialism because it seems to lack emotion or the coherent repetition that draws listeners in. With an understanding of what it is and how it is made, anyone can learn to understand and appreciate serialism.

Schoenberg's publisher, Belmont Music Publishers, offers several videos that chronicle his life and music. One of these videos presents a discussion of Schoenberg's twelve-tone serialism, including when and how he developed it and what it sounds like. For additional insight regarding serialism, watch "Arnold Schoenberg and Twelve-Tone Music."

Neoclassicism

Not all composers wanted to explore new musical territories in the same ways. Several preferred to abide by traditional composing rules and norms while experimenting with ideas inside those rules. This style was called

Figure 6.7 Stravinsky, Bain News Service.

neoclassicism (Walsh). To help traditionally composed music sound more relevant for modern times, composers introduced devices or tools, such as chromaticism and polytonality, into their works. Igor Stravinsky was one such composer. He entered the musical scene with experimental and controversial music but later wrote in a neoclassical style.

Stravinsky was born in Russia and later moved to Switzerland, France, and eventually to the United States. He is known for his ballets *Firebird* (1910), *Petrushka* (1911), and *The Rite of Spring* (1913). These works expressed bold, dissonant sounds that at first repelled listeners. *The Rite of Spring* incited a riot at its first performance in Paris because of the primal nature of the ballet choreography involved. The dancing portrayed violence, a mating scene, and the wildness of nature. Stravinsky's music was remarkably different from other music of the music of the Romantic period, although it was similar to extremes often portrayed by other composers of his era. His music was edgy, intense, and bold. As you listen to an excerpt from *The Rite of Spring*, notice the dissonant harmony and changing, asymmetrical rhythms and meters. The timing will seem inconsistent; look for patterns and change.

Figure 6.8 Andrea Balducci, Le Sacre Du Printemps (The Rite of Spring) performance, August 23, 2009.

Neoclassicism was a movement to return to traditional musical practices. This return doesn't mean the resulting music sounds like a Classical period selection, but the basic forms and structure of earlier periods are used. Stravinsky's more conservative neoclassical pieces include _The Soldier's Tale_ (1918), _Oedipus Rex_ (1927), _Symphony of Psalms_ (1930), and _The Rake's Progress_ (1951). He contributed to the larger musical world by deeply exploring rhythmic expression, irregular meters, and placing emphasis (or accents) in unexpected places to upset audience predictions and keep his works spontaneous. Stravinsky continued the work of extending instrument ranges to extreme high- and low-pitch possibilities that had been explored by several Romantic composers before his time. He also creatively used musical forms and tools employed by Romantic composers.

To learn more about modernism in Stravinsky's music, watch Yale University's Open Yale Courses lecture "Modernism and Mahler" presented by Professor Craig Wright. This presentation includes a discussion of Stravinsky's innovative rhythms, Schoenberg, and other modernist composers. Viewing this lecture content is not required in the APUS MUSI200 Music Appreciation course and is for additional information only.

Electronic Music

The development of recording technology allowed composers to use the recording process as a new musical form. In the 1950s, musicians in Paris experimented with using magnetic tape to manipulate sounds, calling the medium **_musique concrète_**. This term was first used by composer Pierre Schaeffer in 1948. Edgard Varèse (1883-1965) was one composer widely known for exploring this style. He was born in Paris and studied music both there and in Berlin in the early 1900s. His early works were burned in a 1918 fire, shortly after which he moved to New York. Varèse formed the International Composers guild in

1921 and began composing electronic compositions in 1953. His early music interests indicate that he attempted to produce works requiring recorded sound long before the technology was available. Many people followed Varèse's music throughout his life, including Frank Zappa, who is said to have first listened to a record of Varèse's music at age fifteen. Edgard Varèse radio is available online with streaming samples of his work, including a sample of the innovative *Poéme Électronique.*

Other electronic developments in music included the invention of the synthesizer and Musical Instrument Digital Interface (MIDI). Music and instrumental sounds could be created using a computer, allowing composers to control every part of a musical piece by programming the note lengths, dynamics, pitches, and other features into the equipment. Melody, harmony, and texture, as have been presented in this course, do not occur in most electronic compositions the same way they have in music of past centuries. Instead, the tones and sounds are treated as elements to be manipulated and serve as the building blocks of an electronic composition. Pierre Boulez, Arthur Honegger, Lejaren Hiller, and Karlheinz Stockhausen are some noteworthy composers of electronic music.

Chance Music

John Cage (1912-92) challenged the notion that music must be created with tonal sounds. Cage espoused the idea that non-musical sounds, chance noises, and other sounds could be considered music, too. He published many works based on the idea of chance music and prepared instruments. Cage presented a prepared piano work called *The Seasons* in 1947. His *Indeterminacy: New Aspect of Form in Instrumental and Electronic Music* (1959) combined instrumental and vocal sounds with electronic material. The Rozart Mix (1965) presents the unique sounds of piano combined with cassette tape recorders. Cage is most widely known for his unusual piece *4'33",* where the performer prepares the instrument but sits silently for four minutes and thirty-three seconds, while audience and

ambient noises are considered the real "music" of the performance event.

Figure 6.9 David Tudor and John Cage at Shiraz Art Festival, 1971. Courtesy of the Cunningham Dance Foundation Archive.

Learn more about John Cage at his official website, which features a discussion of his

life through his autobiographical statement and a few artifacts from his composed works.

Key Differences between the Romantic Period and Modernism

The Romantic period was a time of breaking the mold, and the twentieth century has

been a time of innovation. In the Romantic era, composers branched out, invented their own

forms if needed, and focused on emotion and expression over restraint. Although Romantic

composers tried smaller and larger forms, some chromaticism, and more complex textures,

the modern period has unleashed a wealth of new scales, ideas, and approaches. The whole-tone scale and other new scales are widely used, and serialism has been developed to systematically involve all twelve notes in an octave. Debussy, Stravinsky, and Schoenberg were pivotal figures who created innovative ways to approach tonality, rhythm, meter, and harmony. Avant-garde composers like Varèse and Cage used instruments and electronics in new ways, developing electronic, minimalist, and chance music and pushing the idea of "serious" music further from the mainstream. Modern composers today, such as Steve Reich, continue these developments.

Critical Listening

While listening to music from the twentieth century, notice the variety of differences from earlier music eras. Focus on listening to identify the specific instruments and sounds produced, and try to describe them. In the case of music from the later 1900s, traditional instruments may have been used in unusual ways to produce sounds that are often unidentifiable, such as a prepared piano that sounds like clicking noises. After listening for instrumentation, notice the volume of the music. Is it loud, soft, or changing? Dynamics vary and may be either static or constantly changing in twentieth-century music. Finally, listen for any harmony that may be present. Are there melodies? Do they have support in other instruments or voices? Do the sounds you hear work together in a pleasing way, or is there a lot of dissonance that sounds grating or chaotic? Some impressionist music includes dissonance, but it is especially common during the modernist period. Use these music analysis skills to explore the assigned listening selections.

Listening Objectives

Listening objectives during this unit are:

1. Listen for instrumentation and timbres, including voices or instruments that are performing.

2. Listen for dynamic and tempo changes, including sudden loud or soft passages and sudden faster or slower sections.

3. Note any harmony or dissonance that may be present.

4. Practice describing these concepts using the music terms instrumentation, timbre, texture, tempo, dynamics, and form.

Key Music Terms

 Instrumentation describes what kind of instrument or voice produced the music. In the twentieth century, voices were used a lot like nonvocal instruments. Sometimes voices were expected to produce sound effects, nontextual noise, and wide leaps as in an expressionist or serial work. Later twentieth century music used traditional instruments in unusual ways, as in the case of the prepared piano employed by composer John Cage.

 Timbre, or tone quality was explored in depth during the twentieth century. Although Romantic-period composers explored a variety of timbres, twentieth-century composers pushed the limits much further. Instruments were used to produce unusual timbres in experimental music and modern works.

Texture is a term that describes what is going on in the music at any moment. In earlier periods, texture included a discussion about melody, harmony, and rhythms. In the twentieth century, texture was no longer the emphasis of a composition but can be discussed conceptually. For example, Schoenberg's *Pierrot Lunaire* is based on serialism, so a clear melody doesn't line up with other musical factors as a particular texture like homophony or polyphony. Instead, one must discuss the twelve-tone row and its role in the overall work.

 Tempo is the speed of the music. Tempo may also be called time. During the twentieth century, composers varied in their use of changing tempos. Stravinsky generally wrote for a fairly regular tempo. In his middle period, however, Schoenberg focused on free-form, non-metered improvisational music called free atonal expressionism.

 Dynamics are volume levels of musical sounds. Changing dynamics were used in previous musical eras to communicate emotion or expression. In the twentieth century, dynamics were used as another manipulative tool, similar to changing a rhythm or a pitch. Dynamics were also used to give the music expression, make it interesting, and add variety.

 Form is the organization and structure of a musical selection. Some twentieth-century composers favored the neoclassical trend of using forms from previous eras: the sonata, the rondo, and other common forms. Experimental and modernist composers favored using no form at all. Sometimes, ideas were through-composed and never repeated.

Composers

Several of the important composers of the twentieth century, Debussy, Stravinsky, Schoenberg, Varèse, and Cage, have been introduced earlier in this chapter. There were

many other great composers throughout the twentieth century, such as Randy Hostetler,
minimalist composer Terry Riley, Aaron Copland, and George Gershwin. Please explore the
additional listening links at the end of this chapter to learn more.

Discussion: How do music concepts from Western concert music apply to popular music?

Listening to popular music and discussing it with music terminology is a great way to
continue developing music appreciation skills. Popular music is generally less complex than
Western concert music from most periods, and listeners are more likely to think about music
with which they are already familiar. Just like Western concert music was shaped by
surrounding political, social, and cultural events, popular music is influenced by many
factors. Pop music is shaped by its own history; earlier songwriters, musicians, and artists
helped shape what is heard on the radio today. Listen to music on CDs, MP3s, the radio, or
over the internet using the skills gained throughout this course. Hopefully, your new music
term vocabulary will continue to be a part of your thoughts about music.

Listeners notice that many of their favorite popular songs have a form like those of
the Classical or Baroque periods. Many songs follow a verse-chorus pattern that can be
analyzed as A A B A B, where A is the verse, and B is the chorus. Listeners can predict that
the next section is coming because the background harmonies change, a cadence occurs
that plays a defining chord at the end of the section, and the music transitions to the next
section.

Closing

The twentieth century included a vast array of music in individualized and often
intellectual styles. Some of these styles include expressionism, serialism, modernism,

electronic music, minimalism, experimental music, and chance music. Many composers from this era are still living and composing, and their music continues to develop. While only a few examples were presented in this chapter, there are many more available that listeners are encouraged to discover. Popular music of the twentieth and twenty-first century was not presented in this chapter, but students are encouraged to apply their listening skills to their favorite tunes. Doing so can help encourage the growth of music analysis skills and abilities.

Music and Technology

This week, watch the video "Music and Technology," part of the Annenberg Learner video series we have been viewing throughout the text.

Guiding Questions

Identify, describe, and provide examples of various types of music from the twentieth century.

1. What are some characteristics of twentieth-century music?

2. What purposes/subject matters are represented in twentieth-century music?

3. How did forms change during the early twentieth century?

Self-Check Exercises

Complete the following self-check exercises to verify your mastery of key music terms presented in this chapter. Check your answers at the bottom of the page.

1. **Which late Romantic period music style involved special scales (such as the whole-tone scale) and lush harmonies?**
   a. Electronic music
   b. Musique concrète
   c. Chance music
   d. Impressionist music

2. **Which composer was responsible for inventing a completely new system of composing music based on twelve pitches?**
   a. Edgard Varèse
   b. Arnold Schoenberg
   c. Claude Debussy
   d. Igor Stravinsky

3. **Who considered all kinds of sounds to be music and composed a three-movement piece called *4'33"* based on silence?**
   a. John Cage
   b. Edgard Varèse
   c. Claude Debussy
   d. Maurice Ravel

4. **Which of the following traits effectively describe modernist music?**
   a. Innovative
   b. Predictable
   c. Orderly
   d. Repetitive

Self-check quiz answers:
1. d. 2. b. 3. a. 4. a.

Additional Resources

Visit the following resources to learn more about twentieth-century music:

Erik Satie music online   *PBS.org: John Cage*

The Charles Ives Society   *Morton Feldman*

Igor Stravinsky music online   *Karlheinz Stockhausen*

Copland House   *John Adams*

Leonard Bernstein   *Steve Reich*

Transcript: "Atonal Music Explained in a Nutshell"

Atonality is the systematic avoidance of permitting any single pitch to sound as a tonal center--the system of going beyond tonality as a basis for musical thought construction. It is the organization of sound without key establishment. Atonality is said to operate within a syntax that favors dissonant formations; and itss organization is based upon shifting intervallic tension or an order of tones.

The various elements in atonal music are tightly knit, usually, by extreme motivic concentration; and reference is constantly made to previous material. And, in many cases in atonality music, especially strict composers, there's little regular rhythmic stamping and no continuous chain rhythms. The rhythmic patterns are usually asymmetrical, and the meter is irregular and often complicated. Of course there are many variations you can do with atonal music. Within your tone row, if you want to add a major third or a minor third, or you get stuck with that in composing your tone row, then you can "go with it." You can go from one extreme to the other; there're so many different variations within that spectrum between atonality and tonality.

The twelve-tone technique, or composition with twelve notes related to one another, is designed to methodically equalize all pitches of the chromatic scale by the following means:

1. A twelve-tone composition is to be based on an arrangement, or series, of the twelve pitches that are determined by the composer. This arrangement is the "tone row," or "set."

2. No pitch may be repeated until all other pitches have been sounded. There is one exception to this restriction. A pitch may be repeated immediately after it is heard. Repetition may also occur within the context of a trill or tremolo figure.

3. The tone row may, within the confines of the system, legitimately be used in retrograde (reversed order), inversion (mirroring of each interval), or retrograde inversion (reversed order in mirrored form).

In this composition I most recently wrote, called *Dissonant Departure,* you'll see that in the first musical row here I have E, B-flat, A, G-sharp, E-flat and so on. These are the pitches that I selected, and I tried to be as dissonant in the interval between each of the notes. If you look at the arrows leading down to where it says "chords," if you're going to use chords, you should use the three notes or five notes in a row, and then the next three, four, or five notes, and then continue on like that. And, of course, the row that you're looking at (the "prime"), is the tone-row. And what I can do is reverse that row, which is on the bottom staff—D, F, C-sharp, G, B, C, and so-on. And that's the "retrograde."

It's nice to have a matrix filled out with the notes you have selected for your tone-row. If you look at the matrix here that's all filled in, the notes on the very top row (the C, G-sharp, E, B-flat, A, and so on), those are the notes that I selected in one of my compositions back in my college days—but this is what the tone row was for *me*. What you do is to also place the numbers in the order that they appear in the chromatic scale, starting with zero as your first note in the row. In this case, I started with Zero, which is "C" and then the next note would be a "C sharp," so that would be the first note. And the next one would be a D, which would be the second, and so on, and so forth.

If you take a look at the matrix, you see the "P" on the far left, that's your prime row, and you can come up with all different kinds of variations. The inversion "I" at the top (of the matrix) is (the prime row) basically mirrored. Then the retrograde to the far right, the "R", means it's just backwards. The melody is being played backwards. The "RI" at the bottom is retrograde inversion.

That should give you a little bit of a start. Thanks for listening!

Works Consulted

Aldridge, Rebecca. *The Sinking of the Titanic*. New York: Infobase Publishing, 2008. Print. Great Historical Disasters.

"Arnold Schoenberg." *AllMusic by Rovi*. Rovi Corp. 2012. Web. 15 May 2012. <http://www.allmusic.com/artist/arnold-schoenberg-mn0000691043>.

Balducci, Andrea. "Le Sacre du printemps 2 – Sirolo." 23 August 2009. *Wikimedia Commons.* Wikipedia Foundation, 16 July 2010. Web. 1 Sept. 2012. <http://commons.wikimedia.org/wiki/File:Le_Sacre_du_printemps_2_-_Sirolo.jpg>.

Beschloss, Michael and High Sidey. *The Presidents of the United States of America*. White House Historical Association, 2009. "Franklin D. Roosevelt." *The White House*. Web. 2 May 2012. <http://www.whitehouse.gov/about/presidents/franklindroosevelt>.

Blackman, Mary Dave. "Arnold Schoenberg and Twelve-Tone Music – OpenBUCS." East Tennessee State University. *YouTube*. 12 Aug. 2013. Web. 15 Apr. 2014. <http://youtu.be/PT2cldbRCNc>.

Botstein, Leon. "Modernism." *Oxford Music Online. Grove Music Online*. Web. 21 June 2012.

Burkholder, Peter J. "Borrowing." *Oxford Music Online. Grove Music Online*. Web. 21 June 2012.

Cage, John. *4'33"*. 1952. *YouTube*. 24 Mar. 2008. Web. 1 Sept. 2012. <http://youtu.be/3fYvfEMUJI8>.

—. *Interdeterminacy: New Aspect of Form in Instrumental and Electronic Music*. 1959. *YouTube*. 23 Oct. 2008. Web. 1 Sept. 2012. <http://youtu.be/AJMekwS6b9U>.

—. *Rozart Mix*. 1965. Perf. Ensemble Musica Negativa. Cond. Rainer Riehn. June 1971. *Music Online: Classical Music Library*. Alexander Street Press. Web. 22 Oct. 2014. <http://ezproxy.apus.edu/login?url=http://search.alexanderstreet.com/view/work/1481824>.

Carpenter, Alexander. "Schoenberg's *Erwartung* and Freudian Case Histories: A Preliminary Investigation." *Discourses in Music*. Vol. 3, No. 2. 2001-2002. Web. 5 Sept. 2012. <http://www.discourses.ca/v3n2a1.html>.

"Computers in Music." *The Oxford Dictionary of Music*. 2nd ed. rev. Eds. Michael Kennedy Joyce Bourne. *Grove Music Online*. Web. 22 June 2012.

Construction tools sign, used with permission from Microsoft. "Images." *Office*. Web. 4 Sept. 2012. <http://office.microsoft.com/en-us/images/results.aspx?ex=2&qu=tools#ai:MC900432556|mt:0|>.

Crouch, Tom D. *Wings: A History of Aviation from Kites to the Space Age*. New York: W.W. Norton & Company, Inc., 2004. Print.

David Tudor and John Cage at Shiraz Art Festival. 1971. Cunningham Dance Foundation Archive. *Wikimedia Commons.* Wikipedia Foundation, 22 Jan. 2011. Web. 1 Sept. 2012. <http://commons.wikimedia.org/wiki/File:TudorCageShiraz1971.jpg>.

Debussy, Claude. "Claire de Lune." *Suite bergamasque.* 1905. Perf. Wolfgang Sawallisch and the Philadelphia Orchestra. Minato-Mirai Hall, Yokohama, Japan. May, 1999. *YouTube.* 24 Oct. 2007. Web. 1 Sept. 2012. <http://youtu.be/gElTKhbnQxU>.

—. *Prelude to the Afternoon of a Faun.* 1894. Perf. L'Orchestre Symphonique de Montréal. Cond. Charles Édouard Dutoit. *YouTube.* 22 Jan. 2011. Web. 22 Oct. 2014. <http://youtu.be/bYyK922PsUw>.

Degas, Edgar. *Ballet Rehearsal on Stage.* 1874. *Wikimedia Commons.* Wikipedia Foundation, 31 May 2011. Web. 1 Sept. 2012. <http://commons.wikimedia.org/wiki/File:Edgar_Germain_Hilaire_Degas_033.jpg>.

Duffy, Michael. *Firstworldwar.com: A Multimedia History of World War One.* 2000. Web. 29 April 2012. <http://www.firstworldwar.com/>.

"Edgard Varèse." *Encyclopaedia Britannica Online Academic Edition.* Encyclopaedia Britannica Inc., 2012. Web. 21 June 2012.

"Edgard Varése." *Last.fm.* 4 July 2012. Web. 21 April 2012. <http://www.last.fm/music/Edgard+Var%C3%A8se>.

Gjourney. "Atonal Music Explained in a Nutshell." *YouTube.* 13 May 2010. Web. 1 Sept. 2012. <http://youtu.be/i5tmK6xcDws>.

Hyacinth at en.wikipedia. "Prime, retrograde, (bottom-left) inverse, and retrograde-inverse." 9 Nov. 2011. *Wikimedia Commons.* Wikipedia Foundation, 10 May 2012. Web. 1 Sept. 2012. <http://en.wikipedia.org/wiki/File:P-R-I-RI.png>.

"Igor Stravinsky." *Encyclopaedia Britannica Online Academic Edition.* Encyclopaedia Britannica Inc., 2012. Web. 21 June 2012.

"Impressionism." *The Oxford Dictionary of Music.* 2nd ed. rev. Eds. Michael Kennedy Joyce Bourne. *Grove Music Online.* Web. 21 June 2012.

"Interview with Arnold Schoenberg." *YouTube.* 8 July 2007. Web. 1 Sept. 2012. <http://youtu.be/Fd61jRM6Chw>.

"Introducing the Pentatonic Scale." *8notes.com.* Red Balloon Technology Ltd., 2000. Web. 9 May 2012. <http://www.8notes.com/articles/pentatonic_scales.asp>.

Ives, Charles. *114 Songs by Charles E. Ives.* 1922. Scott Mortensen. "Songs." *A Charles Ives Website.* 2002. Web. 5 Sept. 2012. <http://www.musicweb-international.com/Ives/WK_Songs.htm>.

Ligeti, György. "Artikulation." 1958. *YouTube.* 28 May 2012. Web. 15 May 2012. <http://youtu.be/71hNI_skTZQ>.

Man, Ray. *Portraitfoto von Arnold Schönberg.* 1927. *Wikimedia Commons.* Wikipedia
     Foundation, 5 May 2012. Web. 1 Sept. 2012.
     <http://commons.wikimedia.org/wiki/File:Arnold_sch%C3%B6nberg_man_ray.jpg>.

Manning, Peter. "Computers and Music." *The Oxford Companion to Music.* Ed. Alison
     Latham. *Grove Music Online.* 22 June 2012.

Moore, Gillian. "Edgard Varése: In Wait for the Future." *The Guardian.* 8 April 2010. Web. 1
     Sept. 2012. <http://www.guardian.co.uk/music/2010/apr/08/edgard-varese-
     national-youth-orchestra>.

"Motion picture." *Encyclopaedia Britannica Online Academic Edition.* Encyclopaedia
     Britannica Inc., 2012. Web. 21 June 2012.

"Music and Technology." *Exploring the World of Music.* Prod. Pacific Street Films and the
     Educational Film Center. 1999. *Annenberg Learner.* Web. 1 Sept. 2012.
     <http://www.learner.org/resources/series105.html>.

"Musique concrète." *The Oxford Companion to Music.* Ed. Alison Latham. *Grove Music
     Online.* 22 June 2012

Naviglec. "12 Tone Serialism." 25 Nov 2009. *YouTube.* Web. 1 May 2012.
     <http://youtu.be/c6fw_JEKT6Q>.

Rose Sanderson. Bain News Service.10 Feb. 1913. George Grantham Bain Collection.
     Library of Congress, Prints & Photographs Division, ggbain12483. *Wikimedia
     Commons.* Wikipedia Foundation, 21 May 2012. Web. 1 Sept. 2012.
     <http://commons.wikimedia.org/wiki/File:Rose-Sanderson-Votes-for-Women.jpeg>.

Samson, Jim. "Avant garde." *Oxford Music Online.* *Grove Music Online.* Web. 21 June 2012.

"San Francisco earthquake of 1906." *Encyclopaedia Britannica Online Academic Edition.*
     Encyclopaedia Britannica Inc., 2012. Web. 21 June 2012.

Schoenberg, Arnold. "Bar 1-5 from Schönbergs Opus 24, 1." 1920-23. Ed. Boris Fernbacher.
     Wikimedia Commons. Wikipedia Foundation, 10 Apr. 2010. Web. 1 Sept. 2012.
     <http://commons.wikimedia.org/wiki/File:Sch%C3%B6nbergOp24-1.png>.

—. "Nacht." *Pierrot Lunaire.* 1912. *YouTube.* 11 Sept. 2007. Web. 1 Sept. 2012.
     <http://youtu.be/u6LyYdSQQAQ>.

"Serialism, Serial Technique, Serial Music." *The Oxford Dictionary of Music.* 2nd ed. rev. Eds.
     Michael Kennedy Joyce Bourne. *Grove Music Online.* Web. 21 June 2012.

Stravinsky. Bain News Service. N.d. George Grantham Bain Collection. Library of Congress,
     Prints & Photographs Division, ggbain 32392. *Wikimedia Commons.* Wikipedia
     Foundation, 13 Oct. 2011. Web. 1 Sept. 2012.
     <http://en.wikipedia.org/wiki/File:Igor_Stravinsky_LOC_32392u.jpg>.

Stravinsky, Igor. *The Soldier's Tale*. 1918. Perf. The Gropius Ensemble. Einav Cultural Center, Tel Aviv, Israel. 23 Apr. 2008. *YouTube.* 23 Apr. 2008. Web. 1 Sept. 2012. <http://youtu.be/uRpg6WTi15s>.

Stravinsky, Igor and Vaslav Nijinsky. *The Rite of Spring*. 1913. Perf. The Joffrey Ballet. 1987. *YouTube.* 30 June 2010. Web. 1 Sept. 2012. <http://youtu.be/jF1OQkHybEQ>.

Taylor, Nick. "A Short History of the Great Depression." N.d. *New York Times.* Web. 7 May 2012. <http://topics.nytimes.com/top/reference/timestopics/subjects/g/great_depression_1930s/index.html>.

Thompson, Kristin, and David Bordwell. *Film History: An Introduction*. 3rd ed. New York: McGraw Hill, 2010. Print.

Walsh, Stephen. "Stravinsky, Igor." O*xford Music Online. Grove Music Online*. Web. 22 June 2012.

Whittall, Arnold. "Serialism." *The Oxford Companion to Music*. Ed. Alison Latham. *Grove Music Online*. 22 June 2012.

"Whole tone scale." *Virginia Tech Multimedia Music Dictionary*. Eds. Richard Cole and Ed Scwartz. 1996. Web. 14 Apr. 2012. <http://dictionary.onmusic.org/terms/3932-whole_tone_scale>.

Wright Aeroplane. 1908. *Wikimedia Commons*. Wikipedia Foundation, 3 Aug. 2012. Web. 1 Sept. 2012. <http://commons.wikimedia.org/wiki/File:Wright-Fort_Myer.jpg>.

Wright, Craig. "Lecture 22: Modernism and Mahler." *Music 112: Listening to Music*. Yale University's Open Yale Courses. 2012. Web. 9 April 2012. <http://oyc.yale.edu/music/musi-112/lecture-22>.

—. "Lecture 21: Musical Impressionism and Exoticism: Debussy, Ravel and Monet." *Music 112: Listening to Music*. Yale University's Open Yale Courses. 2012. Web. 9 April 2012. <http://oyc.yale.edu/music/musi-112/lecture-21>.

"World War II." *Encyclopaedia Britannica Online Academic Edition*. Encyclopaedia Britannica Inc., 2012. Web. 21 June 2012.

"Woman suffrage." *Encyclopaedia Britannica Online Academic Edition*. Encyclopaedia Britannica Inc., 2012. Web. 21 June 2012.

"World War I." *Encyclopaedia Britannica Online Academic Edition*. Encyclopaedia Britannica Inc., 2012. Web. 21 June 2012.

Chapter 7

Jazz

By Bethanie L. Hansen and David Whitehouse

"But jazz music is about the power of now. There is no script. It's conversation. The emotion is given to you by musicians as they make split-second decisions to fulfill what they feel the moment requires."

– Wynton Marsalis (Marsalis and Ward 8)

Figure 7.1 Frisco Jass Band, circa 1917. The Frisco Jass Band was an early U.S. jazz band that recorded for Edison Records in 1917. This publicity shot shows, from left, unknown (drums), Rudy Wiedoeft (clarinet), Marco Woolf (violin), Buster Johnson (trombone), Arnold Johnson (piano), and unknown (banjo).

Jazz is a distinct contribution from the United States on the world's musical stage. More than a century ago, a confluence of musical styles resulted in a way of playing that came to be known as *jazz*. The African musical roots of call and response, syncopation, and polyrhythms formed much of the foundation of jazz music, and improvisation give jazz its energy. It is generally acknowledged that New

Orleans was the place where it all began. In this chapter, readers will learn about the

beginnings of jazz, noteworthy stylistic developments, and significant songwriters and

performers. Given the many styles that have developed within the jazz genre to date,

it would be impossible to present a comprehensive discussion in a mere chapter.

Therefore, readers are encouraged to explore the additional resources at the end of

this chapter for additional study. For an introduction to jazz before reading the

chapter, visit Smithsonian Jazz.

Relevant Historical Events

Known for its distinct cross-cultural and multilingual heritage, New Orleans from the

early 1800s on was a destination for a variety of people of different nationalities. The French

had established the city, the Spanish ruled for a time, and the Americans known as

Kaintucks arrived on flatboats (Shipton 72-73). There were slaves, freemen, and "Creoles of

color," who were progeny of mixed relationships. New Orleans was home to Choctaw and

Natchez American Indians and people from the Balkans including Dalmatians, Serbs,

Montenegrins, Greeks, and Albanians. Chinese, Malays, and Spanish-speaking Filipinos also

added to the mix. Among each group, there were additional distinctions. For instance, some

of the French were descendants of the original settlers, while others came directly from

Canada and France, and still others were French-speaking former slaves from Haiti and

Santo Domingo. Each cultural group brought its own culture and music. This blend of

cultures formed the background of the late nineteenth- and early twentieth-century music

born at the mouth of the Mississippi, called jazz.

Figure 7.2 George Prince, New Orleans, 1919.

Cultural Influences

Throughout the nineteenth century, several types of music permeated New Orleans. At the northern edge of the city, in a grassy area known as Congo Square, blacks gathered on Sunday to dance to drumbeats and music for several hours. They were slaves engaging in the music and dance of their African ancestors. Theaters hosted minstrel shows where various entertainers performed music and skits comprised of original tunes accompanied by banjo, piano, guitar, or tunes heard on the streets of the city and arranged by the performers. As the performance progressed, each player and singer had a chance to be heard in his or her "take" on the words, melodies, and rhythms in what came to be known as *improvisation*. This performance style had its roots on the plantations of the region, as workers used music to make the work bearable.

Funeral ensembles, orchestras, and marching bands eventually found their places in New Orleans. Funerals traditionally included a group of musicians accompanying the deceased and gathered mourners on the way to and from the graveyard. On the way to the burial, the musicians played a simple dirge and then a lighter, festive version on the way back home. By the middle of the 1800s, the city was home to two symphony orchestras and three opera houses. Music brought the people of New Orleans together, as people of all races attended and supported the opera houses. Marching bands, too, played a big part in the musical mix of the city.

Figure 7.3 The Mathews Band of Lockport, Louisiana, 1904. Notice which instruments are present.

Listen to "Jazz Me Blues" by the Original Dixieland Jazz Band, an example of an early New Orleans band. These bands played music influenced by the styles of European military bands and West African folk music. The Onward Brass Band, Excelsior Brass Band, Olympia Brass Band, and the Tuxedo Brass Band were all well-known groups in the late nineteenth and early twentieth centuries in the city. The makeup of the bands varied, but a typical ensemble included at least one cornet, trumpet, trombone, tuba, and snare and bass drums, as shown in Figure 7.3. Other instruments, such as clarinets, violins, guitars, and even stand-up basses, also were included. The designation of "orchestra" and "band" were sometimes interchangeable, always referring to this same instrumentation.

Three different strains of music—ragtime, the blues, and spirituals—were being played at this time in New Orleans that directly influenced the formation of jazz. Ragtime is a style of playing, especially on piano, although entire bands performed in this style too. Ragtime is defined by a steady beat in the pianist's left hand—or the lower instruments of a band—and syncopation of the melody in the pianist's right hand—or the higher melody instruments of a band. No matter in which genre a melody was composed, pianists could make a "rag" out of it by playing the melody in a syncopated way against the steady beat of the accompaniment.

Defining Characteristics of Jazz

One of the key traits of jazz music is *improvisation*, or making up parts of the music as it goes, based on specific rules. In traditional music, a composer wrote down exactly what musicians played, and the musicians did their best to perform precisely by the sheet music provided. In jazz, however, the song is just the beginning, a frame of reference from which musicians can work. Many jazz musicians of the past read music poorly or not at all, but they improvised spontaneously in an energetic, exciting way. Each player in a jazz ensemble showed an elastic, musical mind as he or she "picked up" a tune by ear and followed the progress of a song at the whim of the bandleader. Jazz musicians were capable of making things up as they went along, remaining elastic, ready to do anything spontaneously, and creating new expression in the true spirit of jazz.

Critical Listening

While listening to samples of different jazz styles throughout recent history, consider improvisation as the most common expressive element in jazz. Many arrangements begin with a main melody or "head" tune followed by a looser section of improvised parts played by one or more soloists and accompanied by the rhythm section. This section then is followed by a repeat of the main melody or "head" tune by the ensemble. After identifying which parts of the music are melodies and which parts are improvisations, one is better able to enjoy listening to jazz and describing differences between cohesive and spontaneous parts of the music.

Listening Objectives

Your listening objectives during this unit will be to:

Figure 7.4 Clip art image of a man wearing headphones and seated in front of a computer, used with permission from Microsoft.

1. Identify the primary instruments performing.

2. Listen to the dynamics and tempo of the music and identify whether it is loud or soft or fast or slow.

3. Listen for melody and harmony as well as solo or large-group playing.

4. Identify any special sounds that may give clues about whether the music is swing (a lot of cymbals), rock (a lot of bass drum), latin (a lot of tom toms and clicking sounds), or some other form of jazz.

5. Identify any sections where a musician or musicians seem to be improvising.

Key Music Terms

Instrumentation describes what kind of instrument or voice produced the music. Jazz ensembles can be organized into groups of any instrumentation, but there are some standard arrangements. One of the most common groupings today is the standard big band setup (see Figure 7.5).

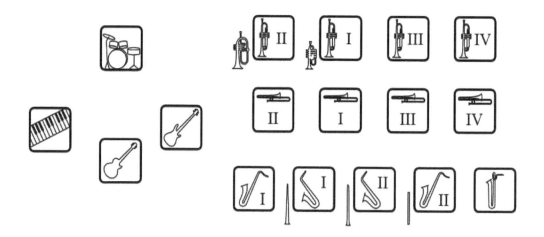

Figure 7.5 This diagram shows a typical seating arrangement for members of a modern-day jazz ensemble. On the left, the rhythm section consists of a drum set, keyboard/piano, electric guitar, and bass guitar. On the right are the horns. The trumpets are in the back row, with the first trumpet sometimes doubling on piccolo trumpet or flugel horn and the second trumpet doubling on flugel horn. In the next row are the trombones, with a bass-trombone playing part IV. In the front row, the five saxophones include two altos, two tenors, and one baritone. Saxophone players sometimes double on other woodwind instruments, such as the soprano saxophone, flute, or clarinet.

Other instrumentation combinations may be larger, as in the case of a jazz orchestra, or smaller, such as the jazz combo or a bebop ensemble. In each case, there is generally a complete rhythm section supporting other musicians comprised of a drum set, piano or synthesizers, guitar, and bass guitar.

Timbre, or tone quality, describes the quality of a musical sound. Timbre is generally discussed using adjectives, like "bright," "dark," "buzzy," "airy," "thin," and "smooth." Jazz musicians explore a wide variety of timbres, including the *wah-wah* of a plunger mute on trumpet or trombone, the buzz of a trumpet Harmon mute, the ocean-wave sounds of "brushes" on a drum set, the unique sounds of cymbals of all sizes and thicknesses, and the occasional doubling of saxophone players on flutes, clarinets, or other woodwind instruments. Some jazz musicians can produce growling or flutter-tonguing sounds on wind instruments, and some keyboard players switch to various synthesized sounds for specific genres and styles within jazz. Timbre is a musical element that is often manipulated in jazz music.

Figure 7.6 This image shows a trumpet with mutes commonly used in jazz.

 Texture is a term that describes what is going on in the music at any moment. Musical texture is the way that melody, harmony, and rhythm combine. The texture in many jazz works is homophonic, with one group playing the melody and other instrument groups playing related chordal accompaniment. In other types of works, such as bebop, more than one melody competes in polyphonic texture. At times, the three brass sections—trumpets, trombones, and saxophones—may all have different competing melodies in polyphony or polyrhythms, or both. Additional chordal notes that do not normally occur in the key often enhance textures in jazz music.

 Melody is a recognizable line of music that includes different notes, or pitches, and rhythms in an organized way. One instrument, an entire section, or the entire ensemble in unison may perform the melody in a jazz piece. Sometimes, a band may pass around a melody, with each player playing a small chunk or motif.

Harmony is created when two or more voices perform together. Jazz harmonies

are known for being colorful, including dissonant notes or widely spaced intervals,

and adding or releasing tension in the music.

When considering musical texture, ask yourself these questions:

- *What instruments or voices am I hearing?*
- *Do I hear one melody or more than one?*
- *Are the extra voices or instruments changing together or at different times?*
- *Is it difficult to identify the melody, perhaps because there are several melodies happening at once?*

 Tempo is the speed of the music. Tempo also may be referred to as "time." One of

the staples in jazz music is syncopation, which shifts the emphasis of rhythms off

the beat and creates anticipation or delays. Some jazz works have a "driving" rhythm that

moves forward quickly with a strong pulse, and other jazz works seem relaxed in "swing"

style, keeping a steady tempo but swinging just a bit behind the beat. Tempo is one factor

that helps listeners identify jazz styles.

 Dynamics are changing volume levels of musical sounds. Sudden dynamic

changes to louder or softer volumes occur frequently in jazz music and add

character to the sound. *Brass kicks* are a common technique used to change dynamics in

jazz. This technique includes sudden loud, punchy notes performed by the bass section

against a quieter background, which surprises listeners and add expression.

 Form is the organization and structure of a musical selection. Many jazz pieces

are organized in AABA or ABA form, with the initial melody returning at the end of

the work. Improvisation sections may be included.

Composers, Performers, and Listening Examples

Early Jazz

Scott Joplin (1868-1917), considered the king of the ragtime style, influenced countless others in the creation of *rags*, music characterized by its syncopated melody or ragged rhythm. Born in Texas, he was the son of laborers and learned to sing and play mandolin and guitar in his youth. Joplin eventually learned piano and became an esteemed composer, writing the popular "Maple Leaf Rag" in 1899. Elements of steady beat and ragged melody were incorporated into this type of jazz. Jazz players were familiar with the style, and when they

Figure 7.7 Portrait of Scott Joplin, 1907. Joplin is considered the king of ragtime composers.

added it to blues and orchestrated it, jazz was the result. Joplin struggled financiaslly before his death from disease-related dementia in 1917 at age 49. He was awarded the Pulitzer Prize posthumously in 1976 after his work, especially the opera *Treemonisha*, gained fame (Forney and Machlis 347). His music also was used in the soundtrack to the movie *The Sting*. Joplin composed forty-four ragtime works, two operas, a musical, a symphony, a piano concerto and a ragtime ballet, much of which has been lost (Berlin).

Figure 7.8 This image shows the cover of the sheet music for Joplin's "Maple Leaf Rag."

Sippie Wallace, born Beulah Thomas (1898-1986), was a singer and songwriter in the early 1900s blues style. Wallace came from a musical Texas family of thirteen children and moved to New Orleans in 1915 then to Chicago in 1923, deeper into the jazz community. Blues, as a musical genre, originated in communities in the Deep South, and entered New Orleans by way of people migrating there from the Mississippi delta. Blues style is defined primarily by the addition of flat tones to a major scale on the third, fifth, and seventh steps. Singers and players can "bend" these notes infinitely, gradually, or greatly, so that the music was even more expressive. They used this device to communicate the pain and the woes of life, and Wallace was very effective at communicating these emotions. Listen as Wallace, one of the most famous jazz singers of the early twentieth century, sings "Devil Dance Blues" (lyrics not necessary for completion of course) and bends the melody notes masterfully.

The second primary defining element of the blues is its form. It has a twelve-bar form that reflects the words. Listen again to "Devil Dance Blues." After a short introduction, Wallace sings the first two lines the same then changes the form on the third line. The total of all music for one verse is twelve bars. This pattern (without the introduction) then repeats itself until a short coda-like passage ends the song.

The same twelve-bar pattern applied to strictly instrumental versions of the blues as well. Listen as the Original Dixieland Jazz Band plays "Livery Stable Blues" (1917). After a short introduction, one can discern when the tonal center changes. Listen closely to hear the same twelve-bar pattern as in "Devil Dance Blues," only at a different pace. Is the tempo in this selection faster or slower than in "Devil Dance Blues"?

Blue notes and twelve-bar form were in the memory and musical ear of every player. In addition, most players could pick up a tune by ear. To teach the band a new tune, the bandleader might play through the tune first alone, then repeating it several times. As the other players picked up the outlines of the melody, they would join in, and soon the entire band would be playing. Players would take solos with a nod of the head from the leader, shifting back to full sound when the solo verse was over. When ready, the bandleader would signal a return to playing the tune at least once more all the way through with the full band and then bring the piece to a close.

Figure 7.9 Robert Runyon, King & Carter Jazzing Orchestra, Houston, Texas, January 1921. Credit: The Robert Runyon Photograph Collection, image number 05019, courtesy of The Center for American History, The University of Texas at Austin.

Louis Armstrong was a well-known jazz trumpet player and singer. Listen as <u>Louis Armstrong and his Hot Five</u> play the song "<u>Heebie Jeebies.</u>" The song shows some of the basic principles of a jazz band, including a lead instrument (in this case trumpet), an accompanying instrument (clarinet), a basic rhythm section (in this case the piano and the banjo), and a bass instrument (trombone).

Other basic jazz principles are:

- an interplay between the
  lead instrument and the
  accompanying instrument(s);

- ragtime technique in the
  piano, banjo, and trombone,
  akin to an *oom-pah* in the
  bass alternating with chords
  on the off beats and
  syncopated melodies on top;

Figure 7.10 William P. Gottlieb, Portrait of Louis Armstrong, Aquarium, New York, N.Y., circa July 1946. Armstrong is a seminal figure in the history of jazz.

- a twelve-bar repeated harmonic structure taken from blues form;

- a lead singer (Armstrong, in this case) with an early example of scat singing;

- varied instrumentation along the way as instruments drop out, play a solo, and
  rejoin the music for the full band; and

- the ability to improvise, even though on a recording the improvisatory nature of
  the performance is not as evident as when it is heard live.

Jelly Roll Morton gave much impetus to the early days of jazz with his solo and group playing and recording, his masterful composing, and his travels. Morton claimed to have single-handedly invented jazz—possibly a tongue-in-cheek claim. Born in New Orleans, Morton was active as a pianist early in life. He engaged in other activities, but piano playing remained his primary profession. He started traveling in 1904 to places including Memphis, Kansas City, and St. Louis, sharing his music along the way. Traveling is one example of how the new jazz style from New Orleans spread not only by Morton but by other solo players and

Figure 7.11 Jelly Roll Morton in his teenage Years, circa 1906. This image is possibly the earliest photograph of Morton.

groups as well. New Orleans is situated at the mouth of the Mississippi River. The steamboats that carried people up and down the river also hired musicians to play. These musicians traveled north to faraway places, spreading the new style and sometimes taking up residence in the cities where the steamboats docked. These visiting musicians gave local musicians a chance to assimilate the jazz style and add their own stylistic elements.

Morton eventually made it to Los Angeles, where, due to his popularity, he remained for five years. In 1922, He moved to Chicago to make recordings of others' and his own music. Five years after moving to Chicago, he recorded with his band, Jelly Roll Morton's Red Hot Peppers. Morton was able to achieve a maximum synthesis between composed music and improvisation. The solos performed by band members on recordings are remarkable because of the flexibility extended by the bandleader, and colors and textures were paramount in Morton's mind.

Other important players who influenced the birth and growth of early jazz include Sidney Bechet (clarinet), Joe "King" Oliver (cornet), Buddy Bolden (cornet), Bunk Johnson (trumpet), and Kid Ory (trombone). These names are only a short list from a plethora of singers, players, dancers, church music directors, marching bands, dance bands, riverboat bands, church bands, duos, trios, quartets, quintets, small bands, large bands, and cultural influences of all types that went into the formation of the jazz style.

Additional early jazz resources:

- Interactive Jazz Timeline

- The Scott Joplin International Ragtime Foundation

- The Red Hot Jazz Archive – A History of Jazz before 1930

- The Mississippi River of Song

- The Blues film series

- The Official George and Ira Gershwin Web Site

- Louis Armstrong House Museum

Later Jazz

Between 1935 and 1948, musicians such as Count Basie, Benny Goodman, and Duke Ellington developed swing bands. One of the most exciting purposes of swing music was to inspire dancing. During the years between World War I and World War II, radio shows featured swing music, and it became even more popular ("Jazz"). Swing bands generally used the same seating arrangement (shown in Figure 7.5) as modern-day jazz ensembles.

Listen to the following examples of swing music:

- Count Basie's "Swingin' the Blues"

- Benny Goodman's "Sing, Sing, Sing"

- Duke Ellington's "Satin Doll"

The bebop phase of jazz music taxed the skills of even the best jazz musicians. Just as concert music in the Romantic period required advanced musical skills for most pieces, the bebop period demanded virtuosity. In the 1940s, the cost of traveling with a full swing band became prohibitive, and musicians reacted by creating smaller bebop ensembles ("Bebop").

These groups consisted of a rhythm section with just a few other musicians, such as one trumpet and/or one saxophone. Improvisation was even more important in bebop, and melodies became less recognizable or familiar and even sometimes unpleasant, reflecting the fear and uncertainty of WWII. Bebop was more challenging to play because of its intricate melodies and fast tempos. New textures were introduced as added notes were included in chords. Bebop in the 1940s paved the way for the modern jazz of today. Charlie Parker, Lester Young, Thelonius Monk, and Dizzy Gillespie are some well-known bebop musicians (Hodeir).

Listen to the following examples of bebop:

- Charlie Parker's "Sessions"

- Lester Young's "Mean to Me"

- Thelonius Monk's "Straight No Chaser"

- Dizzy Gillespie's "A Night in Tunisia"

As a reaction to the fast tempos and challenging techniques of the bebop trend, a new jazz style emerged in the 1950s called *cool school*, or *West Coast jazz*. This style included the same type of small ensembles as bebop, namely the jazz combo, but played music that was more laid back, slower, and melodically pleasing. Cool school music brought back some of the older European concert-music forms, such as the rondo and the waltz, with a focused sound and tone quality. Dave Brubeck and Miles Davis are two musicians from this philosophy.

Listen to following examples of cool school:

- The Miles Davis Quintet's "It Never Entered My Mind"

- The Dave Brubeck Quartet's "Take Five"

The next movement in jazz, known as *free jazz*, lasted roughly thirteen years, from about 1956 to 1969 ("Free Jazz"). The free jazz genre used odd chord progressions, unpredictable forms, awkward structure, and avant-garde moods. The primary purpose of free jazz was to express sounds, not melody nor form. This particular type of jazz is more radical than bebop or any other style of jazz music. Listening to this type of jazz takes focused attention and active listening. John Coltrane composed his later works in free jazz style (Gammond).

Listen to the following example of free jazz:

- An excerpt from John Coltrane's *Ascension*

After jazz developed through the swing, bebop, cool school, and free jazz styles, modern performers developed *fusion,* a style of music based on modes rather than scales and a combination of other techniques from earlier jazz. Using modes meant that a few raised or lowered pitches to fit into a different kind of musical scale altered the set of notes for a given piece. In fusion jazz, musicians often used different and nontraditional combinations of instruments, sometimes including ethnic instruments not normally included in jazz ("Jazz-Rock Fusion").

Listen to an example of fusion jazz using a few Korean instruments:

- Oriental Express' "Monsoon"

Additional later jazz resources:

- Jazz Review.Com: Where people talk about jazz

- Miles Davis' Official Website

- John Coltrane's Official Website

- All About Jazz – Current reviews, free MP3 downloads, and links

Closing

Jazz music consists of a mixture of early styles and modern genres. One of the defining features of jazz music is improvisation, or spontaneous music making, at an individual level. There are many styles within the genre of jazz music, including swing, bebop, cool jazz, free jazz, and fusion. In addition to these styles, there are many others, including jazz ballads, funk, and Latin jazz, which have not been discussed in this chapter. As jazz continues to develop in the present era, more techniques and styles may emerge while old ideas are continually reused. Explore jazz music to determine which styles you enjoy, and seek out new and interesting examples. If you wonder whether jazz bands exist and perform today, look no further than your local high school jazz ensemble. If you prefer a more adult ensemble, consider investigating Gordon Goodwin's Big Phat Band that regularly performs in Los Angeles and on movie soundtracks like Disney's *The Incredibles.*

For more information about Gordon Goodwin's Big Phat Band, visit www.bigphatband.com.

Composers and Improvisers

This week, watch the video "Composers and Improvisers," part of the Annenberg Learner

video series we have been viewing throughout the text.

Guiding Questions:

Identify, describe, and provide examples of jazz music.

1. What are some characteristics of early jazz?

2. What purposes/subject matters does jazz represent?

3. How did jazz styles change during the early twentieth century?

4. What are some of the noteworthy pieces that were composed during this period?

5. Who are some of the significant jazz composers?

Self-Check Exercises

Complete the following self-check exercises to verify your mastery of key music terms presented in this chapter. Check your answers at the bottom of this page.

1. **Which of the following phrases could describe early jazz music?**
   a. Based on African call-and-response pattern
   b. Influenced by African spirituals
   c. Began in New Orleans
   d. All of the above

2. **Which early style combined ragged melody with a steady bass part?**
   a. Swing
   b. Bebop
   c. Ragtime
   d. Funk

3. **What is the most important basic element of jazz music?**
   a. Fast tempos
   b. Melody played by the saxophone section
   c. Reading music
   d. Improvisation

4. **Which performer both sang and performed jazz on the trumpet?**
   a. Louis Armstrong
   b. Sippie Wallace
   c. Jelly Roll Morton
   d. None of the above

Self-check quiz answers:
1. d, 2. c, 3. d, 4. a

Additional Listening Examples

Swing

"Jeepers Creepers" by Louis Armstrong and Jack Teagarden

"How High the Moon," by Louis Armstrong

"Caravan" by Duke Ellington

Bebop

"Leap Frog" by Charlie Parker and Dizzy Gillespie

Theater

"Summertime," from the opera *Porgy and Bess*, by George Gershwin

Fusion

"Cantaloupe Island" by Herbie Hancock

"Chameleon" by Herbie Hancock

Works Consulted

Armstrong, Louis. "How High the Moon." 1947. Live in Australia, March, 1963. *YouTube*. 29 Nov. 2009. Web. 1 Sept. 2012. <http://youtu.be/XzOvJ8wYA1l>.

Armstrong, Louis and Jack Teagarden. "Jeepers Creepers." 1958. *YouTube*. 24 Nov. 2008. Web. 1 Sept. 2012. <http://youtu.be/2jbZrocd6vs>.

Basie, Count. "Swingin' the Blues." 1941. *YouTube*. 15 Oct. 2008. Web. 1 Sept. 2012. <http://youtu.be/TYLbrZAko7E>.

"Bebop." Encyclopaedia Britannica Online Academic Edition. Encyclopaedia Britannica Inc., 2012. Web. 27 June 2012.

Berlin, Edward A. A Biography of Scott Joplin. 1998. "Biography." The Scott Joplin International Ragtime Foundation, 2004. Web. 5 Sept. 2012. <http://www.scottjoplin.org/biography.htm>.

Coltrane, John. Ascension. 1965. Perf. New Zealand School of Music. 4 June 2009. YouTube. 23 July 2009. Web. 1 Sept. 2012. <http://youtu.be/-Ox1jsVuduU>.

"Composers and Improvisers." Exploring the World of Music. Prod. Pacific Street Films and the Educational Film Center. 1999. Annenberg Learner. Web. 1 Sept. 2012. <http://www.learner.org/resources/series105.html>.

Construction tools sign, used with permission from Microsoft. "Images." Office. Web. 4 Sept. 2012. <http://office.microsoft.com/en-us/images/results.aspx?ex=2&qu=tools#ai:MC900432556|mt:0|>.

Ellington, Duke. "Caravan." 1937. *YouTube*. 8 Nov. 2010. Web. 1 Sept. 2012. <http://youtu.be/r95flkZciJE>.

—. "Satin Doll." 1953. *YouTube*. 30 Oct. 2006. Web. 14 Apr. 2014. <http://youtu.be/TrytKuC3Z_o>.

"Free Jazz." Encyclopaedia Britannica Online Academic Edition. Encyclopaedia Britannica Inc., 2012. Web. 27 June 2012.

Frisco Jazz Band. Circa 1917. Wikimedia Commons. Wikipedia Foundation, 26 Mar. 2010. Web. 4 Sept. 2012. <http://commons.wikimedia.org/wiki/File:Friscojazzbandc1917.jpg>.

Forney, Kristine, and Joseph Machlis. The Enjoyment of Music: An Introduction to Perceptive Listening. 11th ed., shorter version. New York: W.W. Norton, 2011. Print.

Gammond, Peter. "Free Jazz." The Oxford Companion to Music. Ed. Alison Latham. Grove Music Online. Web. 27 June 2012.

Gershwin, George. "Summertime." Porgy and Bess. 1935. *YouTube*. 24 Mar. 2009. Web. 1 Sept. 2012. <http://youtu.be/faiG6Ssvpyc>.

Gillespie, Dizzy. "A Night in Tunisia." 1942. *YouTube*. 28 Jan. 2008. Web. 14 Apr. 2014.
<http://youtu.be/BQYXn1DP38s>.

Goodman, Benny. "Sing, Sing, Sing." Hollywood Hotel. 1937. *YouTube*. 29 Jan. 2006. Web. 1
Sept. 2012. <http://youtu.be/3mJ4dpNal_k>.

Gottlieb, William P. Portrait of Louis Armstrong, Aquarium, New York, N.Y. Circa July, 1946.
"Performing Arts Encyclopedia." The Library of Congress. 8 Dec. 2010. Wiki*media
Commons*. Wikipedia Foundation, 19 Jan. 2012. Web. 5 Sept. 2012.
<http://commons.wikimedia.org/wiki/File:Louis_Armstrong.jpg>.

Hancock, Herbie. "Cantaloupe Island." 1964. *YouTube*. 1 Aug. 2006. Web. 1 Sept. 2012.
<http://youtu.be/XrgP1u5YWEg>.

—. "Chameleon." 1973. *YouTube*. 12 Aug. 2011. Web. 1 Sept. 2012.
<http://youtu.be/onbKsXUnl4c>.

Hodeir, André. "Bop." O*xford Music Online. Grove Music Online*. Web. 27 June 2012

"Jazz." *Encyclopaedia Britannica Online Academic Edition*. Encyclopaedia Britannica Inc.,
2012. Web. 27 June 2012.

"Jazz-Rock Fusion." *The Oxford Companion to Music*. Ed. Alison Latham. *Grove Music Online*.
Web. 27 June 2012.

Jelly Roll Morton in his Teenage Years. Circa 1906. *"Oh, Mister Jelly": A Jelly Roll Morton
Scrapbook*. Copenhagen: Jazz Media, 1999. *Wikimedia Commons*. Wikipedia
Foundation, 4 Aug. 2012. Web. 5 Sept. 2012.
<http://commons.wikimedia.org/wiki/File:TeenagedJellyRollMorton.jpg>.

Joplin, Scott. "Maple Leaf Rag." 1899. Cond. Zachary Brewster-Geisz. Perf. Garritan Personal
Orchestra's sample library. 1 June 2006. "Community Audio." *Internet Archive*. 10
Mar. 2011. Web. 1 Sept. 2012. <http://archive.org/details/MapleLeafRag>.

Louis Armstrong and His Hot Five. "Heebie Jeebies." 1926. *YouTube*. 6 Jan. 2009. Web. 1
Sept. 2012. <http://youtu.be/ksmGt2U-xTE>.

Mako098765. *Trumpet Mutes. Wikimedia Commons*. Wikipedia Foundation, 23 August
2006. <http://en.wikipedia.org/wiki/File:TrumpetMutes.jpg>.

Man working at computer and listening to headphones, used with permission from
Microsoft. "Images." *Office*. Web. 4 Sept. 2012. <http://office.microsoft.com/en-
us/images/results.aspx?qu=listening%20to%20headphones&ctt=1#ai:MP9004225
41|mt:2|>.

Maple Leaf Rag. Wikipedia: The Free Encyclopedia. 19 Apr. 2009. Web. 5 Sept. 2012.
<http://en.wikipedia.org/wiki/File:Maple_Leaf_Rag.PNG>.

Marsalis, Wynton and Geoffrey Ward. *Moving to Higher Ground: How Jazz Can Change Your
Life*. New York: Random House, 2008. Print.

Monk, Thelonius. "Straight, No Chaser." 1951. Perf. Thelonius Monk Quartet. The Best of Thelonius onk: The Blue Note Years. 1991. *YouTube.* 3 Feb. 2009. Web. 22 Oct. 2014. <http://youtu.be/qVb9e1DgKJ4>.

Oriental Express. "Monsoon." 2007. Korean Traditional Instrument and Fusion Jazz Concert, Seoul, South Korea, 2007. *YouTube.* 27 June. 2008. Web. 1 Sept. 2012. <http://youtu.be/oXtrD9Oz2eE>.

Original Dixieland Jazz Band. "Jazz Me Blues." 1921. "National Jukebox." *Library of Congress.* Web. 14 Apr. 2014. <http://www.loc.gov/jukebox/recordings/detail/id/7835/>.

—.. "Livery Stable Blues." 1917. "National Jukebox." *Library of Congress.* Web. 14 Apr. 2014. <http://www.loc.gov/jukebox/recordings/detail/id/4668/>.

Parker, Charlie. "Sessions." N.d. *YouTube.* 6 Feb. 2007. Web. 1 Sept. 2012. <http://youtu.be/DjElQ6Ekr9o>.

Parker, Charlie and Dizzy Gillespie. "Leap Frog." 1950. *YouTube.* 12 Dec. 2009. Web. 1 Sept. 2012. <http://youtu.be/1aMCviqO95k>.

Prince, George. *New Orleans, 1919.* 17 Nov. 1919. "American Memory." *The Library of Congress.* Web. 4 Sept. 2012. <http://memory.loc.gov/cgi-bin/query/D?pan:9:./temp/~ammem>.

Portrait of Scott Joplin. American Musician. 17 June 1907. Performing Arts Reading Room, The Library of Congress, Washington, D.C. *Wikimedia Commons.* Wikipedia Foundation, 19 Dec. 2011. Web. 1 Sept. 2012. <http://commons.wikimedia.org/wiki/File:Scott_Joplin_19072.jpg>.

Runyon, Robert. *King & Carter Jazzing Orchestra, Houston, Texas, January 1921.* Robert Runyon Photograph Collection. The Center for American History and General Libraries, University of Texas at Austin. "The South Texas Border, 1900-1920." *The Library of Congress,* 30 Aug. 2012. Web. 1 Sept. 2012. <http://hdl.loc.gov/loc.award/txuruny.05019>.

Shipton, Alyn. *A New History of Jazz.* New York: Continuum International Publishing Group, 2001. Print.

The Dave Brubeck Quartet. "Take Five." *Time Out.* 1959. *Jazz Casual.* 1961. *YouTube.* 15 Feb. 2008. Web. 1 Sept. 2012. <http://youtu.be/PQLMFNC2Awo>.

The Mathews Band of Lockport, Louisiana. 1904. *Wikimedia Commons.* Wikipedia Foundation, 1 Jan. 2010. Web. 4 Sept. 2012. <http://commons.wikimedia.org/wiki/File:MathewssBandLockport.jpg>.

The Miles Davis Quintet. "It Never Entered My Mind." *Workin' with the Miles Davis Quintet.* 1956. *YouTube.* 29 Sept. 2010. Web. 14 Apr. 2014. <http://youtu.be/GPdszbuqnnl>.

Wallace, Sippie. "Devil Dance Blues." 1925. "78 RPMs & Cylinder Recordings." *Internet Archive*. 10 Mar. 2001. Web. 1 Sept. 2012. <http://archive.org/details/SippieWallace-DevilDanceBlues1925>.

Wilson, Matthew D. *Diagram showing a typical seating arrangement for members of a jazz ensemble*. 26 Nov. 2008. *Wikimedia Commons*. Wikipedia Foundation, 27 Nov. 2008. Web. 15 May 2012. <http://en.wikipedia.org/wiki/File:Jazz_ensemble_-seating_diagram.svg>.

Young, Lester. "Mean to Me." N.d. *Art Ford's Jazz Party*. Danmarks Radio. 25 Sept. 1958. *YouTube*. 20 July 2010. Web. 1 Sept. 2012. <http://youtu.be/9wvAjA-ovhs>.

Chapter 8

Music of the World

By Cathy Silverman

"The curious beauty of African music is that it uplifts even as it tells a sad tale. You may be poor, you may have only a ramshackle house, you may have lost your job, but that song gives you hope."

-- Nelson Mandela

Fig. 8.1: Smkphotos, Dr. Cheng Yu playing the P'ipa, 2008.

Many indigenous cultures believe in the power of music to interact with cosmic energy. This knowledge has traditionally been used throughout history by indigenous peoples to maintain harmony with the universe, both in the past and continuing today. Around the world, sound is often seen as having the ability to interact with unseen energy forces. Although music therapy is a new concept in the West, music has been used for thousands of years by animistic societies. Animistic cultures utilize traditional healers, known as shamans to interact with the physical and spiritual realms. These societies use music, art, theater, and dance to bring balance to the community and its environment.

Often, the main purpose of music in traditional indigenous cultures is to maintain harmony. Sacred sounds are used to invoke energy forces. Some types of sacred music and rhythms affect brain waves in the range four to eight hertz, which are called theta waves. This is a type of brainwave connected to creativity, dreaming, and memory. Theta waves are produced during meditation, prayer and spiritual awareness, which can induce a trance state ("The Science of Brainwaves").

From a traditional perspective, through the use of rituals, cosmic energy is released that keeps the universe and humans in harmony. Around the world, sacred sounds are used for many purposes—spirituality, healing, controlling the weather, bringing good fortune, and others. Numerous cultures studied sound as a science and developed music to a high level of advancement. Sound was used as an intermediary between the material and non-material realms.

Most evidence of the use of music in primitive/archaic cultures demonstrates that music was primarily used in sacred ritual created for various purposes, such as attracting the attention of the spirits of nature, healing the sick, bringing good fortune, and repelling negative forces. Essentially, the shaman is humanity's original multimedia artist, utilizing music, dance, visual art, and theater to interact with the forces of the universe with the intention of bringing balance and harmony to both the community and the environment. Shamans around the world do not perceive music as something merely for entertainment; instead, music is seen as having the ability to interact with seen and unseen reality.

Numerous cultures studied the interaction of sound with the physical and spiritual worlds as a science and developed that science's potential to amazingly advanced levels of understanding and expression. In the twentieth and twenty-first centuries, physicists and other scientists are arriving at the conclusion that all matter is composed of energy or vibration. The power of music is not solely abstract, but is also physical. The air vibrations of sound are not only real and measurable, but they are also capable of affecting the physical world. An excellent example of this effect is the ability of an opera singer to cause glass to shatter by singing a high note. Music and other forms of sound can cause various sympathetic vibratory resonances within objects at a distance (sympathetic vibration is a phenomenon in which a vibration produced in one object produces the same vibration in another object). Contemporary research into sounds with frequencies below the threshold for human hearing suggests that nausea or headache may be caused by sounds emitted by machinery at a distance. Rhythm also can be a powerful force. For centuries, military experience has held that when troops marching in unison need to cross a bridge, the commanding officer should give the order to break step. The effect of marching in step has more than once led to the collapse of bridges, such as the <u>Angers Bridge collapse</u>.

The power of intention when combined with music is another concept understood well by the ancients that is beginning to be recognized by modern science. The power of intention refers to the understanding that sound has the ability to transmit the intention of the one creating the sound to the one receiving it. Intention, this belief claims, is part of the energy behind the sound. This concept has been tested by kinesiology demonstrations theorizing that an angry or negative thought coupled with sound causes the body to weaken; conversely, a positive intention results in strengthening. The belief in the power of intention is one reason why music is often used in healing rituals around the world.

Traditional peoples express their deep respect and connection to their environment through the use of music and intention within a ritualized context. These rituals reflect an extraordinary understanding of the nature of vibration, the local ecology, and their effects on the human mind and body. These concepts can be embodied in the Hindu Sanskrit saying, "Nada Brahma," which means "The world is sound." This idea is embraced by almost every indigenous culture in the world, which will be further explored in this chapter.

Listening Objectives

Your listening objectives during this chapter will be to:

1. Identify different traits found in the different world music styles.

2. Listen for instrumentation and timbres, including voices or instruments that are performing.

3. Observe small motifs in music and listen for their repetition, manipulation, change, and overall presentation throughout a piece; this includes the return of familiar musical sounds and/or melodies that could signal a repeated section in the larger form of the work.

4. Listen for dynamic and tempo changes, including sudden loud or soft passages and sudden faster or slower sections.

5. Practice describing these observed concepts using the music terms instrumentation, timbre, texture, tempo, dynamics, and form.

Key Music Terms

This chapter will not use the "tool" icon as has been used in other chapters, except to highlight a few instrumentation descriptions. By now, readers should have developed some confidence identifying and describing timbre or tone quality, texture, tempo, dynamics, and form. These terms are included as needed in each world music discussion that follows.

Fig. 8.2: Bill Brindle, *During the rain dance in Corroboree,* 2005. This photo depicts a traditional Aboriginal corroboree, a ceremony with songs and symbolic dances.

Australia

Australian Aborigines represent one of the

oldest continuous cultures living on earth today, tracing their history back more than fifty thousand years ("Aboriginal People"). Upon the arrival of Europeans in the eighteenth century, there were approximately one million Aborigines living in Australia. These Aborigines represented five hundred distinct tribes speaking more than two hundred languages (Chatwin 21). In general, the Europeans did not treat the indigenous peoples of Australia with respect or kindness. By the mid-twentieth century, the Australian Aboriginal population was reduced to sixty thousand members ("Aboriginal People"). These remaining people were forced to speak English and were moved to government camps. Children were taken away from their families in order to be raised in white homes. Although Australian Aborigines were forced to assimilate into Western culture, they were not granted citizenship until 1967 (Cameron). Land rights were not extended until the Aboriginal Land Rights Act of 1976 ("The Aboriginal Land Rights Act"). Today, most Australian Aborigines have been acculturated into modern Australian society. However, they face many of the same problems experienced by other colonized indigenous peoples, including high rates of unemployment and substance abuse, and continued discrimination within their respective societies ("Aboriginal Issues").

Traditionally, Australian Aborigines are hunter-gathers, and represent one of the few cultures on earth that did not undergo the Neolithic Revolution—meaning the indigenous peoples of Australia did not engage in agriculture or settle into permanent villages. They also did not domesticate large animals or accumulate many material objects. The central focus of traditional Australian Aboriginal culture is to re-affirm the energy of the land, thereby guaranteeing its continued existence. Aboriginal religion is an expression of cultural knowledge preserved in memory and enacted through music and dance.

The Dreamtime and Songlines

The foundational principles of Australian religion, music, and culture are based upon the ***Dreamtime.*** During this period, Ancestral Beings "dreamed" the land and heavens into existence, using music and dance to "sing" the world into creation. The Dreamtime knows no time; it is eternal. Therefore, Aboriginal existence is part of eternal existence. The Dreamtime is not a dream in the Western sense; rather, it is an ongoing process with the earth regarded as a conscious creation that nurtures seen and unseen reality. Australian Aboriginal music, dance, and ritual are expressions of these concepts, which are based upon songs received from the Dreamtime.

Legends are sung and danced daily; each series of stories creates a path (or "*songline*") that connects locations of mythic episodes. Songlines are maps of specific locations and experiences, serving as a network of communication and cultural exchange that guides all of the nomadic movements of Australian Aborigines; they can find their way simply by knowing the song of a geographic area. These songlines cover the Australian continent. Specific tribes "own" a section of the songlines, and have the responsibility of maintaining it. Through these songlines, the entire continent of Australia can be seen as a sort of musical score (Chatwin 43).

Songlines are not only ritualistic; they also serve an important practical purpose—survival. Australia has a multiplicity of microclimates. A person from one area would have detailed knowledge of its flora and fauna, land formations, streams, and other geographic features. By naming all of the details of a particular area through a song, a person could survive (interestingly, birds also sing their territorial boundaries). It is fascinating to note that songlines also correspond to subtle lines of magnetic energy that flow around the earth. Aborigines, along with many other native peoples, see these magnetic lines as the blood of the gods. Initiated men and women learned to travel these lines using their "spirit" bodies, and claimed to gain the ability to communicate between people separated by vast distances (Chatwin 47).

Traditionally, songlines, rather than things, were the principal focus of trade within Australian Aboriginal culture. Songs were inherited, serving as deed to territory. These songs could be lent and borrowed, but they could never be sold. Songs were traded through "walkabouts," which always traveled a specific songline inherited through totemic association (a totem is an animal, plant or natural object that serves as the symbol of a specific clan or kinship group). Walkabouts are ritual journeys tracing the footprints of the Ancestors. From an Aboriginal perspective, land must continue to be sung because land that is no longer sung will die—considered a great crime within Aboriginal culture. In addition, singing a song incorrectly or in an improper order is believed to have the ability to cause reality to cease to exist. The singing of songs on a walkabout is conceptually and literally recreating creation, linking past and present, and connecting singers to an ancient continuum (Chatwin 51).

Songlines do not convey information through words, but rather through melody, rhythm, or both. Songs are associated with totemic lines. A song will follow a particular melodic structure, even when the songline is thousands of miles long. Therefore, even if a person does not know the language, a songline and its totemic line can be recognized based upon the melodic pattern of a particular song. This recognition has deep significance due to the strong connection of Aborigines to their totemic line (Chatwin 52).

Australian Aboriginal Instruments

For the Australian Aborigine, observation of nature immediately requires state of empathy, which leads to imitative expression. Traditionally, Aboriginal music is influenced by animal sounds—the flapping of wings, the thump of feet on ground—and other sounds in nature—wind, thunder, trees creaking, water running, and more. These sounds are reflected in the instruments used in Aboriginal music, such as the didgeridoo, which can produce sounds that imitate those found in the natural environment.

Traditional Aboriginal music consists mainly of singing supported by a few instruments. Traditional Aboriginal instruments are usually percussive and are commonly mixed with sounds created by using the body, such as hand claps, body slapping, or the hitting of boomerangs or clapsticks (two sticks struck together). The ***didgeridoo*** (or yidaki) is probably the most recognizable of the Australian Aboriginal instruments. It is a wind instrument made from a log hollowed by termites. It produces a constant drone that includes a wide variety of rhythmic patterns and accents. It can produce many different tone colors, which are created by the performer through altering the shape of the mouth and the position of the tongue. An advanced didgeridoo player uses a circular breathing technique that does not require pausing to take a breath. Didgeridoos also can produce two different notes simultaneously that are alternated to produce complex rhythms. Watch this video for an example of the Aboriginal didgeridoo.

Fig. 8.3: Thomasgl. *Image of didgeridoo,* 2003.

Another interesting instrument used in Australian Aboriginal music is the ***bullroarer***, which is a piece of wood attached to a long string that is swung to produce a roaring sound. Bullroarers are often used before a sacred ceremony to produce a sound that serves to warn the uninitiated to not approach the ceremony and as a method of cleansing the area ("Aboriginal Artefacts").

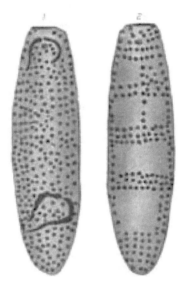

Fig. 8.4: William Aflred Howitt, The Narrang-ga bull-roarer, 1904.

For more information about Australian Aboriginal music and culture, visit the <u>Aboriginal Australia Art & Culture Centre.</u>

Sub-Saharan Africa

Music and dance are the lifeblood of African culture. There are dozens of tribes in sub-Saharan Africa, each with unique forms of music, dance, and ritual. The following are a few styles found in western and central Africa.

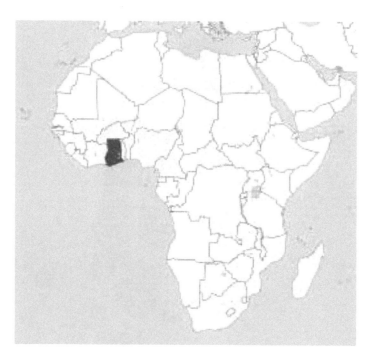

Fig. 8.5: TUBS, Ghana in Africa, 2011. In this map of Africa, the country of Ghana is highlighted in red.

Music of the Dagomba, Ghana

The Dagomba live in northeastern Ghana and speak a language called Dagbani. The main performers of Dagomba music are *lunsi*, who are from a hereditary clan of drummers. Lunsi are responsible for many aspects of Dagomban life, serving as historians, cultural experts, genealogists, and counselors to royalty. Lunsi perform at many Dagomban festivals and ceremonies.

The primary instrument in Dagomban music is the *luna,* a cylindrical, carved drum with a snare on each of its two heads. By squeezing the leather cords strung between its two heads, a player can change the tension and thus the pitch of the drum tone. In the

Fig. 8.6: Cathy Silverman, Dagomban musicians leading First Lady of Surinam into Voices of African Mothers Conference, 2010.

hands of an expert, the luna's sound closely resembles the Dagomban language. Many types of Ghanaian music relate to speech. In Dagomban music, the connection between music and language is direct, and it is possible for an instrument to play music that conveys the verbal language. The luna, also known as the talking drum, is the main feature of this music. Talking drums are used to send messages and relate stories because they imitate the sound of speech (Silverman and Spezzacatena). Watch a demonstration of the talking drum.

Fig. 8.7: Cathy Silverman, Luna, 2010. Fig. 8.8: Cathy Silverman, Gungon, 2010.

The other main instruments in Dagomba music include the ***gungon***, a medium-sized, barrel-shaped drum with a single head that is played with a curved stick and carried by a strap around the neck. Another common instrument is the ***gonje***, a one-string bowed lute (a string instrument with a neck and a pear-shaped body) mounted on a calabash gourd covered with crocodile or alligator skin. The gonje is traditionally used to extol the majesty, valor, and good deeds of the chief or king (Silverman and Spezzacatena).

Fig. 8.9: Cathy Silverman, Gonje, 2010. The photo depicts a traditional Dagomban musician playing the gonje.

Listen to "Chief Installation," an example of traditional Dagomban music.

Damba

Festivals in Ghana are conducted for purification, dedication, thanksgiving, and reunion. One of their important functions is to maintain a link between the living and their ancestors, who are believed to guide all human activities (Silverman and Spezzacatena). The most important festival of the Dagomba is Damba, which is observed in all Dagomba villages where a paramount chief lives. The Damba festival begins during the third month of the

Dagomba lunar calendar and lasts for seven days. The Damba festival began in the

sixteenth century during the reign of the first Muslim Ya-Naa, or paramount chief, in Yendi, Ghana (Kinney 258). Islam was introduced to northern Ghana in the ninth century ("Pre-Colonial Period"). Therefore, today rituals of the Dagomba often combine both Dagomba and Islamic elements.

Damba is traditionally a time for the Dagomba to celebrate chieftainship. During the ceremony, chiefs participate in processions wearing elaborate regalia. Lesser chiefs show homage to their superiors up to the

Fig. 8.10: Nico Spezzacatena, Ya-Na Yakubu Andani II, Dagomban Paramount Chief, 1999.

Ya Naa, or paramount chief. The Dagomba gather and participate in a demonstration of respect and to hear singers articulate Dagbon oral history and sing praise songs to the chief. Damba is also an occasion for most people to exchange gifts and buy new clothes. Men dress in colorful, handwoven smocks called *batakari* that are designed for a style of dancing that includes many spins and twirls. Women wear expensive jewelry and a traditional, handwoven cloth wrapped around their waists. Damba also is a time for feasting, displaying horsemanship skills, and shooting rifles (Silverman and Spezzacatena).

This video, *Damba Festival,* highlights the events of the Damba festival. In the morning, the chiefs and other elders come to the palace where a bull is slaughtered according to ancient ritual. Then, there is a procession of the chief and elders accompanied by drummers, gonje players, and other musicians. Later, the chief is led back to his home by singers and drummers. The end of the video features gonje singers. This particular Damba ceremony was held on July 3, 1999, in Yendi, Ghana. The largest Damba ceremonies are held here because it is the seat of the Ya Naa.

Ewe Music, Ghana

The Anlo-Ewe occupy southeastern Ghana and the southern parts of neighboring Togo and Benin. Dance-drumming is fundamental to Ewe culture as a way to focus community energy. The veneration of ancestors is a central part of this process because ancestors are a considered a source of wisdom to be consulted (K. Ladzekpo).

Ewe dance-drumming music is polyrhythmic, usually combining 4/4 and 6/8 meters. The music is accompanied by traditional songs and dancing. The drum language is secret and known only by the drummers (A. Ladzekpo). If there are no organized performances, community elders do not encourage the playing of drums, as it is seen as a disturbance when drums are played without the dancers and entire musical ensemble. Open-air performances provide Anlo-Ewe youth the only opportunity to learn the music by listening and forming syllables from the drum language. During a performance, if lead drummers need a vacant instrument to be played, they beckon to any youth, traditionally a boy. If the chosen person already knows the part, he doesn't need any instructions. If he doesn't know the part, the lead drummer demonstrates the drum pattern and hand him sticks to play. If he plays correctly, he continues to play. If he fails, the lead drummer takes instrument and gives it to someone else (A. Ladzekpo).

Fig. 8.11: Nico Spezzacatena, Anlo-Ewe dance-drumming ensemble, 1999.

Ewe music is played in an ensemble that usually features a lead drum, supporting drum, rattles, and bell. The lead drum is the ***atsimevu,*** which is carved from a log and measures four to five feet in length. The drum head is usually made from the skin of a deer or antelope. It is played using a combination of sticks and hands.

Supporting drums include the ***sogo, kidi,*** and ***kaganu.*** The individual phrases of the supporting drummers are usually relatively simple. However, playing them in an ensemble is surprisingly hard.

The ***gankogui*** (bell) is the timekeeper and must be played steadily and without error. Promising young drummers often are given the responsibility of playing the bell in an ensemble.

The ***axatse*** (rattles) are made from large gourds covered in a web of beads and are used to accent beats in the rhythm. The axatse players are usually also part of the chorus.

Visit the Virtual Drum Museum at Dancedrummer.com to see photos and demonstrations of the main instruments in an Anlo-Ewe dance-drumming ensemble.

Agbekor or The Great Oath

There are many different pieces found in the Anlo-Ewe musical repertoire. This section will examine Agbekor or "the great oath."

In 1957, my father, Kofi Zate Ladzekpo, told me meaning of "Atsiagbekor" or "Agbekor" drum language. Agbekor is Anlo-Ewe war music called "Atamga" meaning "the great oath." It is the oath the ancestors took before they went to war to defend their tribe. The drum's statements are admonishments from a father to his two sons who crave war. He plays calls on lead drum for dancers to demonstrate what goes on in war. Agbekor expresses the enjoyment of life.

--Alfred Ladzekpo

Agbekor is a classic call and response piece. It is practiced in seclusion and learned through direct teaching and guidance rather than listening/performing as in many other forms of Ewe music. Players learn long sequences, and the music is not strictly formalized. No one knows what is going to happen next (A. Ladzekpo).

Watch a video excerpt featuring "Atsiagbekor," which is the opening section of "Agbekor." This example features an excerpt from a performance played during the video *Husunu's Durbar* and shows a traditional Anlo-Ewe ensemble, including a few American dance-drumming students who were invited to perform with the ensemble. The entire video depicts a celebration of the anniversary of the death of Husunu Ladzekpo, a revered leader of the Ewe people.

Listen to "Atsiagbekor" featuring lead drummer Agbi Ladzekpo.

Kwamivi Tsegah's Funeral, Anyako, Ghana

This excerpt from the video *Kwamivi Tsegah's Funeral* features the Anyako Woeto group performing "Afa," a piece always played at the beginning of a performance that is integral to get blessings and ensure that the performance goes well. Afa is the god of divination and a widespread religion that is open to anyone. This piece features the sogo as the lead drum, and almost every rhythm has a specific meaning, demonstrating a communication technique similar to the talking drum of the Dagomba (ladada). The instrumentation in this performance includes sogo, kidi and kaganu, axatse, and the gankogui. The Woeto group's colors for this performance are blue and white. Those who are not wearing those colors are from other areas in the community. They can be invited to dance, but cannot play the drums or lead songs (Liner Notes, *Kwamivi Tsegah's Funeral*).

Another section of "Afa" is "Axatsevu." *Axatse* is the Ewe name for rattle, and *Vu* means drum, hence rattle drum, a style of music dominated by rattles. "Axatsevu" is unique because it is the only Ewe piece with two songs happening simultaneously. The men and women have completely different song repertoires. The *shoshi* (the tail of a horse) is held by the song leader/s of the group. In most instances, there is more than one song leader so it doesn't get boring. If the group is large, it is easier to identify the songs that the song leaders establish. When a person becomes a *heno* (song leader) of a group, a special horse tail is handed down in a private ceremony (Liner Notes, *Kwamivi Tsegah's Funeral*).

Political Music in Africa: Fela Kuti and Thomas Mapfumo

Fig. 8.12: Nico Spezzacatena. Anlo-Ewe axatse ensemble, 1999.

Music in Africa has traditionally been a method of communication that includes the transmission of history, religion, genealogy, social and political issues, and more. Music often is used to offer commentary on contemporary society and politics, and many musicians in Africa rose to prominence in the struggle for independence from Great Britain colonization, which began in the 1960s. This section will discuss two of the most influential and popular political musicians in West Africa: Fela Kuti of Nigeria and Thomas Mapfumo of Zimbabwe.

Fela Kuti

Nigerian saxophonist, keyboardist, and vocalist Fela Kuti is a mythic figure in the African popular music tradition. In the late 1960s, Kuti traveled to the United States and was inspired by the civil rights movement (*Music is the Weapon*). He returned to Nigeria in 1971 and pioneered Afrobeat, a style of political protest music that combined funk, jazz, and highlife, a style of music originating in Ghana in the early twentieth century that combines indigenous melody and rhythm with the use of Western instruments. Through his music and public statements, Kuti challenged Nigeria's military rulers and portrayed the suffering of the Nigerian people. He created a counterculture in the city of Lagos through using song to criticize political leaders, declaring his compound an independent nation, and surviving numerous attacks by the Nigerian authorities (Veal 77-92). In 1979, he formed the Movement of the People (M.O.P.) political party and ran for president, although his party was disqualified from the elections by the ruling powers due to his outspoken criticism of political leaders. Kuti died in August 1997 due to complications from AIDS. Kuti "arguably combined elements of pure artistry, political perseverance, and a mystic, spiritual consciousness in a way that no other individual ever has" (Kambui). The fact that Kuti was able to flourish for three decades despite extreme pressure from authorities reflects the widespread affection many Nigerians held for Kuti and his work (Veal 243). Visit PBS's *Fela Kuti: Black President* to learn more about Fela Kuti and hear samples of his music.

Thomas Mapfumo

Thomas Mapfumo was born in 1945 and is known as "the Lion of Zimbabwe" due to his use of music to boldly criticize political leaders in Zimbabwe and his role as both a developer and leader of traditional music of the Shona people, the largest indigenous group in Zimbabwe. As a youth, Mapfumo modeled American and English music, but later, in the 1960s, he began to translate protests songs into the Shona language. In 1972, Mapfumo formed the Hallelujah Chicken Run Band and began to explore traditional Shona folk music, which features the *mbira*, a type of thumb piano that is the main instrument in Shona music. Together with the band's guitarist, Joshua Dube, Mapfumo transcribed the tonal scale used by the mbira for the guitar and added traditional drums (Eyre).

Mapfumo's lyrics reflected the concerns of his people, such as the hardships suffered in rural areas, young men fighting in the bush, and a rising outrage against white rulers who systematically devalued and attacked traditional Shona culture. Mapfumo named his new music style *chimurenga*, the Shona word for "struggle" and the name taken by guerrilla freedom fighters in Zimbabwe (Eyre).

Mapfumo was seen as a troublesome political leader by the white regime in Zimbabwe that tried to block the release of his music and forbade playing Mapfumo's music on the radio. He was imprisoned without trial, which led to violent protests that eventually led to his release. After Zimbabwe's independence, the ban against Mapfumo's music was lifted and in 1980, his group performed with Bob Marley and the Wailers at an event marking Zimbabwe's independence. Mapfumo continued to write politically motivated music that criticized the corruption and misuse of power by the post-colonial leaders of the newly independent Zimbabwe.

In the 1990s, Mapfumo changed his focus to criticizing the new leaders of independent Zimbabwe, who he believed had failed the people. By summer 2000, the conditions in Zimbabwe had deteriorated badly, partially due to Robert Mugabe's aggressive and violent policies. Mapfumo's music was unofficially banned from state-controlled television and radio. Due to this pressure from the government, which included threats and false charges of theft, Mapfumo relocated his family to the United States in 2000, though Mapfumo continued to return to Zimbabwe despite the risks until 2004 to continue to speak out against corruption and greed within the political leadership ("Thomas Mapfumo"). Today, Mapfumo continues to sing and speak out for the poor and disenfranchised people of Zimbabwe.

Watch this video of Thomas Mapfumo and the Blacks Unlimited performing "Moyo Wangu" in 1994.

North Africa and the Middle East

"What we call music in our everyday language," according to the great master of the Sufi sect of Islam Hazrat Inayat Khan, "is only a miniature, which our intelligence has grasped from that music or harmony of the whole universe which is working behind everything, and which is the source and origin of nature. It is because of this that the wise of all ages have considered music to be a sacred art. For in music the seer can see the picture of the whole universe ..." (Shelquist).

Figure 8.13: Justinian-of-Byzantium, Middle East map in full, 2011. In this map, the Middle East is highlighted in green.

The origins of Arabic music are in the distant past and emerged during pre-Islamic times in the Arabian Peninsula. Many elements of music, such as the tonal system, rhythmic patterns, musical forms, compositional techniques, and performance practices, are essentially the same in all Arab countries (Touma 8).

Arabic Melody and Rhythm

Fig. 8.14: Aleppo Music Band, 1915. This photo depicts a traditional Arabic musical ensemble.

Melody in Arabic music is quite different from Western melody. Arabic music most commonly uses scales consisting of seventeen, nineteen, or up to twenty-four equal quartertones—smaller intervals than those found in Western music, half the length of half-steps or semitones. Quartertones are also sometimes referred to as microtones. Arabic melody is based upon over fifty-two modes called *maqamat*, which means "place or situation." A *maqam*, or melody, utilizes selected notes from a specific maqamat with a certain tendency of movement. A maqam is "something more than a scale, yet something less than a tune" (Spencer). An Arabic melody must use the notes of a specific maqam and incorporate the melodic fragment into the melody line with an emphasis on ornamentation, a technique in which a musical note is embellished by adding notes or changing the rhythm. The maqam helps create the mood for a particular piece of music (Touma, preface).

Arabic music has a monophonic texture with one central melodic line and does not utilize harmony. When multiple instruments play, one instrument carries the primary melody with the other instruments layering melodies and rhythms over it. This is different from

Western music, which usually includes harmony and chords. Soloists in Arabic music often improvise during a performance. This structure reflects Arabic music's nomadic traditions and its use of caravan songs. Traditionally, Arabic music is not notated, rather it is learned by listening ("The Arabic Maqam").

The rhythm of Arabic music can be quite complex with patterns up to forty-eight beats called *iqa'at*. Arabic rhythms typically include several downbeats (*dums*) or principal accented beats, upbeats (*taks*) or unaccented beats that precede the downbeats, and rests or silences. The dum, or downbeat, is usually a deeper tone created from striking the center of the drum. The *tak*, or upbeat, generally has a higher and crisper timbre and is creating by hitting the drum near the rim. Much like Indian music, which will be explored in the next section, Arabic musicians usually play a basic pattern ornamented with improvisations that can be compared to the performance style found in jazz (Montford).

Arabic music performance traditionally reflects the response of the audience, which is expected to react during a performance verbally or with applause. If an audience is quiet, this often means the audience is disinterested or dislikes the music. The audience is an active participant in determining the length of a performance, and it shapes the music by encouraging musicians to repeat a section or move to the next one (Danielson).

Classical Arabic music is based upon the *takht*, a small ensemble consisting of the oud, qanoun, nay, violin, and percussion without vocal accompaniment (Dimitriadis).

An *oud* is a pear-shaped instrument with two to seven strings with its origin in ancient Egypt (Dimitriadis). The *qanoun* is a plucked zither with strings made of gut or nylon. The *nay* is an open end-blown flute traditionally made from bamboo that can be either vertical or horizontal. The main Arabic percussion instrument is the *riq*, a small tambourine with its head made from goat or fish skin. Around the frame of a riq are paired brass cymbals that create a jingling sound ("Arabic Musical Instruments"). Each region in the Arab world has its own distinctive style, instrumentation, rhythmic pattern, modal structure, and performance technique; these create an art form that extends across a large geographic area and an artistic

Fig. 8.15: Catrin, Egyptian riqq, 2006. This photo depicts a traditional Arabic riq.

tradition that evolves while maintaining its traditional heritage.

Listening Examples

- *"Maqam Bayati" (played on the oud)*

- *"A Journey with the Oud"*

South Asia

Classical Indian Music

Indian music has religious roots. Indian mythology asserts that music was brought to the people of India from the celestial plane and is used to free the self

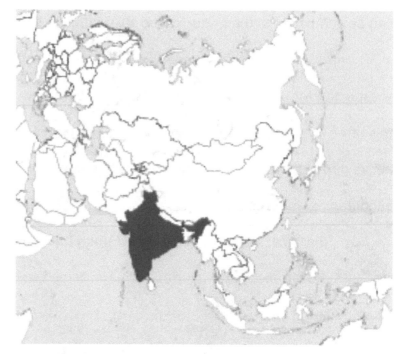

(*atman*) from mind and matter. This enables a merger between

Fig. 8.16: TUBS, India in Asia, 2011. This map of Asia depicts the country of India, which is highlighted in red.

the atman and the cosmic forces of the universe. This concept is expressed in the following passage from *The Natya Shastra*, an ancient Indian text on the performing arts:

Once, a long time ago, during a transitional period between two Ages it so happened

that people took to uncivilized ways, were ruled by lust and greed behaved in angry

and jealous ways with each other and not only gods but demons, evil spirits, ... and

such like others swarmed over the earth. Seeing this plight, Indra [the Hindu God of

thunder and storms] and other Gods approached god Brahma [God of Creation] and

requested him to give people a toy (Kridaniyaka), but one which could not only be

seen but heard and this should turn out a diversion (so that people would give up

their bad ways). It was determined to give the celestial art of sangeet to mankind.

(Courtney)

This was the origins of **sangeet**, a Sanskrit term used for the traditional Indian performing

arts, which include vocal music, instrumental music, and dance. The aesthetic basis of

sangeet is formed by the nine fundamental emotions from which all complex emotions can

be produced. This reflects Hindu concepts about how mood and its creation of energy can

affect the mind and body. Through classical Indian music, every feeling and emotion can be

expressed and experienced. The purpose of classical Indian music is to activate energy

centers (*chakras*) and connect humans to higher levels of consciousness (Shankar).

In India, music is seen as a spiritual discipline that leads to self-realization and

enlightenment. This is based upon the traditional teaching that sound is God, or that

vibration is the source of the universe. This belief is known in Sanskrit as "Nada Brahma":

"the world is sound." In texts from the Vedic culture of ancient India, there are two types of

sound. One is a vibration in the celestial plane, known as "Unstruck" sound (*Anahata Nad*),

which can only be heard by enlightened yogis. The other sound, known as "Struck" sound

(*Ahata Nad*), is the vibration found in the earthly realm. This includes sounds in nature and manmade sounds, both musical and non-musical (Shankar).

The introduction of music to humans by the divine was the first step; it then had to be taught. The inherent divine qualities of Indian classical music require the following prerequisites:

1. Guru (teacher): Indian music is orally transmitted and is considered the highest form of knowledge. A guru is essential to the learning process.

2. Humility: Indian classical music is a sacred art requiring not only technical but also spiritual development. If a student lacks humility, then he or she will not be able to learn.

3. Discipline: Music is a highly evolved and complex art form, which requires disciplined practice. This discipline applies to both technical and spiritual learning. Discipline is essential to mastering Indian classical music (Courtney).

Basic Components of Classical Indian Music

Indian classical music typically has three layers:

1. *Drone*: The drone is an unchanging tone or tones that underlies the melody. The drone marks the tonal center of a piece. Usually a plucked tambura or a sruti box plays the drone (a sruti box is a type of organ that creates its sound using hand-pumped bellows that force air through reeds) (Titon and Fujie 212).

2. *Raga*: A raga is the melodic form upon which the musicians improvise. Ragas are not based upon harmony, counterpoint, modulations, or other melodic elements found in Western music. A raga is based upon a particular scale and specific movements of

the melody. One raga is differentiated from another by subtle differences in the order of the notes, or omission or emphasis on a dissonant note, slide, or microtone. Ornamentation and intonation are central aspects of the performance of a raga. The phrase *"Ranjayathi iti Raga"* is found in ancient Indian texts. This description of ragas is translated as "that which colors the mind," and is an expression of the inner spirit of an artist (Titon and Fujie 212).

3. *Tal*: The rhythm and drumming in India are among the most complex in the world. Many common rhythmic patterns are centered on repeating patterns of beats. Drummers memorize hundreds, and sometimes thousands, of rhythmic patterns. Talas can range from three to one hundred eight beats and are played in many different complex meters (9, 11, 13, 17, 19). The most advanced musicians play some rhythms on only rare occasions. Playing a tal requires constant calculation to determine how different patterns fit with the tala cycle. These rhythms can be expressed vocally as well, which is called *solkattu*. Indian classical rhythms differ in how the beats are divided and accented. They are expressed with subtle variations, such as the use of pauses, accelerandos, and ritardandos, and are reflective of the infinite variety represented in the Hindu faith (Titon and Fujie 214).

It is estimated that there are over six thousand ragas and that up to ninety percent of Indian classical music is improvised. Ragas are used to create psychological states and are associated with times of day, seasons, planets, moods, or certain magical properties. This divine quality of music is expressed through *nad siddha*, the ability to perform miracles by playing specific music (Shankar). Tansen, a musician from North India who lived in the sixteenth century, was the most famous miracle-making musician and was said to be able to create fire and rain through the singing of specific *ragas* (Courtney). Ragas are utilized for

myriad mystical purposes, including healing the sick, affecting the weather, summoning

spirits, charming cobras, and many more. It is not possible to notate a raga because it is

never the same twice: there are many variations in length, rhythm, intonation, and

embellishment.

The structure of Indian Classical Music

A traditional recital of Indian classical music begins with the *alap*, a section that

explores the melody of the chosen raga without a clearly defined rhythm. After this slow and

introspective beginning, the music moves onto the *jar*. This is when the rhythm enters and

develops without the accompaniment of a drum. This section evolves into the *gat*, which is

the fixed composition of the raga. In the gat, the drum joins the main structure of the raga

and the tal. The gat becomes the basis for improvisation; musicians are free to improvise

within the basic structure of the raga and tal. It requires years of practice and discipline to

be an effective improviser (Shankar).

When performing Indian classical music, musicians take into consideration the

setting, the mood of the audience, the time allowed, the time of day and season, and other

factors. The goal is to maximize that particular moment. Musicians have great flexibility in

shaping a performance, and concerts can last several hours (Shankar). It is also important

to recognize that the interpretation and expression of the raga and tal are not the same

throughout India. Today, there are two main traditions within Indian classical music: the

South Indian Carnatic tradition and the North Indian Hindustani tradition.

Carnatic Music, South India

The *Carnatic* tradition reflects a more orthodox Hindu tradition. All Carnatic music is based upon a song. Even if there is no vocalist, the words are known to those with an understanding of the music. The first composers of the Carnatic tradition served as musicians to the ancient raja courts and are from the Brahmin caste. The caste system is a traditional method of stratification used in India. Membership in a caste is hereditary. Brahmin is the highest caste and its members are often priests or scholars.

 The main instruments of the Carnatic tradition are the *veena, mridangam*, and *tambura*. The *veena* is an instrument with four playing strings and three drone strings. Along the neck are brass frets set in wax that are curved to allow the player to bend the strings. There are many complex fingerings, slides, and ornaments utilized by the musician to express the character of a specific raga.

Fig. 8.17: Gringer and Sreejithk2000, Veena, 2010. Fig. 8.18: Domtw, Mridangam, 2010.

The *mridangam* is a barrel-shaped double-headed drum. The heads of the drum are made from leather and are connected to the body of the drum by leather straps attached to moveable tuning pegs. The lower (untuned) head has a circle of soft wheat paste in the center that creates a booming sound when struck. The higher head is tuned to the tonic note of the raga, which is the central note upon which the raga is based, and has a hard black spot in the center that creates a high pitched, sharp sound. The complexity of the drumheads combined with the sophisticated fingering techniques used by mridangam players makes it possible to play more than fifteen distinct sounds through varying combinations of drum strokes.

The *tambura* is a plucked instrument with four strings. It is held vertically and functions as a drone. It is tuned to the tonic note of the raga, or the natural fourth or perfect fifth above or below the tonic note.

Listen to "Raga Narayani" performed by D.K. Jayaraman and D.K. Pattammal, traditional Carnatic singers (second song on the list). Please note that for this chapter, transcripts of song and music lyrics are not necessary to gain an understanding of the material.

Hindustani Music, North India

The North Indian *Hindustani* style of music utilizes the same ragas and talas, but has been more influenced by Persian and Islamic culture than the Carnatic style. The main instruments found in Hindustani music are the *sitar* and *tabla*.

The *sitar* is a complex and beautiful string instrument. A sitar has eighteen strings, including several drone strings located under the moveable frets, which are bars set across the fingerboard on the neck, that vibrate sympathetically when the main strings are played. The drone strings are also periodically struck to provide an atonal base (atonal music is music without a

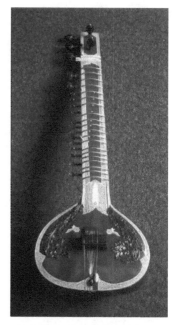

Fig. 8.19: Jan Kraus, Sitar, 2008.

tonal center). Most of the playing on a sitar is done on one string.

The *tabla* is a set of two drums, one of which is smaller than the other. Tablas are tuned by tightening the pegs and strings. Wheat paste in the center of one drum produces a deep, booming sound.

Fig. 8.20: Ankitchd26, Historycal Musical instruments, 2011. This photo depicts the tabla, the traditional drum played in Hindustani music.

Listening Examples

"Tabla solo in Teentala" Nikhil Ghosh, tabla

"Raga Kaushi Kanada" (second track on list) Nikhil Banerjee, sarangi

Bollywood Music

The rise of Hindi film music in the 1930s influenced many styles of music around the world. One of the most prolific Indian film music styles is Bollywood. This popular music, written and performed for Indian cinema, is a modern evolution of traditional Indian forms of entertainment that feature music as a central aspect of the performance (Wohlgemuth). Rather than singing themselves, the film actors in Bollywood films usually lip-sync music sung by accomplished singers. Bollywood music soundtracks account for the majority of popular music sales in India. In fact, most Indian people go to the movies for the songs

("Bollywood Music"). Bollywood music has a nationalistic quality, representing India as a whole and incorporating styles from many Indian musical traditions (Carnatic and Hindustani classical music, religious and folk music) (Wohlgemuth). Today, the Bollywood film industry consists of many genres and styles.

For an example of Bollywood film and music, watch "[Maiya Yashoda]()," an excerpt from the Bollywood film Hum Saath Saath Hain. *Please note that for this chapter, transcripts of song and music lyrics are not necessary to gain an understanding of the material.*

Southeast Asia

The Southeast Asian country of Indonesia is the home to myriad musical traditions. Over thousands of years, some of these forms remained indigenous and localized, whereas others evolved through interaction with neighboring, and sometimes invading, cultures to produce various syncretic styles (syncretism in music is a combination of musical elements from individual cultures that creates a new style of music).

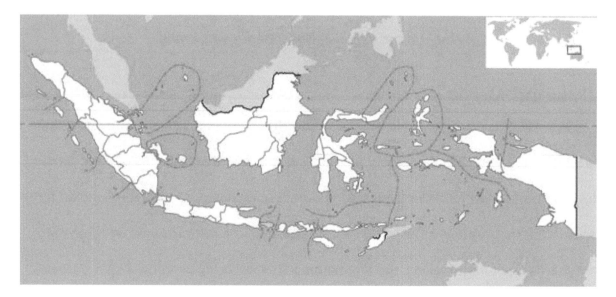

Fig. 8.21: Anonylog, Indonesia, Bali, 2008. This photo depicts the archipelago of Indonesia. The island of Bali is highlighted in green.

Balinese and Javanese orchestral music represent some of the most complex styles of music found in the Indonesian archipelago. This section will explore the more lively style of Balinese orchestral music called the *gamelan*.

Balinese Music and Dance

Almost everyone participates in artistic activity in Bali. The arts are directly connected to Bali-Hindu religion, a religion based upon indigenous practices combined with Hinduism and elements of Buddhism. Dances and dramatic performances are seen as an integral part of Balinese religion and culture, and serve as an expression of devotion to the gods and as a method of reinforcing cultural values. The essence of Balinese culture rests in the village, where most ceremonies are held. Each village in Bali has differing ceremonies, performance techniques, and specialties with seemingly endless and mind-boggling variation.

The main type of music found in Bali is **gamelan** music. A gamelan is an orchestra comprised of a variety of instruments including drums, gongs, and cymbals. These instruments are ornately decorated with symbols and gods from Bali-Hindu religion and mythology. The instruments are tuned in pairs (male and female) with one tuned slightly higher than the other to create a shimmering sound. Instruments are regarded as highly sacred and are played only after proper offerings and rituals have been completed. The instruments serve as the most important elements to reach God.

Balinese music is constantly evolving with old styles falling out of favor and new styles emerging. There are seemingly infinite styles of gamelan music found in Bali, an island only two hundred miles wide. These include *semar peguliligan* (the love gamelan), *gambuh* (a nine-hundred-year-old style featuring very large vertical bamboo flutes) (Spies and de Zoete 75), *jegog* (gamelan instruments made from bamboo), *gong gede* (prevalent in

Fig. 8.22: Cathy Silverman, Village gamelan, Luwus, Bali, 2008.

early 1900s) (Brunet), *kebyar* (a twentieth century style), the marching gamelan, and many, many more. The most sacred of all gamelans is *gamelan selonding*, which is the oldest type of gamelan dating back two thousand years, (Lewiston and Burger) and is made from iron rather than the bronze found in modern gamelans (Bakan 355).

Balinese gamelan music is playful and frenetic with sudden stops and starts, dramatic changes in volume, precise syncopated playing, and complicated counterpoint. A gamelan has no real conductor; the music is usually led by one or two experienced drummers who control its pace and signal changes to the musicians. Members of a village gamelan orchestra are not professional musicians—they have normal family responsibilities, jobs, and village obligations.

Gamelan music is played from memory, which is quite extraordinary considering the length and complexity of many gamelan compositions. The music is heard from birth and is learned through listening and repetition. The musical parts interlock, which creates the impression that the music is performed more quickly than it actually is. Gamelan melodies are based upon two primary equal temperament scales: *slendro* (a five-note pentatonic scale) and *pelog* (a seven-note scale). According to a legend of the Bali Aga, who are the original inhabitants of Bali, the gods provided the first gamelan notes.

Gamelan Instruments

There are many types of gamelan instruments—too many to address here—however, we will highlight the instruments commonly found in a Balinese gamelan orchestra, The most common type of gamelan ensemble consists mainly of *gongs* and *gender*s, a type of xylophone instrument that is struck with mallets. ***Genders*** have bronze keys suspended over bamboo resonators and are tuned in pairs, each at a slightly different frequency, which create a shimmering sound when played together. The ***gongs*** are also made from bronze, although in the past the gongs and genders were made from iron. There are three types of gongs: single-hanging and lying gongs played by one person that accent the central melody, sets of gongs on a frame played by one

Fig. 8.23: Cathy Silverman, Gamelan factory, Tihingin, Bali, Indonesia, 2005.

person that plays the central melody, and larger gong sets played by two to four people used to embellish the central melody.

Fig. 8.24: Cathy Silverman, Balinese gongs, 2008. Fig. 8.25: Cathy Silverman, Balinese drummers, 2005.

The gamelan orchestra is conducted by the *kendang*, a pair of double-headed drums, one with a higher pitch than the other. The gamelan also often includes the *suling* (bamboo flutes), a *rebab* (a two-string violin), and the *chang-chang* (a set of cymbals). Gamelans are tuned to themselves and therefore instruments from one gamelan cannot be used in another gamelan.

Balinese music has a remarkable quality: the lower instruments in a gamelan ensemble play lower-pitched, slower tempo parts, while the higher instruments play higher-pitched, faster parts. This interestingly reflects the way sound waves resonate scientifically (lower frequencies resonate in long, slow waves, whereas higher frequencies resonate in short, fast waves). How the ancient Balinese knew this without the use of scientific equipment is a mystery yet to be solved.

Watch a gamelan performance at <u>Pitra Yadnya</u>, a Balinese funerary ceremony.

Listen to "<u>Gamelan selonding</u>" from the Bali Arts Festival.

In addition to the more common bronze and iron gamelans, there are also gamelans made from bamboo called *jegog* that are traditionally found in Western Bali.

Fig. 8.26: Cathy Silverman, Jegog instruments, 2010.

Listen to "Jegog" performed by the Surya Metu Reh ensemble, Negara, Bali.

Genjek

Genjek is a unique form of music found in Bali. Genjek is the vocalization of gamelan music, using voices instead of instruments. It is a secular style of music, often performed at parties and social gatherings. Genjek singers sit in a circle and intersperse the genjek songs with the drinking of *arak*, a type of liquor made from palm.

Listen to "Genjek" from a performance in Candidasa, Bali.

The Relationship Between Balinese Music & Dance

Dance and music are inextricably connected within Bali-Hindu culture and are performed primarily as an offering to the gods. Balinese dances bring to life ancient stories.

There are hundreds of accompanying dance styles in Bali, including Sangyang trance

dances, Legong (young girls dance), Baris (young men's dance), Calonarang, Joget, Janger,

the popular Barong & Rangda (a dance that restores the balance between good and evil),

and dozens more. Of particular interest are the masked dances, such as Topeng and Jauk.

These two dance styles are unique: the dancers lead the gamelan, rather than the gamelan

leading the dancers as is found in other forms of Balinese dance. Topeng and Jauk, both

forms of masked dance, are more spontaneous and improvised than other forms of

Balinese music and dance.

East Asia

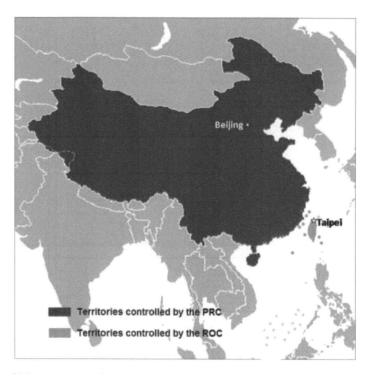

Fig. 8.27: Hmh 2001, China map updated, 2011. This map of China depicts both the PRC (People's Republic of China) and the ROC (Republic of China, also known as Taiwan).

The music of East Asia has a long and varied history. Traditionally, the Chinese

believed that sound influenced the harmony of the universe. Interestingly, one of the first

duties of the emperor in a new dynasty was to seek out and establish the true standard of pitch for the dynasty. Harmony within Chinese society, both spiritual and communal, was not

determined by economics or other material measurements, but was based upon music. This

represented the philosophy of Confucius, who believed that music was a means of

controlling negative emotions, rather than merely a form of entertainment. Music was

thought to have the ability to connect humans to higher levels of consciousness through the

principle of harmonic resonance: "right" music had a harmonious effect on people and their

environment, maintaining balance between the physical and spiritual worlds and creating

health, harmony, prosperity, and peace. "Wrong" music, however, would create illness,

economic problems, and war. In China, music is seen as having the ability to affect the

human body and psyche, leading to personal development and later, spiritual

enlightenment. Music represents a

connection and mode of

communication between heaven

and earth (Eaton).

Most Chinese music is

based upon just intonation,

compared to the equal

temperament system of tonality

developed in the Baroque era that is

utilized in Western music. The

difference between these two types

of tuning systems is that just

intonation reflects the way sound

Fig. 8.28: Bagdadani, Ancient Chinese instrumentalists, 2008.

resonates naturally and therefore is harmonic with the natural environment. In contrast, equal temperament is essentially a man-made system developed in Europe in the early eighteenth century that is harmonic within itself, but is dissonant (or clashes) with the harmonics of the natural environment and the basic resonances of the human body. The Chinese have always refused to completely adopt the equal temperament scale because they believe disharmonious music can cause problems in society and nature (Eaton).

The Pentatonic Scale

The primary scale used in traditional Chinese music is the five-tone, or pentatonic scale, which is a scale found in many types of sacred music around the world. Five is a significant number in Chinese cosmology, representing the five elements of the visible world: the four elements and the center. This concept of the number four is reflected in the four cardinal directions, the four seasons, which arise from the fifth celestial element (*Akasa*), or the central principle (Eaton).

The five notes of the pentatonic scale, according to Chinese theory, are the only ones with the ability to create true harmony on the physical plane. Comparisons can be made between musical harmony and the proportions of sacred architecture, and those of the human body, colors, time, and concepts found in fractal geometry (Winn). Here is an excellent example of a pentatonic scale demonstrated by Bobby McFerrin at the World Science Festival in a symposium entitled "Notes and Neurons: In Search of the Common Chorus" (transcript available).

Melody and tone color are prominent expressive features of Chinese music, with great importance placed on proper articulation of each tone (Fang).Traditionally, Chinese instruments are classified according to the materials used: stone, metal, wood, clay, bamboo, and other natural materials. The oldest instruments in China include flutes,

zithers, panpipes, mouth organs, and percussion instruments such as bells, gongs, clappers,

and drums. A flute carved from the wing bone of a crane found in China dated c. 7000 BCE

is the world's oldest still playable instrument.

Classical Chinese Court Music

Chinese music is not a single, unified tradition, but rather reflects the many different

ethnic groups found in China. An example is the traditional music of Amoy, a city in the

southeastern province of Fujian situated on the Taiwan Strait. The traditional music of Amoy

is known as *nan-kuan* (southern pipes) and is believed by Chinese musicologists to have

preserved a type of classical Chinese court music that reached its peak during the Tang

Dynasty (Lieberman).

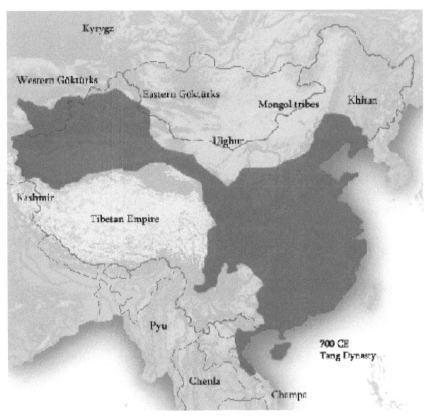

Fig. 8.29: Ian Kiu, Tang dynasty circa 700 CE, 2007.

Listen to "<u>Fei Fei Shih Shih (Rainy Weather)</u>" (number three on the list). This piece

features the *hsiao* (or xiao), a vertical bamboo flute that traditionally has five holes, although

today it often has six holes. Performers must master dozens of complicated fingerings to

successfully play the hsiao. This composition also features the *pipa*, a pear-shaped lute with

a crooked neck and four to five strings that are plucked. The pipa is a commonly used solo

instrument in ensembles and Chinese orchestras (Lieberman).

Central Asia

Central Asia includes some of the oldest
forms of music found on earth, dating back
several thousand years. Traditional music in
central Asia is based upon nature, and reflects
an ancient shamanistic tradition in which all
things and phenomena have a spiritual
counterpart. For example, the spirituality of
rivers and mountains manifests through
physical shape, but also through the sounds
they produce. Humans are believed to have the
ability to access the energy (and
consciousness) of nature, assimilating the

Fig. 8.30: Voodooisland, Tuvan People's
Republic, 2010. This image depicts the Republic
of Tuva, which is highlighted in green.

power of nature by imitating its sounds, a practice called "sound mimesis." There are many

types of stylistic variations used to imitate the calls and other sounds made by wild and

domesticated animals (Levin and Edgerton).

Khöömei - Throatsinging of Tuva

For the semi-nomadic herders living in Tuva, a central Asian republic in southern Siberia, the natural soundscape inspires a form of music that resonates with the environment creating a blend of natural and human sounds. Of the many ways Tuvans use sound to interact with the environment, one of the most distinct is their use of throat singing, a remarkable technique found primarily in central Asia in which one vocalist produces two or more separate tones simultaneously. In Tuva, singers state that the origins of this method can be traced far back in history; shamans used it and a variety of sounds as tools for spiritual and physical healing (Levin and Edgerton).

In Tuvan throat singing, one of the tones produced is a low, sustained drone and the other tone is a series of higher pitches that could be described as representing the song of a bird, the gurgling of a mountain stream, or the rhythm of a cantering horse. The term for this type of singing is called *khöömei*, which is the Mongolian word for throat. Throat singers are able to manipulate their vocal folds in a way that enables them to create a whistle-like pitch while simultaneously creating the underlying low drone (Levin and Edgerton).

Rather than taught formally, khöömei is learned like a language. There are many styles found within the khöömei tradition, including *sygyt*, *kargyraa*, and *barbang-andyr*. Khöömei is sung in separate phrases with pauses between each phrase. Tuvan musicians conceive of each phrase as an independent sonic image.

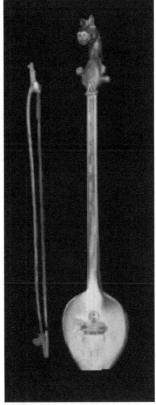

Fig. 8.31: Kovitz, Johanna, Igil front view, 2007. This photo depicts the igil, a traditional Tuvan string instrument.

The pauses give singers time to listen to the ambient sounds in the natural environment and create a sonic response (Levin and Edgerton).

Tuvan Instruments

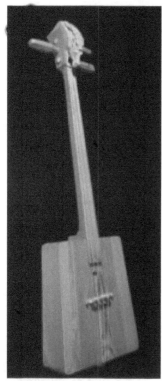

There are also many types of instruments used in Tuvan music. The *tungur* is a frame-drum used also in shamanic rituals. The *igil* is a fiddle with a horse head at the top of the neck; it has one or two strings made from horsehair. The *doshpuluur* is a three-stringed instrument with an unfretted neck that is plucked or strummed. The *xachyk* is a rattle made from bull testicles, and the *tuyug* is a percussion instrument made from horse hooves. The *xomuz* is a jaw harp used to recreate natural sounds like water, and human sounds, including speech. Good xomuz players can encode spoken language in a way that can be understood by an experienced listener ("Tuva: Among the Spirits").

Fig. 8.32: Kovitz, Johanna, Doshpuluur made by Marat Damdyn, 2007. This photo depicts the doshpuluur, also known as a horse head fiddle.

Today, khöömei is performed both as it always has been in its natural environment, and also in concerts and competitions. A wonderful film entitled *Genghis Blues* documents a throat singing competition in Tuva. It features Paul Pena, a famous blues singer and one of the few Westerners to master the throat singing technique.

Here is an example of sygyt performed by Kaigal-ool Kovalyg, a member of the traditional Tuvan throat singing group Huun-Huur-Tu (transcript

Fig. 8.33: Tosha, Kamuz, 2007. This photo depicts the xomuz, also known as a jaw harp.

<u>available).</u> Also, listen to an example of <u>kargyraa</u>, a form that creates undertones rather than overtones, performed by the same group.

Native American Music

The indigenous music of Native Americans is both fascinating and diverse: it represents over five hundred distinct tribes, each with its own unique musical tradition. As Natalie Curtis states in *The Indians' Book: Songs and Legends of the American Indians,* "To the Indian, song is the breath of the spirit that consecrates the acts of life" (xxiv). Throughout North and Central America, song, ceremony, and prayer are central aspects of healing ceremonies conducted by Native American shamans and medicine men. In the past and

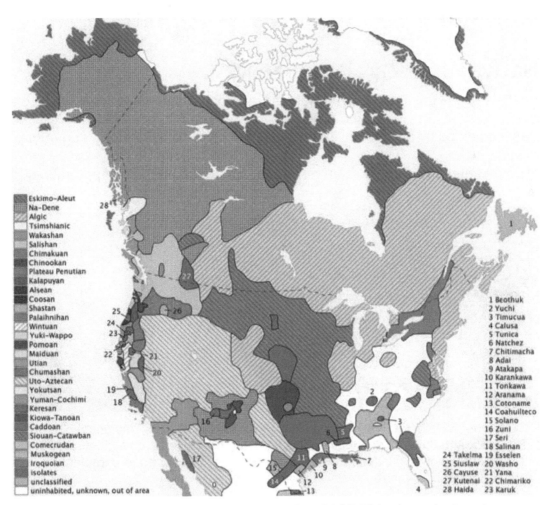

Fig. 8.34: Ish Ishwar, Languages Native America, 2005. This photo depicts the many Native American languages found in North America.

continuing today, music and drama are an inseparable part of the religious, social, and

military activities of Native American people. Music and dance are used to celebrate the

relationship between humans, nature, and spirits, and traditional rituals are used to connect

the present, past and future.

During the eighteenth and nineteenth centuries, the U.S. government's official policy

towards Native Americans was forced assimilation. Children were taken from their families

and placed in schools with the goal of assimilating the children into white American culture.

Native children were not permitted to speak their indigenous languages, which included

singing their culture's songs and music. This has had a significant detrimental effect on the

survival of Native American musical traditions over the course of time (Honani).

Native American Instruments

The voice is the central instrument in traditional Native American music, often

accompanied by dance. Vocals generally are powerfully rhythmic, sometimes

featuring shouts and animal calls. Rattles, drums, and flutes are also important instruments

Fig. 8.35: Beesnest McClain, LACMA Tairona brownware ocarina, 2009., This photo depicts a zoomorphic clay flute. Fig. 8.36: Alfred Mc Garr, Pueblo Indians making hollow log drums, 1930-1945. Fig. 8.37: Franco Altirador, Antlers of fallow deer, 2007. This photo depicts deer antlers traditionally used as percussion instruments by a variety of Native American peoples.

within the Native American musical tradition. Some of the instruments include turtle shell rattles, zoomorphic (representing an animal form) clay and bone flutes, gourd trumpets, log drums, and deer antlers.

Most Native American instruments have symbolic meaning, such as the rattle. The body of the rattle, often a gourd, represents the female aspects of nature. The handle represents male attributes. When joined together, they represent the unity and transcendence of dualism (one thing having two parts, such as night and day or male and female). Stones are generally put inside the gourd to create a rattle's sound; these too have symbolic meaning. Worldwide, stones are believed to be receptacles for ancient wisdom. This is because stones are the oldest objects on the planet and are thought to have been absorbing the energy around them for millions of years. It is believed that when a rattle is shaken, the sound created by the stones hitting each other is the material manifestation of the release of ancient wisdom (Honani).

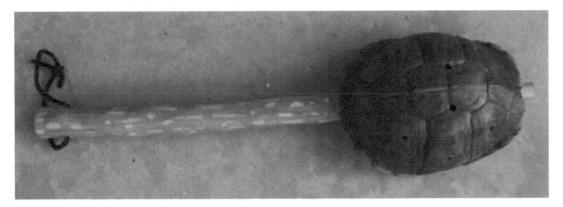

Fig. 8.38: Tommy Wildcat, Turtleshell rattle, 2009.

The following example, "Grass Dance Song," features the traditional singing of the Blackfoot tribe, which has traditionally lived next to the Rocky Mountains in Montana ("We Come From Right Here"). Dancing is a central aspect of Blackfoot spirituality. The Grass

Dance expresses how traditionally young men would trample the grass before setting up camp; this dance demonstrates how to do so ("The Blackfoot: Dancing").

Fig. 8.39: John C. Grabill, Indian Warriors, 1890. This photo depicts traditional Blackfoot dancers after a performance of "Grass Dance."

Watch *"Men's Grass Dance"* performed by Blackfoot Crossing Historical Park Dance Group.

Powwow Drumming

The term "powwow" was originally used to refer to healing ceremonies. Over time it has come to refer generally to Native American gatherings. In a Native American context, the word "powwow" today refers to a secular event featuring singing and social dancing by members of various tribes. Although many elements of the powwow remain traditional, today they are dynamic

Fig. 8.40: Danielle Lorenz, Colors of the Sun, 2010. This photo depicts a powwow dancer in traditional costume.

expressions of Native American identity and pride, serving as pantribal events featuring a variety of songs, dances, games, and contests. Although secular in nature, there is always an observance of spiritual elements. Participants come to powwows to reflect and pray, as well as to dance and compete ("What is a Powwow?").

Fig. 8.41: Dori, Native American PowWow, 2008. This photo depicts the feather headdress of a powwow dancer.

Listening Example

"Owashtinong Chungaming Drumming"

Mayan Music of Mexico & Central America

The Mayans were an advanced civilization living in Mesoamerica that can be traced back to approximately 1500 BCE. They are known for their complex calendar system and sophisticated pyramids. One cannot explore the music of the ancient Maya without addressing the astounding sonic attributes of Mayan architecture. For example, El Castillo pyramid at Chichen Itza in Mexico's Yucatan peninsula has interesting acoustic properties. As people climb the colossal stairs of the pyramid, their footsteps create sounds that mimic the sound of falling rain. It has been recently theorized by researchers that these sounds were created and used to communicate with Chac, the Mayan rain god (Franks).

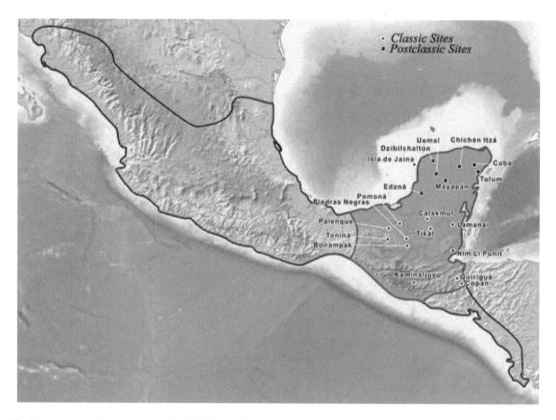

Fig. 8.42: Kmusser, Maya map, 2006. This photo depicts the locations of ancient Mayan archeological sites.

Scientists have also demonstrated that the tiered steps of Castillo create sounds that mimic the quetzal bird, a sacred bird in Mayan mythology. Clapping at the base of the pyramid creates this chirping sound. An analysis of the pyramid's acoustics demonstrated that the chirping sounds were made by a variety of complex sonic factors, such as a natural acoustical filter created by the pyramid's steep steps (Ball). Also, a person standing on the top step speaking at a normal volume can be heard by those on the ground at some distance. This attribute is also found at one of the pyramids at Tikal and among its various Mayan ball courts that have survived to modern times ("The Acoustics of Mayan Temples").

The remarkable sonic attributes of Mayan architecture reflect a technology and understanding that continues to baffle researchers. Even today, there is no clear understanding of how Mayan buildings were constructed to create sound.

To hear one example of this amazing acoustical phenomenon, listen to this recording of a "Quetzal chirp" created by clapping at the base of Kukulkan pyramid at Chichen Itza.

Fig. 8.43: Brian Snelson, El Castillo, 2007. This photo depicts El Castillo, an ancient Mayan pyramid located at Chichen Itza in the Yucatan peninsula in Mexico.

The Maya maintain a strong connection to their ancestors and history through rituals and mythology. Fiestas, dancing, and traditional music remain central aspects of Mayan culture. There are many ceremonies and celebrations occurring throughout the year, during which dancers, singers, and musicians wear elaborate costumes and masks (Franco). This section examines two popular dances found in the highlands of Guatemala where Mayan traditions are still observed.

Fig. 8.44: Frank Vassen, Resplendent Quetzal, 2007. This is a photo of a quetzal bird, a sacred bird in ancient Mayan religion. Fig. 8.45: Ptcamm, Quetzalcoatl, 2007. This is a picture of a sixteenth-century drawing of Quetzalcoatl, a central god in ancient Mayan religion.

"Palo Volador" is an extremely old, and rare, dance. In this dance, participants swing from a sixty-foot pole reenacting the descent of the Hero Twins into the Underworld as described in the sacred Mayan text, *Popul Vuh.* The dancers originally hung from their ankles while playing rattles and other instruments. It is a dangerous dance that has resulted in numerous deaths over its long history (Liner Notes, *Palo Volador*).

Fig. 8.46: TUBS, Guatemala in North America, 2007. This image depicts North and Central America with the country of Guatemala highlighted in red.

The "Dance of the Conquistadores" is an entertaining dance that serves as a type of social commentary. It developed after the colonial period as a way to make fun of the colonists. Observe how the dancers wear colonial-type costumes and dance in an erratic and ungraceful manner bumping into each other. This dance features music of the marimba, an instrument that migrated with African slaves to the Americas (Liner Notes, *Dance of the Conquistadores*).

Closing

This chapter has explored a variety of world music styles, from the songlines of the Australian Aborigines to throat singing in Central Asia. It has covered many new types of instruments and some that evolved into Western instruments, such as the mbira, which is an ancestor of the piano. It is interesting to note that the concepts and use of music are very similar cross-culturally. All over the world, music is used for healing, spiritual understanding, interacting with the universe, and much more. Music is truly universal. It is a medium that transcends language and something all cultures have in common.

Guiding Questions

1. What are the similarities and differences found between various types of world music?

2. How does indigenous music reflect culture and geography?

3. Can you identify Western relatives of instruments found around the world?

4. How do the sounds of various world music styles differ from the sounds of Western music?

Self-Check Exercises

Complete the following self-check exercises to verify your mastery of key music terms presented in this chapter. Check your answers at the bottom of the page.

1. **What is a maqam?**
   a. A dance from India
   b. A melodic fragment in Arabic music
   c. A style of music from China
   d. All of the above

2. **The gungon is a traditional instrument of what peoples?**
   a. Australian Aborigines
   b. Tuvans
   c. The Dagomba
   d. The Inuit

3. **Traditional Chinese music is based upon what type of scale?**
   a. Equal temperament heptatonic
   b. Just intonation pentatonic
   c. Major/minor scale
   d. Mixolydian mode

4. **Which of the following statements are true of Australian Aboriginal songlines?**
   a. They serve as a repository of cultural knowledge.
   b. They are maps of specific geographic locations.
   c. They are the principal medium of exchange.
   d. All of the above

Self-check quiz answers:
1.b. 2.c. 3.b. 4.d.

Additional Resources

Aboriginal Studies WWW Virtual Library

Agawu, V. Kofi and Kofi Agawu. *African Rhythm: A Northern Ewe Perspective.* Cambridge: Cambridge University Press, 1995. Print.

al Faruqi, Lois Ibsen. *An Annotated Glossary of Arabic Musical Terms.* Hartford, CT: Greenwood Press, 1981. Print.

Australian Institute of Aboriginal and Torres Strait Islander Studies

Balfour, Mark. "Sacred Sites: Sacred Sounds." In *Song of the Spirit: The World of Sacred Music. New Delhi, India:* Varanasi, India: Tibet House, 2000. Print.

"Balinese Dancing in the Period of Modern Society." ModernSociety.com, n.d. Web. 12 Oct. 2004.

Bebey, Francis. *African Music: A People's Art.* Lawrence Hill Books, 1999. Print.

Belo, Jane. *Trance in Bali.* New York, NY: Columbia University Press, 1960. Print.

Berliner, Paul F. *The Soul of Mbira: Music and Traditions of the Shona People of Zimbabwe.* Chicago: University of Chicago Press, 1993. Print.

Bhattacharya, Dilip. *Musical Instruments of Tribal India.* New Delhi: Manas Publications, 1999. Print.

Chernoff, John. *African Rhythm and African Sensibility: Aesthetics and Social Action in African Musical Idioms.* Chicago: University of Chicago Press, 1981. Print.

Cope, Jonathan. *How to Khöömei and Other Overtone Singing Styles.* London: Sound for Health, 2004. Print.

Courtney, David R & Courtney Chandrakantha. "Antiquity in Indian Music: Facts Factoids, and Fallacies." *Sruti Ranjani: Essays on Indian Classical Music and Dance*, 156-171. The India Music and Dance Society, 2003.

Coutts-Smith, Mark. *Children of the Drum.* Hong Kong: Lightworks Press, 1997. Print.

Cutis, Natalie, ed. *The Indians' Book.* Avenel, NJ: Gramercy Books, 1987. Print.

Danielou, Alain. *Ragas of North Indian Music.* London: Berrie and Rockliff, 1968. Print.

Danielson, Virginia. *The Voice of Egypt.* Chicago: University of Chicago Press, 1997. Print.

Diallo, Yaya and Mitchell Hall. *The Healing Drum: African Wisdom Teachings.* Rochester, VT: Destiny Books, 1989. Print.

Didgeridoo Cultural Hub

Eiseman, Fred & David Pickell, eds. *Bali: Sekala & Niskala*, Vol. 1. London: Periplus Editions, 1995. Print.

Elkin, A.P. *Aboriginal Men of High Degree*. Queensland, Australia: University of Queensland Press, 1977. Print.

Elkin, A, P. *The Australian Aborigines*. 3rd ed. Garden City, N.Y.: Doubleday and Co., 1964. Print.

Erlmann, Veit. *Nightsong: Performance, Power, and Practice in South Africa*. Chicago: University of Chicago Press, 1996. Print.

Farmer, Henry George. *Historical Facts for the Arabian Musical Influence*. London: Arno Press, 1978. Print.

Farmer, Henry George. *A History of Arabian Music*. London: Luzac & Co., Ltd, 1973. Print.

Furst, Dan. "Didgeridoos and Trance States." *Sacred Sounds,* 2006. Web. 17 Jan. 2012.

Hale, Thomas. *Griots and Griottes: Masters of Words and Music.* Bloomington: Indiana University Press, 2007. Print.

James, J. Alison. *The Drums of Noto Hanto*. NY, NY: DK Publishing, Inc. 1999. Print.

Jegede, Tunde. *African Classical Music: The Griot Tradition.* London: Diabate Arts, 1994. Print.

Kaufmann, Walter, *Tibetan Buddhist Chant: Musical Notations and Interpretations of a Song Book by the Bkah Brgyud Pa and Sa Skya Pa Sects.* Bloomington: Indiana University Press, 1975. Print.

Le Mouël, Jean- François. *Music of the Inuit: The Copper Eskimo Tradition.* UNESCO, 1983. CD & notes.

Leonard C., J. Holvik & H. Bailey. *Japanese Music: Another Tradition, Other Sounds.* Richmond, Indiana: Earlham College Press, 1990. Print.

Levin, Theodore. *Where Rivers And Mountains Sing: Sound, Music, And Nomadism in Tuva And Beyond.* Bloomington: Indiana University Press, 2006. Print.

Lubman, David. "An archaeological study of chirped echo from the Mayan pyramid of Kukulkan at Chichen Itza." *Acoustical Society of America* meeting. Norfolk, VA. October 12-16, 1998.

Malm, W.P. *Music Cultures of the Pacific, the Near East, and Asia.* Upper Saddle River, NJ: Prentice-Hall, Inc, 1977. Print.

Malm, W.P. *Six Hidden Views of Japanese Music.* Berkeley, CA: University of California Press, 1984. Print.

McPhee, Colin. *A House in Bali.* Hong Kong: Oxford University Press, 1972. Print.

Native American Audio Collections

Nico F. Declercq, Joris Degrieck, Rudy Briers, Oswald Leroy. "A theoretical study of special acoustic effects caused by the staircase of the El Castillo pyramid at the Maya ruins of Chichen-Itza in Mexico." *Journal of the Acoustical Society of America.* 116(6), 3328-3335, 2004.

Rosenthal, Ethel. *Story of Indian Music and Its Instruments.* New Delhi: Oriental Book, 1973. Print.

Sankaran, Trichy. *The Rhythmic Principles & Practices of South Indian Drumming.* Toronto: Lalith Publishers, 1994. Print.

Shehadi, Fadlou and E.J. Brill. *Philosophies of Music in Medieval Islam.* Leiden, Netherlands: Brill Academic Publishers, 1995. Print.

Spies, Walter & Beryl de Zoete. *Dance & Drama in Bali.* London: Faber & Faber, 1938. Print.

Stock, Jonathan P. *Huju: Traditional Opera in Modern Shanghai.* Oxford, UK: Oxford University Press, 2003. Print.

Suryani, Luh Ketut & Gordon D. Jensen. *Trance and Possession in Bali.* Oxford, UK: Oxford University Press, 1993. Print.

Thomas, T. Ajayi. *History of Juju Music: A History of an African Popular Music from Nigeria.* Self-Published, 1992. Print.

Touma, Habib Hassan. *The Music of the Arabs.* Portland: Amadeus Press, 1996. Print.

Trance 1: Sufi Dervish Rite, Tibetan Overtone Chant, Indian Druphad. Musical Expeditions, 1995. Mixed Media.

Unikkaat Sivunittinnit: Messages from the Past

Van Tongeren, Mark C. *Overtone Singing: Physics and Metaphysics of Harmonics in East and West.* Amsterdam: Fusica, 2002. Print.

Wafer, Jim. *Vibrational Healing with the Didgeridoo.* Chicago, IL: Inma-Ku, 1989. Print.

Wang-Ngai, Siu and Peter Loverick. *Chinese Opera: Images and Stories.* Seattle: University of Washington, 1997. Print.

Whidden, Lynn. "Ritual Powwow Music: Its Power and Poetics." *Canadian Journal for Traditional Music,* 1983. Web. 6 Feb. 2012.

Yidakiwuy Dhäwu Miwatjnurunydja: Didgeridu Story from Far Northeast Arnhem Land

The Yirrkala Art Centre & The Mulka Project

Transcript: "Example of Pentatonic Scale"

[In this video, Bobby McFerrin demonstrates the power of the pentatonic scale while participating in the event "Notes & Neurons: In Search of a Common Chorus" at the 2009 World Science Festival. His point is that people intuitively understand the pentatonic scale.]

"We're talking about expectations. Expectations. Watch."

Bobby McFerrin has audience repeat a note in the pentatonic scale. He is pretending there are piano keys on the floor. For each note, McFerrin jumps and says, "Ba."

"Ba." "Ba." "Ba." "Ba." "Ba. Ba. Ba. Ba. Ba. Ba."

Bobby McFerrin demonstrating higher note by jumping to stage left.

"Ba." "Ba." "Ba."

Then Bobby is jumping back and forth alternating between first two notes:

"Ba." "Ba." "Ba." "Ba." "Ba. Ba. Ba. Ba. Ba. Ba. Ba."

Then McFerrin unexpectedly goes to an even higher note. The audience responds with "Ba." Laugher and clapping follows because the audience sang the correct new note right without prompting from McFerrin.

Bobby McFerrin then leads the audience to sing a melody by jumping from note to note on the imaginary piano keys.

"Ba, Ba, Ba, Ba, Ba, Baaaa." "Ba, Ba, Ba, Ba, Ba, Baaaa."

Then, Bobby McFerrin starts to scat (do a vocal improvisation) on top of the melody sung by the audience. The audience is singing the notes that correspond with the notes indicated by Bobby McFerrin's jumping on the imaginary piano keys on stage.

McFerrin then continues with the scale exercise including new lower and higher notes that the audience sings correctly.

At the end of this exercise, McFerrin says, "Yeah!" to audience applause and cheering and sits down with the rest of the panel participants.

Bobby McFerrin: "What's interesting to me about that is regardless of where I am, anywhere, every audience gets that. It doesn't matter. You know. That's just the pentatonic scale for some reason."

Panel participant: "If you are looking for a job in neuroscience...."

Audience laughter.

Transcript: "Sygyt"

[The traditional Tuvan throat singing group Huun-Huur-Tu is on stage during a performance at the 2006 Philadelphia Folk Festival. Sayan Bapa, one of the members of Huun-Huur-Tu, is introducing the following demonstration.]

"Throat singers and musicians. And now I ask of my friend (unintelligible name of performer) singing one of our best and beautiful throat singing style. We are calling this style sygyt, which means "whistle." Usually herder men singing this style sit in front of the river and singing about the nation (unintelligible) and about our country called Tuva."

Demonstration of sygyt begins. Please note that for this chapter, transcripts of song and music lyrics are not necessary to gain an understanding of the material.

At the end of the demonstration, there is audience cheering and applause.

Works Consulted

"Aboriginal Artefacts." *Aboriginal Arts*. Aboriginal Arts, n.d. Web. 5 Feb. 2012.
        <http://aboriginalarts.co.uk/artefacts.htm>.

"Aboriginal Issues." *Centre for Social Justice*. Centre for Social Justice, 2012. Web. 11 Jan.
        2012. <http://www.socialjustice.org/index.php?page=aboriginal-issues>.

"The Aboriginal Land Rights Act." *Central Land Council*. Central Land Council, n.d. Web. 11
        Jan. 2012. <http://www.clc.org.au/articles/info/the-aboriginal-land-rights-act>.

"Aboriginal People." *Survival International*. Survival International, n.d. Web. 11 Jan. 2012.
        <http://www.survivalinternational.org/tribes/aboriginals>.

"The Acoustics of Mayan Temples." *The Lucky Mojo Esoteric Archive*. LuckyMojo.com.,
        2011. Web. 4 Feb. 2012.
        <http://www.luckymojo.com/esoteric/interdisciplinary/architecture/ecclesiastical/m
        ayanacoustics.html>.

Aleppo Music Band. 1915. Postcard. *Wikimedia Commons*. Wikipedia Foundation, 18 Mar.
        2012. Web. 2 Feb. 2012. <http://commons.wikimedia.org/wiki/File:Aleppo-
        MusicOBand.jpg>.

"Angers Bridge (1850)." *Bridges of Dublin*. Dublin City Council. Web. 14 Apr. 2014.
        <http://www.bridgesofdublin.ie/bridge-building/disasters/angers-bridge-france-
        1850>.

Ankitchd26. *Historycal Musical Instrument. Tabla*. 10 Oct. 2011. *Wikimedia Commons*.
        Wikipedia Foundation, 20 Apr. 2012. Web. 2 Feb. 2012.
        <http://commons.wikimedia.org/wiki/File:Historycal_Musical_instrument.jpg>.

Anonylog. *Indonesia, Bali*. 14 Sept. 2008. *Wikimedia Commons*. Wikipedia Foundation, 20
        Nov. 2009. Web. 2 Feb. 2012.
        <http://commons.wikimedia.org/wiki/File:IndonesiaBali.png>.

Anyako Woeto, perf. "Afa." *Kwamivi Tsegah's Funeral*. Nada Brahma Foundation, 1999.
        Video.

"The Arabic Maqam." *Maqam World*. Maqam World, 2007. Web. 15 Feb. 2012.
        <http://www.maqamworld.com/maqamat.html>.

"Arabic Musical Instruments." *Maqam World*. Maqam World, 2007. Web. 15 Feb. 2012.
        <http://www.maqamworld.com/instruments.html>.

ArcturusCmn. *Quanoun*. 4 Oct. 2007. *Wikimedia Commons*. Wikipedia Foundation, 18 Sept.
        2009. Web. 18 Sept. 2012.
        <http://commons.wikimedia.org/wiki/File:Quanoun_19eme_siecle.jpg>.

Arent. *Tambura*. 9 Aug. 2005. *Wikimedia Commons*. Wikipedia Foundation, 3 Jan. 2012.
        Web. 18 Sept. 2012. <http://commons.wikimedia.org/wiki/File:Tambura.jpg>.

"Atamga (Atsiagbekor)." Perf. Agbi Ladzekpo. Nada Brahma Foundation, 2007. MP3.

"Atamga (Atsiagbekor)." Husunu's Durbar. Perf. Agbi Ladzekpo. Nada Brahma Foundation, 2007. Video.

Atirador, Franco. *Antlers of fallow deer*. 2 June 2007. *Wikimedia Commons*. Wikipedia Foundation, 5 June 2007. Web. 4 Feb. 2012. <http://commons.wikimedia.org/wiki/File:Antlers_fallow_deer.jpg>.

Bagdadnani. *Ancient Chinese instrumentalists*. 20 Feb. 2008. *Wikimedia Commons*. Wikipedia Foundation, 13 May 2012. Web. 2 Feb. 2012. <http://commons.wikimedia.org/wiki/File:Ancientchineseinstrumentalists.jpg>.

Bakan, Michael B. *World Music: Traditions and Transformations*. New York: McGraw-Hill, 2007. Print.

Ball, Philip. "Quetzal Echo at Chichen Itza 2004." *Nature News*. 14 Dec. 2004. *Archaeo-Acoustics*. Lab for Ultrasonic NDE, 16 Sept. 2012. Web. 20 Sept. 2012. <http://www-old.me.gatech.edu/declercq/laboratory/research-topics/periodic-structures/archaeo-acoustics--chichen-itza/index.php>.

Banerjee, Nikhil, perf. "Raga Kaushi Kanada." *Vijaya Parrikar Library*. Rajan Parrikar Music Archive, 2012. Web. 18 Sept. 2012. <http://www.parrikar.org/vpl/?page_id=177>.

"The Blackfoot: Dancing." *The Blackfoot*. Calgary Board of Education, 2003. Web. 6 Feb. 2012. <http://projects.cbe.ab.ca/ict/2learn/mmspeight/blackfoot/html/powwow.htm>.

Blackfoot Crossing Historical Park Dance Group, perf. "Men's Grass Dance." 23 July 2011. *YouTube*. 24 July 2011. Web. 20 Sept. 2012. <http://youtu.be/8C5swdaL6QY>.

"Bollywood Music." *Indianetzone*. Indianetzone, 7 Feb. 2012. Web. 9 Feb. 2012. <http://www.indianetzone.com/2/bollywood_music.htm>.

Brindle, Bill. *During the rain dance in Corroboree*. 28 Jan. 2010. *Wikimedia Commons*. Wikipedia Foundation, 9 Aug. 2012. Web. 2 February 2012. <http://commons.wikimedia.org/wiki/File:Corroborree.jpg>.

Brunet, Jacques. Liner notes. *Lelambatan*. Galloway Records,1975. CD.

Cameron, Kate. "Aboriginal people struggle for citizenship rights." *Discovering Democracy*. Australian Broadcasting Corporation, 2000. Web. 11 Jan. 2012. <http://www.abc.net.au/civics/democracy/struggle.htm>.

Catrin. *Egyptian riqq*. 2 June 2006. *Wikimedia Commons*. Wikipedia Foundation, 9 Apr. 2012. Web. 2 February 2012. <http://commons.wikimedia.org/wiki/File:Riqq.jpg>.

Chatwin, Bruce. *The Songlines*. New York: Viking Books, 1987. Print.

"Chief Installation." Nada Brahma Foundation, 1999. MP3.

Construction tools sign, used with permission from Microsoft. "Images." Office. Web. 4 Sept. 2012. <http://office.microsoft.com/en-us/images/results.aspx?ex=2&qu=tools#ai:MC900432556|mt:0|>.

Courtney, David. "Mythological Origins of Sangeet." *Chandra & David's Homepage.* Chandra & David's Homepage, n.d. Web. 20 Feb. 2012. <http://chandrakantha.com/articles/indian_music/myth_origin.html>.

Curtis, Natalie. *The Indians' Book: Songs and Legends of the American Indians.* Mineola, NY: Dover Publications, 1907. Print.

Danielson, Virginia. "Arab Music." University of Colorado Boulder, n.d. Web. 15 Feb. 2012. <http://autocww.colorado.edu/~toldy2/E64ContentFiles/MusicAndTerms/ArabMusic.htm>.

Dimitriadis, Nikos. "Oud & Ud." *Oud.gr.* Oud.gr, n.d. Web. 15 Feb. 2012. <http://www.oud.gr/about_oud.htm>.

Domtw. *Mmridangam.* 31 Aug. 2010. *Wikimedia Commons.* Wikipedia Foundation, 6 Oct. 2010. Web. 2 Feb. 2012. <http://commons.wikimedia.org/wiki/File:Wiki-mridangam.jpg>.

Dori. *Native American Powwow.* 6 Sept. 2008. *Wikimedia Commons.* Wikipedia Foundation, 7 Sept. 2008. Web. 4 Feb. 2012. <http://commons.wikimedia.org/wiki/File:Native_American_PowWow_9488.jpg>.

Eaton, David. "The Influence of Music on Self and Society." *International Conference on the Unity of the Sciences.* Seoul, Korea. February 2000. Conference Presentation.

Eyre, Banning. "Thomas Mapfumo." *National Geographic Music.* National Geographic, 2012. Web. 5 Feb. 2012. <http://worldmusic.nationalgeographic.com/view/page.basic/artist/content.artist/thomas_mapfumo_1760/it_IT>.

Fang, Liu. "Liu Fang's Passionate Pipa." Interview by Paula E. Kirman. *Inside World Music.* Philmultic.com, June 24, 2001. Web. 15 Feb. 2012. <http://www.philmultic.com/liufang/interviews/world_music.html>.

"Fei Fei Shih Shih (Rainy Weather)." Prod. Liang Tsai-ping. *An Anthology of the World's Music.* Anthology. Society for Ethnomusicology. Taiwan, 1969.

Fela Kuti: Black President. Prod. Cassandra Herrman. *Sound Tracks: Music without Borders.* Public Broadcasting Service, 2012. Web. 18 Sept. 2012. <http://www.pbs.org/soundtracks/stories/black/>.

Franco, Samuel. Personal interview. 10 Aug. 2000.

Franks, Sevaan. "Ancient Mayans made pyramids to make music for rain god." 24 Sept. 2009. *A Blog About History.* 2012. Web. 20 Sept. 2012. <http://www.ablogabouthistory.com/2009/09/24/ancient-mayans-made-pyramids-to-make-music-for-rain-god/>.

"Gamelan selonding." Bali Arts Festival, Indonesia. Nada Brahma Foundation, 2005. MP3.

"Genjek excerpt." Nada Brahma Foundation, 2003. MP3.

Ghosh, Nikhil, perf. "Tabla solo in Teentala." *Vijaya Parrikar Library*. Rajan Parrikar Music Archive, 2012. Web. 18 Sept. 2012. <http://www.parrikar.org/vpl/?page_id=251>.

Grabill, John C. Indian Warriors. Mr. Bear-that-Runs-and-Growls, Mr. Warrior, Mr. One-Tooth-Gone, Mr. Sole (bottom of foot), Mr. Make-it-Long. 1890. Library of Congress. Prints & Photographs Division. John C. Grabill Collection. LC-DIG-ppmsc-02521. 2012. Web. 4 Feb. 2012. <http://www.loc.gov/pictures/item/99613805/>.

Gringer and Sreejithk2000. *Veena*. 26 Oct. 2010. *Wikimedia Commons*. Wikipedia Foundation, 19 May 2012. Web. 18 Sept. 2012. <http://commons.wikimedia.org/wiki/File:Veena.png>.

Hmh. *Map of China.* 30 July 2011. *Wikimedia Commons*. Wikipedia Foundation, 13 Aug. 2011. Web. 2 Feb. 2012. <http://commons.wikimedia.org/wiki/File:China_map_updated.png>.

Honani family. Personal interviews. Sept.- Dec. 2001.

Howitt, Alfred William. *The Narrang-ga bull-roarer*. 1904. *Wikimedia Commons*. Wikipedia Foundation, 17 Sept. 2011. Web. 2 Feb. 2012. <http://commons.wikimedia.org/wiki/File:Native_tribes_of_South-East_Australia_Fig_40_-_Narrang-ga_bull-roarer.jpg>.

Huun Huur Tu, perf. "Prayer." *The Orphan's Lament*. 1994. *YouTube.* 18 Jan. 2008. Web. 19 Sept. 2012. <http://youtu.be/B-20tFVLSOw>.

Iadadada, Dzogbone. Personal interview. 26 June 2000.

Imoro, Sulley. "Sulley Imoro demonstrating the talking drum." *YouTube*. 24 Sept. 2009. Web. 17 Sept. 2012. <http://youtu.be/0W55kNtDS8I>.

Ishwar, Ish. *Languages of Native America.* 2005. *Wikimedia Commons*. Wikipedia Foundation, 1 Mar. 2009. Web. 2 Feb. 2012. <http://commons.wikimedia.org/wiki/File:Langs_N.Amer.png>.

Jadue, Yuseff. "Taksim Oud Maqam Bayati." *YouTube.* 21 Apr. 2012. Web. 21 Sept. 2012. <http://youtu.be/_Tv-WEY61_I>.

"Jauk." Nada Brahma Foundation, 2004. Video.

Jayaraman D.K., and D.K. Pattammal, perf. "Raga Narayani." *Vijaya Parrikar Library*. Rajan Parrikar Music Archive, 2012. Web. 18 Sept. 2012. <http://www.parrikar.org/vpl/?page_id=850>.

"Jegog excerpt." Perf. Surya Metu Reh ensemble. Negara, Bali. Nada Brahma Foundation, 2010. MP3

A Journey with the Oud. Internet Archive. Internet Archive, n.d. Web. 18 Sept. 2012.
<http://archive.org/details/oudkandi>.

Justinian-of-Byzantium. *Middle East map in full*. 18 Nov. 2011. *Wikimedia Commons*.
Wikipedia Foundation, 17 Aug. 2012. Web. 2 Feb. 2012.
<http://commons.wikimedia.org/wiki/File:Middle_east_map_in_full.png>.

Kambui, Jacuma. "Fela Anikulapo-Kuti." *TheTalkingDrum.com*. TheTalkingDrum.com, 2003.
Web. 18 Sept. 2012. <http://www.thetalkingdrum.com/fela.html>.

Kinney, Sylvia. "Drummers in Dagbon: The Role of the Drummer in the Damba Festival."
Ethnomusicology 14.2 (1970): 258-265. Print.

Kiu, Ian. *Tang Dynasty circa 700 CE*. 27 Aug. 2008. *Wikimedia Commons*. Wikipedia
Foundation,12 Dec. 2010. Web. 2 Feb. 2012.
<http://commons.wikimedia.org/wiki/File:Tang_Dynasty_circa_700_CE.png>.

Kmusser. *Maya Map*. 20 July 2006. *Wikimedia Commons*. Wikipedia Foundation, 26 Aug.
2012. Web. 4 Feb. 2012. <http://commons.wikimedia.org/wiki/File:Mayamap.png>.

Kovalyg, Kaigal-ool, perf. "Huun Huur Tu at Philadelphia Folk Festival, August 2006." 2006.
YouTube. 15 Sept. 2006. Web. 19 Sept. 2012. <http://youtu.be/RxK4pQgVvfg>.

Kovitz, Johanna. *Doshpuluur made by Marat Damdyn*. 2007. *Wikimedia Commons*.
Wikipedia Foundation, 3 June 2010. Web. 2 Feb. 2012.
<http://commons.wikimedia.org/wiki/File:Doshpuluur_made_by_Marat_Damdyn.gif
>.

Kovitz, Joanna. *Igil Front View*. 2007. *Wikimedia Commons*. Wikipedia Foundation, 1 May
2009. Web. 2 Feb. 2012.
<http://commons.wikimedia.org/wiki/File:Igil_oktober_saya_front_view.gif>.

Kraus, Jan. *Sitar*. 7 Feb. 2009. *Wikimedia Commons*. Wikipedia Foundation, 7 Oct. 2009.
Web. 2 Feb. 2012. <http://commons.wikimedia.org/wiki/File:Sitar_full.jpg>.

Ladzekpo, Alfred. "RE: Agbekor question." Message to Cathy Silverman. 11 Feb. 2001. E-
mail.

Ladzekpo, Kobla. Personal interview. 22 Apr. 2007.

Levin, Theodore, and Michael Edgerton. "The Throat Singers of Tuva." *Scientific American*.
Scientific American, 20 Sept. 1999. Web.
<http://www.scientificamerican.com/article.cfm?id=the-throat-singers-of-tuv>.

Lewiston, David, and Julian Burger. Liner notes. *Voices of Forgotten Worlds: Traditional
Music of Forgotten Peoples*. Ellipsis Arts, 1996. CD.

Lieberman, Fredric, ed. Liner notes. *An Anthology of the World's Music: China II*. Rounder
Records, 1998. CD.

Lorenz, Danielle. *Colours of the Sun.* 26 July 2010. *Wikimedia Commons.* Wikipedia Foundation, 22 June 2011. Web. 4 Feb. 2012. <http://commons.wikimedia.org/wiki/File:Colours_of_the_sun.jpg>.

"Maiya Yashoda". *Hum Saath Saath Hain.* 1999. Dir. Sooraj R. Barjatya. Rajshri Productions. *YouTube.* 17 Sept. 2009. Web. 18 Sept. 2012. <http://youtu.be/jOjgKr-GeGl>.

Mandela, Nelson. Long Walk to Freedom: the Autobiography of Nelson Mandela. Boston: Back Bay, 1995. Print.

Mapfumo, Thomas. "Moyo Wangu." 2004. Perf. Thomas Mapfumo and the Blacks Unlimited. *YouTube.* 30 Sept. 2008. Web. 18 Sept. 2012. <http://youtu.be/yMC_5FxdULY>.

McClain, Beesnest. *LACMA Tairona Brownware Ocarina.* Feb. 2009. *Wikimedia Commons.* Wikipedia Foundation, 3 Jan. 2010. Web. 4 Feb. 2012. <http://commons.wikimedia.org/wiki/File:WLA_lacma_Tairona_brownware_ocarina.jpg>.

McFerrin, Bobby. "World Science Festival 2009: Bobby McFerrin Demonstrates the Power of the Pentatonic Scale." *YouTube.* 23 July 2009. Web. 19 Sept. 2012. <http://youtu.be/ne6tB2KiZuk>.

Mc Garr, Alfred. *Pueblo Indians making hollow log drums.* Postcard. 1930-1945. *Wikimedia Commons.* Wikipedia Foundation, 17 Aug. 2011. Web. 4 Feb. 2012. <http://commons.wikimedia.org/wiki/File:Pueblo_Indians_making_hollow_log_drums.jpg>.

Montford, Matthew. "Arabic Rhythmic Patterns." *AncientFuture.com.* AncientFuture.com, n.d. Web. 15 Feb. 2012. <http://www.ancient-future.com/arab.html>.

Music is the Weapon. Dir. Jean Jacques Flori and Stéphane Tchalgadjieff. Universal Import, 2004. DVD.

Nada Brahma Foundation. *Damba Festival. YouTube.* 27 Oct. 2009. Web. 17 Sept. 2012. <http://youtu.be/nhA4ewbBbNQ>.

Najarian, Viken. *Oud.* 3 Mar. 2006. *Wikimedia Commons.* Wikipedia Foundation, 27 Sept. 2007. Web. 18 Sept. 2012. <http://commons.wikimedia.org/wiki/File:Oud.jpg>.

O'Sullivan, Kevin. "Virtual Drum Museum." *Dancedrummer.com.* Dancedrummer.com, 2001. Web. 17 Sept. 2012. <http://www.dancedrummer.com/museum.html>.

Owashtinong Chungaming. "Owashtinong Chungaming drumming." *Internet Underground Music Archive Collection.* Internet Archive, 2001. Web. 20 Sept. 2012. <http://archive.org/details/iuma-owashtinong_chung>.

"Pitra Yadnya." Nada Brahma Foundation, 2004. Video.

"Plucked-Stringed Instruments." *China People Promotions.* China People Promotions, n.d. Web. 20 Sept. 2012. <http://chinesemusic.co.uk/index.php/traditional-chinese-instruments/plucked-string-instruments>.

"Pre-Colonial Period." *GhanaWeb.* GhanaWeb, 2012. Web. 4 Feb. 2012. <http://www.ghanaweb.com/GhanaHomePage/history/pre-colonial.php>.

Ptcamn. *Quetzalcoatl.* Sixteenth Century. *Codex Magliabechiano.* 3 Apr. 2007. *Wikimedia Commons.* Wikipedia Foundation, 29 May 2012. Web. 4 Feb. 2012. <http://commons.wikimedia.org/wiki/File:Quetzalcoatl_magliabechiano.jpg>.

"The Science of Brainwaves." *Neurohealth Associates.* Neurohealth Associates, 2004. Web. 11 Sept. 2012. <http://www.nhahealth.com/science.htm>.

Shadkala Govinda Marar. 30 Oct. 2010. *Wikimedia Commons.* Wikipedia Foundation, 2 Aug. 2012. Web. 18 Sept. 2012. <http://commons.wikimedia.org/wiki/File:Shadkala_Govinda_Marar.jpg>.

Shankar, Ravi. "On Appreciation of Indian Classical Music." *RaviShankar.org.* Ravi Shankar Foundation, 2011. Web. 20 Feb. 2012. <http://www.ravishankar.org/indian_music_frame.html>.

Shelquist, Wahiduddin Richard. "The Music of the Spheres." *The Mysticism of Music, Sound and Word.* Wahiduddin's Website, 23 Oct. 2005. Web. 15 Feb. 2012. <http://wahiduddin.net/mv2/II/II_10.htm>.

Silverman, Cathy. *Balinese Drummers.* 2005. Used with permission of Nada Brahma Foundation.

—. *Balinese Gongs.* 2008. Used with permission of Nada Brahma Foundation.

—. Dagomban musicians leading First Lady of Surinam into Voices of African Mothers Conference. 2010. Accra, Ghana. Used with permission of Nada Brahma Foundation.

—, ed. *Dance of the Conquistadores (excerpt).* Nada Brahma Foundation, Aug. 2000. DVD.

—. *Gamelan factory, Tihingin, Bali, Indonesia.* 2005. Used with permission of Nada Brahma Foundation.

—. *Gonje.* 2010. Used with permission of Nada Brahma Foundation.

—. *Gungon.* 2010. Used with permission of Nada Brahma Foundation.

—. *Jegog instruments.* 2010. Used with permission of Nada Brahma Foundation.

—. Liner Notes. *Palo Volador.* Nada Brahma Foundation, 2000. DVD.

—. Liner Notes. *Dance of the Conquistadores.* Nada Brahma Foundation, 2000. DVD.

—. *Luna.* 2010. Used with permission of Nada Brahma Foundation.

—, ed. *Palo Volador (excerpt).* Nada Brahma Foundation, Aug. 2000. DVD.

—. *Village gamelan, Luwus, Bali*. 2008. Used with permission of Nada Brahma Foundation.

Silverman, Cathy and Nico Spezzacatena. Liner notes. *Damba in Yendi*. Nada Brahma Foundation, 2007. DVD.

Smkphotos. *Dr. Cheng Yu playing the P'ipa*, 30 Nov. 2010. *Wikimedia Commons*. Wikipedia Foundation, 17 Feb. 2012. Web. 20 June 2012. <http://commons.wikimedia.org/wiki/File:Cheng_Yu.jpg>.

Snelson, Brian. *El Castillo*. 8 Nov. 2007. *Wikimedia Commons*. Wikipedia Foundation, 14 Feb. 2008. Web. 4 Feb. 2012. <http://commons.wikimedia.org/wiki/File:El_Castillo.jpg>.

Spencer, Mimi. "Middle Eastern Music: An Introduction." *Shira.net* . Shira.net, n.d. Web. 11 Sept. 2012. <http://www.shira.net/music/music-intro.htm>.

Spezzacatena, Nico. *Anlo-Ewe axatse ensemble*. 1999. Used with permission of Nada Brahma Foundation.

—. *Anlo-Ewe dance-drumming ensemble*. 1999. Used with permission of Nada Brahma Foundation.

—. Liner notes. *Kwamivi Tsegah's Funeral*. Nada Brahma Foundation, 2007. DVD.

—. *Ya-Na Yakubu Andani II, Dagomban Paramount Chief*. 1999. Used with permission of Nada Brahma Foundation.

Spies, Walter, and Beryl de Zoete. *Dance & Drama in Bali*. London: Faber & Faber, 1938. Print.

Teosoet. "Quetzal chirp from Kukulkan's piramid [sic] at Chichen Itza." *YouTube.* 20 Sept. 2011. Web. 20 Sept. 2012. <http://youtu.be/sb4c3rTxh2g>.

"Thomas Mapfumo." *Walters Music Agency*. WaltersMusicAgency.com, n.d. Web. 5 Feb. 2012. <http://www.waltersmusicagency.com/mapfumo/>.

Thomasgl. *Image of a didgeridoo*. 16 June 2005. *Wikimedia Commons*. Wikipedia Foundation, 11 June 2007. Web. 2 Feb. 2012. <http://commons.wikimedia.org/wiki/File:Didgeridoo.jpg>.

Titon, Jeff Todd & Linda Fujie. *Worlds of Music*. Belmont, CA: Schirmer Books, 2005. Print.

Touma, Habib Hassan. The Music of the *Arabs*. Portland: Amadeus Press, 1999. Print.

"Topeng." Nada Brahma Foundation, 2005. Video.

Tosha. *Kamuz.* 10 Mar. 2007. *Wikimedia Commons*. Wikipedia Foundation, 5 Aug. 2012. Web. 2 Feb. 2012. <http://commons.wikimedia.org/wiki/File:Kamuz.jpg>.

TUBS. *Map of Ghana in Africa*. 7 Apr. 2011. *Wikimedia Commons*. Wikipedia Foundation, 21 May 2012. Web. 2 Feb. 2012.

<http://commons.wikimedia.org/wiki/File:Ghana_in_Africa_%28-mini_map_-rivers%29.svg>.

—. *Map of Guatemala in North America*. 26 Mar. 2011. *Wikimedia Commons*. Wikipedia Foundation, 21 May 2012. Web. 4 Feb. 2012. <http://commons.wikimedia.org/wiki/File:Guatemala_in_North_America_%28-mini_map_-rivers%29.svg>.

—. *India in Asia*. 6 Apr. 2011. *Wikimedia Commons*. Wikipedia Foundation, 21 May 2012. Web. 2 Feb. 2012. <http://commons.wikimedia.org/wiki/File:India_in_Asia_%28de-facto%29_%28-mini_map_-rivers%29.svg>.

"Tuva, Among the Spirits: Sound, Music and Nature in Sakha and Tuva." *Xiami.com*. Smithsonian Folkways, 1999. Web. 20 Feb. 2012. <http://www.xiami.com/album/349240>.

Vassen, Frank. *Resplendent Quetzal*. 7 Dec. 2007. *Wikimedia Commons*. Wikipedia Foundation, 5 Mar. 2011. Web. 4 Feb. 2012. <http://commons.wikimedia.org/wiki/File:Resplendent_Quetzal,_Mirador_de_Quetzales,_Costa_Rica.jpg>.

Veal, Michael. *Fela: Life and Times of an African Musical Icon*. Philadelphia: Temple University Press, 2000. Print.

Voodooisland. *Tuvan People's Republic*. 10 Aug. 2011. *Wikimedia Commons*. Wikipedia Foundation, 25 July 2012. Web. 2 Feb. 2012. <http://commons.wikimedia.org/wiki/File:Tuva_map.png>.

Walley, Richard. "Australian Aboriginal Music: Song with Didgeridoo." *YouTube*. 7 Nov. 2007. Web. 14 Sept. 2012. <http://youtu.be/dFGvNxBqYFI>.

"We Come From Right Here." *Blackfeet Nation*. Blackfeet Nation, 2012. Web. 6 Feb. 2012. <http://www.blackfeetnation.com/about-the-blackfeet/our-history.html>.

"What is a Powwow?" *The Nanticoke Indian Tribe*. The Nanticoke Indian Tribe, 2011. Web. 6 Feb. 2012. <http://www.nanticokeindians.org/what_powwow.cfm>.

Wildcat, Tommy. *Turtleshell Rattle*. 2009. *Wikimedia Commons*. Wikipedia Foundation, 22 Dec. 2009. Web. 4 Feb. 2012. <http://commons.wikimedia.org/wiki/File:Cwy_turtleshell_rattle.jpg>.

Winn, Michael. "Magic Numbers, Planetary Tones and the Body: The Evolution of Daoist Inner Alchemy into Modern Sacred Science." *International Daoism Conference*. Boston University, 2003.

Wohlgemuth, Jill. "Brief History of Bollywood." *Bollywood & Libraries*. The Jillbrary, n.d. Web. 9 Feb. 2012. <http://jillbrary.wordpress.com/bollywood-and-libraries/brief-history-of-bollywood/>.